The First Space Race

D1240170

Number Eight:
Centennial of Flight Series
Roger D. Launius, *General Editor*

The First Space Race

Launching the
World's First Satellites

Matt Bille and
Erika Lishock

Foreword by James A. Van Allen

Texas A&M University Press ■ *College Station*

The paper used in this book meets the minimum requirements
of the American National Standard for Permanence
of Paper for Printed Library Materials, Z39.48-1984.
Binding materials have been chosen for durability.
⊗

Library of Congress Cataloging-in-Publication Data

Bille, Matt, 1959–
    The first space race : launching the world's first satellites / Matt Bille and
Erika Lishock ; foreword by James A. Van Allen — 1st ed.
        p. cm. — (Centennial of flight series ; no. 8)
    Includes bibliographical references and index.
        ISBN 1-58544-356-5 (cloth : alk. paper) —ISBN 1-58544-374-3 (pbk. : alk. paper)
        1. Artificial satellites—United States—History. 2. Artificial satellites—Soviet Union—
History. 3. Space race.   I. Lishock, Erika.   II. Title.   III. Series
TL796.5.U5 B54 2004
629.46'0973—dc22
                                                        2003026809

To Deb, Corey, and Lauryn Bille—
the present and the future—
and to the "rocket men" of the 1950s,
who built the foundation for both
—Matt Bille

To all people in ages past, present, and future,
who continue to dream and seek to do the impossible
—Erika Lishock

Contents

Foreword
James A. Van Allen

This book is an entrancing account of the technological and political race between the United States and the Soviet Union to launch satellites of the Earth.

On the one hand, it is a well-written and readily readable story of the clashes of strong minded personalities, of heroes and their rivals, of competing organizations within each nation, and of failures and successes. It develops the subject as an international mystery tale, which a reader is reluctant to lay aside lest the next few pages reveal crucial elements of the unfolding plot.

On the other hand, it is a scholarly work of undeniable authenticity. It may well be the definitive chronicle of the "first space race." The authors have woven together material from an evenhanded and comprehensive scrutiny of primary documents and from personal interviews with surviving participants. These sources are footnoted unobtrusively, yet thoroughly, and suggestions for further reading are offered.

Even participants in the famous space race, as I was, will gain a much improved context for their own fragmentary knowledge. The authors convey a detailed perspective of grand aspirations and heroic endeavors. Above all, the authors provide participants and non-participants alike, as well as their progeny, with insight into a prominent feature of the U.S./U.S.S.R. Cold War and into the way that the space race served as a peaceful proxy for destructive military conflict.

In 1686, Sir Isaac Newton published a clear explication of the physical principle of propelling objects into orbit about the Earth. He would have treasured this book on how the feat was eventually accomplished.

Preface

It is always challenging to attempt a definitive account of a bygone era. Many disagreements and discrepancies creep into records of historical events, even those within living memory. Despite the best efforts of the authors and their many collaborators, some ambiguities remain concerning certain details of events in this narrative.

Some of those we interviewed will find accounts here that do not match their recollections. We apologize to anyone who thinks his or her word was not accepted. We never had the slightest doubt about the veracity of anyone we talked to. When memories differ, though, judgments must be made. We have done our best to weigh contemporary documentation, eyewitness accounts, photographs, and other evidence to produce what we believe is the most accurate record possible of the events leading up to the opening of the frontier beyond Earth's atmosphere.

Four other notes about the book are in order.

First, there are various ways of spelling Russian names rendered in the English alphabet. We have generally adopted the spellings used by NASA. The correct pronunciation is not always obvious from these spellings. For example, "Korolev" is pronounced as if spelled "Korolyov." English speakers may look at "Tsiolkovsky" and assume the "T" is silent, when in fact the Cyrillic character beginning this name is pronounced "Ts."

Second, Sputnik, Explorer, and Vanguard satellite designations vary between Roman and Arabic numerals, depending on the source cited (this is true even in official documents produced while these programs were underway). To confuse things further, the U.S.S.R. never gave its first satellite any real name, referring to it by the acronyms PS-1 or 1-Y ISZ ("first artificial Earth satellite"). For standardization, we opted to keep the common term *Sputnik* for early Russian spacecraft and use Arabic numbers on all satellites.

A number of abbreviations and acronyms have been used throughout the book. A list follows the acknowledgments.

Finally, all cost figures in this book, unless otherwise specified, are given in then-year dollars (that is, quoted as they were in the year they appeared, rather than being adjusted for inflation).

Acknowledgments

Any book on history, even recent history, requires a great deal of assistance. Countless people made contributions to this volume.

Among those we felt the need to single out were the space program veterans who were interviewed in person or by telephone. They included:

For Explorer—Walter Downhower, Albert Hibbs, William Pickering, Charles Stelzried, Ernst Stuhlinger, James Van Allen.

For NOTSNIK—Dick Boyd, Frank Cartwright, Frank Knemeyer, Frank St. George, Robert G. S. Sewell, Bill "Woody" Woodworth.

For Vanguard—Edgar Dix, Roger Easton, Milt Rosen, Marty Votaw, Ron Potts.

There were dozens of other contributors. These people included historians, writers, "old hands" from several organizations, and reviewers. They shared memories, sent documents, found information, arranged for photographs, gave advice, and otherwise helped make this book possible. Our alphabetical list of people to thank includes Pete Alway, Barb Anderson (Jet Propulsion Laboratory [JPL]), John Bluth (JPL/Sherikon Space Systems), Skip Bradley (Air Force Space Command [AFSPC]), Len Cormier (formerly of the National Academy of Sciences), Arnie Crouch, James A. Davis, Dwayne Allen Day (National Air and Space Museum [NASM]), Leroy Doig (Naval Weapons Center), Chuck Donaldson, Amy Downing (Naval Research Laboratory [NRL]), Fred Durant (former President, American Rocket Society), Curtis Emerson (Goddard Space Flight Center), Joanne Gabrynowicz (Center for Law and Remote Sensing), Al Hartmann (Cape Canaveral Air Station [CCAS] Museum), Linda Greenway (NRL), R. Cargill Hall (National Reconnaissance Office), George W. Hoover II, Kaylene

Hughes (Army Aviation and Missile Command [AMCOM]), Robert Jacques (NASA Marshall Space Flight Center), Pat Johnson (MEI), Stephen B. Johnson (*Quest* magazine), Jeff Joyce, Hansen Kalak, Robyn Kane (MITRE Corp.), Roger Launius (NASM), Cliff Lethbridge (CCAS Museum), Andrew LePage, David Livingston (The Space Show), Skip Macaw (Booz Allen Hamilton), Jonathan McDowell (Harvard Center for Astrophysics), Henry Magill, Earl Mayfield (formerly of the Naval Weapons Center), Claus Martel (AMCOM), Jim McDade (Moonshot Web), Ron Miller, Donna McKinney (NRL), Thomas Moore (Johns Hopkins University), Mike Neufeld (National Air and Space Museum), Wes Oleszewski, James Oberg, Peter Pesavento, Joel Powell, Ted Soros, Andreas Schulz, Peter Stickney, Asif Siddiqi, Rick Sturdevant (AFSPC), Brian Wilcox (JPL), and David van Keuren (NRL), plus the staff at Texas A&M University Press.

From Matt: In addition to Erika, my friend and collaborator, I give special thanks to my employer, Booz Allen Hamilton, and the people there who have encouraged my work—Tony Williams, Dave Shiller, Lisa Reed, Vic Villhard, Dave Snyder, Kurt Stevens, Harry Kingsbery, and Glen Bruels, among others. Thanks are also due to my former colleagues from ANSER, Pat Johnson, John Haaren, Les Hamlin, Chuck Schwalier, and Jim Wilson. I especially thank Robyn Kane for her friendship and support. Finally, I owe a great deal of appreciation to my wife, Deb, for her patience and encouragement.

From Erika: Special thanks and appreciation to Matt Bille for his never-ending enthusiasm and steadfast belief in this project. Thanks also to my many friends, who have supported me throughout all of my endeavors, and to James and Loren Ridinger, for showing me how to turn my occupation into my avocation. I love you all.

Acronyms and Abbreviations

A-4	Aggregat (Aggregate) 4
AAF	Army Air Forces
ABL	Allegheny Ballistics Laboratory
ABMA	Army Ballistic Missile Agency (formerly Army Ordnance Guided Missile Center)
AFMTC	Air Force Missile Test Center
AOMC	Army Ordnance Missile Command
APL	Applied Physics Laboratory
ARDA	Astronautical Research and Development Agency
ARPA	Advanced Research Projects Agency
ARS	Advanced Reconnaissance System
ARS	American Rocket Society
ASAT	Antisatellite
ASROC	(Navy) Anti-submarine Rocket
BIS	British Interplanetary Society
BuAer	(Navy) Bureau of Aeronautics
BuOrd	(Navy) Bureau of Ordnance
CEP	Committee on Educational Policies
CIA	Central Intelligence Agency
COPUOS	Committee on the Peaceful Uses of Outer Space
CSAGI	Special Committee for the International Geophysical Year (from French initials)
DARPA	Defense Advanced Research Projects Agency
DoD	Department of Defense
DOVAP	Doppler, Velocity, and Position

ESV	Earth Satellite Vehicle
fps	feet per second
GALCIT	Guggenheim Aeronautical Laboratory at California Institute of Technology
GDL	Gas Dynamics Laboratory
GE	General Electric Company
GIRD/MosGIRD	
	Group for studying Reaction Propulsion / Moscow GIRD
GNP	Gross National Product
GPS	Global Positioning System
HATV	High Altitude Test Vehicle
Hi-Hoe	Hydrogen, Helium, and Oxygen Experiment
HOTROC	NOTS designed motor for Navy's ASROC (Anti-submarine Rocket)
IAF	International Astronautical Federation
ICBM	Intercontinental Ballistic Missile
IGY	International Geophysical Year
Institut Rabe	
	German-Russian Group (abbreviation for German terms for rocket manufacturing and development)
IRBM	Intermediate Range Ballistic Missile
I_{sp}	"specific impulse" (energy per mass of propellant expended)
JATO	Jet Assisted Take-off
JPL	Jet Propulsion Laboratory
KIK	Soviet satellite tracking system
LEO	Low Earth Orbit
lox	liquid oxygen
MHz	megahertz
MOUSE	Minimum Orbital Unmanned Satellite of the Earth
NAA	North American Aviation
NACA	National Advisory Committee on Aeronautics
NAS	National Academy of Sciences
NASA	National Aeronautics and Space Administration
NAVSPASUR	
	Naval Space Surveillance System
NDEA	National Defense Education Act
NII-4	Scientific-Research Artillery Institute of Rocket-Propelled Armaments (Soviet Union)
NII-88	Scientific Research Institute #88 (Soviet)

NKVD   Peoples Commissariat for Internal Affairs (Soviet secret police)

NOTS EV-2   NOTS Exoatmospheric Vehicle 2

NOTS   Naval Ordnance Test Station

NOTSNIK   Naval Ordnance Test Center (NOTS) + "nik" (from *Sputnik*)

NRL   Naval Research Laboratory

NSC   National Security Council

NSF   National Science Foundation

OKB-1   Special Design Bureau 1 (Soviet Union)

OKB-46   Special Design Bureau 46 (Rocket Engine Development Center)

ONR   Office of Naval Research

PARD   Pilotless Aircraft Division

Project SCORE
            Signal Communication by Orbiting Relay

Project ORDCIT
            JPL contract with Army Ordnance (ORD for Ordnance; CIT for California Institute of Technology)

RAND   Research and Development

RASCAL   Rapid Access, Small Cargo, Affordable Launch

RCA   Radio Corporation of America

RMI   Reaction Motors, Inc.

RNII   Reactive Science Research Institute (Soviet Union)

RTV   Reentry Test Vehicle

RV   Reentry Vehicle

SAC   (U.S. Air Force) Strategic Air Command

SAMOS   Satellite and Missile Observation System (or Satellite)

SIP   Solar Instrument Probe

SLV   Space Launch Vehicles (Project Vanguard)

SolRad/GRAB
            Solar Radiation/Galactic Radiation and Background

SS   Schutzstaffel (Nazi secret police)

STL   Space Technology Laboratories

TiPS   Tether Physics Experiment

TIROS   Television Infrared Observation Satellite

TPESP   Technical Panel for (or on) the Earth Satellite Program

TsKB-1   Central Design Bureau 1

TVs   Test Vehicles (Project Vanguard)

U.S.S.R.   Union of Soviet Socialist Republics

UDMH   Unsymmetrical dimethyl hydrazine

UFOs   Unidentified Flying Objects
USNC   U.S. National Committee
V-2   Vergeltungswaffe ("vengeance weapon") 2
VfR   Verein für Raumschiffahrt (Society for Space Travel)
VOG   Vanguard Operations Group
VP-1   Vertical Probe-1; recoverable Earth photography experiment
WAC   Without Attitude Control (Corporal)
WGEI   Working Group on External Instrumentation
WGII   Working Group on Internal Instrumentation
WS-117L   Weapon System 117L

The First Space Race

Introduction
The Race to Valhalla

The term "space race" is a cliché by now. Everyone knows how the United States and the Union of Soviet Socialist Republics (U.S.S.R.) pitted their technical prowess against one another in an epic battle to reach the Moon, a contest that ended with the triumphant words "The Eagle has landed."

The grandeur of the lunar adventure has almost wiped from popular history the importance of another contest: the first race into space. From 1955 to 1958, three dedicated, talented teams of engineers—two American, one Soviet—were locked in a race to capture the world's imagination. The Soviets knew little of the Americans. The Americans knew even less about the Soviets. And the two American teams knew about each other all too well. The race to Valhalla—the mythical hall of immortality in the sky—ushered in the Space Age with a tumultuous saga of science, politics, technology, engineering, militarism, and human dreams.

In today's era of space shuttles, Mars rovers, and the International Space Station, it is difficult to imagine just how challenging the first steps into space really were. In 1955, the concept of an artificial satellite had been demonstrated only on paper. No one knew just where the atmosphere ended, or what the cosmic-radiation environment would be above it. The theory of satellites was well understood, but would it work in practice?

The first nation to answer this question would gain advantages in areas as diverse as science, international politics, the Cold War propaganda contest, and the military balance. Visionaries such as America's Wernher von Braun and Russia's Sergey Korolev knew that all these fields of endeavor would be affected by an artificial Earth satellite. Moved by patriotism, inquisitiveness, and pride, countless people on both sides of the Iron Curtain worked diligently to make that satellite a reality.

Some aspects of this story are famous. Some, like the U.S. Navy's NOTSNIK satellite project, were secret at the time and remain almost unknown today. Even some details of well-known programs, such as the appearance of America's pioneering *Explorer 1* satellite, are generally misrepresented in the history books and museums devoted to this pivotal era.

This book is our attempt to tell the whole story of the first space race. The tale begins with the origins of space-flight theory and continues through the military and political events that engendered the massive government support needed to turn the ideas of the space and rocket pioneers into reality. At the end of the race, not only had the satellite programs themselves been accomplished, but the technology developed in the process was opening up space to new applications that would forever change life on Earth.

In recounting this saga, we have tried to fill in the gaps between the better-known events and personalities, introducing some overlooked but important parts of the story and correcting some misconceptions. We invite the reader to journey back with us to those uncertain, frantic times of the 1950s, when space travel of any kind was still a dream and those who believed in it were often ridiculed as hopelessly impractical. The deep space probes, broadcast satellites, and lunar landings that came afterward were possible only because of the perseverance of those dreamers. Their story was part of the shaping of our modern world, and it deserves to be remembered.

Chapter 1

Laying the Foundations
From Kepler to the Cold War

Every revolution has its herald. The Aviation Age was announced by the coughing roar of the Wright airplane's homebuilt gasoline engine. The Atomic Age arrived with a stupendous explosion, accompanied by the light of an earthbound sun. By comparison, the Space Age crept most innocuously into being, heralded by nothing more than the electronic "beep" of a small satellite.

That revolutionary satellite—*Sputnik 1*—was not much to look at, either. It was a simple metal sphere with four trailing antennas, measuring only 23 inches in diameter and weighing just 184 pounds. Yet never in history has a more profound and lasting wave of change been set off by so insignificant a device.

The idea of placing an artificial satellite in orbit about the Earth was not a twentieth-century concept. In 1869, American writer Edward Everett Hale published a science-fiction story concerning a large, manned satellite. Hale's satellite was a communications station built of brick, and the story was appropriately titled "The Brick Moon."

How could Hale have come up with such a notion? The basics of orbital mechanics had been worked out in the early 1600s by German astronomer Johannes Kepler (1571–1630). While working in Prague in 1609, Kepler published *Astronomia Nova* (New Astronomy), which contained the mathematical laws explaining how elliptical

orbits worked. In 1610, Kepler coined the word "satellite" to describe the small bodies Galileo had discovered orbiting Jupiter.

In 1686, Sir Isaac Newton finished his landmark work on physical science, *Philosophiae naturalis principia mathematica* (Mathematical Principles of General Philosophy). Newton realized that Kepler's laws permitted, in theory, the development of an artificial satellite of the Earth. He offered the illustration of a cannonball fired from a mountaintop on a path parallel to the ground. As gravity attracted the cannonball, it would describe an arc carrying it down to the ground. The higher the initial velocity of the cannonball, the farther it would travel before striking the Earth. This was true not only because of its own speed but because the surface of the Earth curved away from it. If the projectile could be given sufficient velocity, the trajectory it described would not bring it back to the surface at all, but would keep it in a continual "falling" path around the planet.

The seed planted by Johannes Kepler and nourished by Newton would, three centuries later, give life to the world's first three major rocketry programs: one in Germany, one in the Union of Soviet Socialist Republics, and one in the United States.

In order to grow from the Keplerian inspiration, each program needed a visionary to provide roots and a builder to turn theories into machinery. In Russia, Konstantin Tsiolkovsky would be that visionary, and Sergey Korolev would lead the practical men who would build hardware on the foundation of Tsiolkovsky's theories and equations. In Germany, the theorist was Hermann Oberth, the builder Wernher von Braun. In America, the dreamer and the first major builder were both present as one man, Robert H. Goddard.

Any study of humanity's reach for space must begin with Konstantin Edvardovich Tsiolkovsky (1857–1935). Tsiolkovsky was not a university professor or a government-paid expert. He was a poor, almost totally deaf rural mathematics teacher, fired by an imagination that made him stay up nights working out the details of travel beyond the atmosphere. He also proposed jet aircraft and designed improved dirigibles, even building a miniature wind tunnel in his home in the town of Kaluga to test airship models.[1]

Tsiolkovsky followed Newton and Kepler to work out what actually could be done to build satellites and spaceships. He wrote about the possibility of an artificial satellite in 1895 and discussed the basics of space flight and orbital mechanics in two articles, one published in 1903 and the other in 1911. Tsiolkovsky expanded on Newton's thinking by applying the knowledge of gravity, atmospherics, and propulsion gained since Newton's time.

He was able to flesh out Newton's conjectures and calculate the velocity needed to propel an object so the balance of motion and gravity would keep it in a continuous circle above the atmosphere. For example, a satellite maintaining an orbital altitude of 300 miles requires a speed of 17,000 miles per hour (mph). (Due to atmospheric resistance, the perigee, or lowest altitude, of a stable orbit must be at least 100 miles above the Earth's surface.)

Tsiolkovsky realized that a giant rocket was the only practical machine that could boost a satellite above the atmosphere. He analyzed possible rocket-engine designs and propellants, finally concluding that a combination of liquid hydrogen and liquid oxygen (now commonly called "lox") would provide the greatest power and the highest efficiency. This was an impressive deduction at a time when all rockets were small, short-range devices, and when no one had yet built a rocket engine using any type of liquid propellants. Tsiolkovsky went on to derive the "rocket equation," the fundamental mathematical statement explaining a rocket's acceleration and showing how such a device could propel a spacecraft at high speed. The equation itself was not new, but Tsiolkovsky was the first to show how it could be applied to rockets used for space travel.[2] Among his many other ideas, Tsiolkovsky speculated on the means for keeping humans alive in space, designed large rockets and space stations, and developed his theory of the "rocket train"—the multistage rocket, one of the keys to space exploration.

Tsiolkovsky was little-known in his homeland until after the Bolshevik Revolution of 1918. The new government took notice of his pioneering work, as it helped promote the notion that the emergence of Communist society would foster a wave of technological progress. (It helped that Tsiolkovsky enthusiastically approved of Vladimir Lenin's regime.) In 1919, Tsiolkovsky was elected to the Russian Socialist Academy. In 1921, he was granted a lifetime pension. Until his death in 1935, Tsiolkovsky was supported and honored by the Soviet government, and more than fifty of his articles and books were published at government expense.[3]

As time would prove, Tsiolkovsky's explanation of how to orbit a satellite was perfectly correct. However, much additional information, such as the effective limit of the atmosphere, had to be obtained before the theory could be put into practice. Even more important, someone had to perfect a rocket capable of imparting the necessary direction and velocity to any object destined to become an artificial moon.

The rocket, like the satellite, was an old concept. Indeed, it was far older: the use of rockets in China dates back at least to 1045 A.D. In subsequent centuries, rocket use spread into Russia, Europe, and America. Most rockets were used for military purposes (bombardment or signaling), and all were built on the same basic design: a tube filled with solid propellant, streamlined at the nose and ignited at the tail.

Initially, all rockets were made by stuffing the tube with some variety of compacted gunpowder. Improvements made over the centuries included using nitrocellulose-based "smokeless powder" and other compounds as fuels and casting the propellant grain with an empty channel through the center to allow for faster, more even burning of the propellant. Still, the propellant force generated by these primitive rockets was orders of magnitude below that required to lift a body into Earth orbit. Much greater advances, mainly involving liquid-propellant rockets, would be needed for space flight.

While Tsiolkovsky's work was not widely circulated outside the U.S.S.R., he inspired a generation of Russian engineers and designers whose names would someday be enshrined with his in the pantheon of Soviet heroes. Three of these, all destined to play important roles in the birth and growth of space flight, were Valentin Glushko, Mikhail Yangel, and Frederich Tsander. A fourth, who would eventually lead the Soviet Union and the world into space, was Sergey Pavlovich Korolev.

Korolev was born in 1907 in the town of Zhitomir in northern Ukraine. When he saw an airplane demonstration flight in 1913, his course in life was chosen. He designed a glider at age seventeen, graduated early from the Moscow Higher Technical School, and went to work on gliders and powered aircraft, some of which he flew himself.

Korolev was still in his twenties when he caught the "rocket bug." He was inspired by the work of Tsiolkovsky, although it is not certain whether the two ever met. In 1930, while living in Moscow, Korolev joined an amateur enthusiast society named the Group for Studying Reaction Propulsion, known by its Russian initials as GIRD (sometimes also called MosGIRD to distinguish it from sister organizations in other cities). He worked on airplanes during the day and joined GIRD's leader, Frederich A. Tsander, in developing a liquid-fuel rocket engine in his spare time.

Tsander (1887–1933) had been writing about space travel and rockets since 1908. He was a successful aircraft designer who believed the future of aviation lay in rocket-powered airplanes, which would eventually take the first steps into space. (His children were named Astra and Mercury.) While his designs were impractical, Tsander developed ideas about aircraft-rocket hybrids that foreshadowed the space shuttles of today.[4]

Valentin P. Glushko was another key player in early rocket design. In

1923, at fifteen, he was already such a rocket enthusiast that he began corresponding with Tsiolkovsky. By 1928, he was working as an engineer with the Gas Dynamics Laboratory (GDL) in Leningrad. Here he developed artillery rockets, designed liquid-propellant engines, and even built working models of electrical propulsion systems—an idea decades ahead of its time.[5]

In 1932, with Tsander's health failing, Korolev assumed leadership of the Moscow GIRD.[6] Korolev's legendary determination was already visible. On one occasion, he outfitted a GIRD member with a fake Red Army officer's uniform and sent him to requisition a lathe from the Heavy Industry Commissariat.[7] Around that time, Marshal Mikhail Tukhachevsky, the Army's chief of armaments, took an interest in GIRD's work and began to supply it with modest financial support (as he had already been doing for GDL).[8]

In August 1933, another GIRD enthusiast, thirty-two-year-old Mikhail K. Tikhonravov, took center stage. Like many other early rocketeers, Tikhonravov, a 1925 graduate of the Zhukovsky Air Force Academy, was an aircraft engineer. On August 17, he led the GIRD team that launched the world's first hybrid-propellant rocket. The 40-pound device used lox with a semi-solid fuel (gelled gasoline, similar to napalm). In December of the same year came the successful flight of the all-liquid GIRD X. This was a sleek, modern-looking rocket using a motor based on a design by Tsander.[9] It was slightly over seven feet tall and weighed 66 pounds. Two years later, Tikhonravov launched Russia's first instrument-carrying meteorological rocket.

Before anyone outside the U.S.S.R. became familiar with Tsiolkovsky, other researchers, notably Germany's Hermann Oberth and America's Robert Goddard, independently duplicated much of his work.

Hermann Oberth was born in 1894 in Hermannstadt in what was then Austria-Hungary. As a boy, he read Jules Verne's *From the Earth to the Moon* until he had it memorized. He realized Verne's idea of space travel via a giant cannon was impossible, and he began to think seriously about how such travel could be accomplished. This led him into the study of rockets. After World War I, Oberth began studies in physics. In 1922, he submitted his thesis at the University of Heidelberg. It was rejected because the topic—the use of rockets for space travel—was deemed impractical and outlandish. Undaunted, Oberth turned the thesis into a short book called *The Rocket into Interplanetary Space.* Although some experts continued to dismiss Oberth's ideas, his book sparked widespread discussion of rocketry by academics and scientists who had previously ignored this immature field of technology.

The Rocket into Interplanetary Space also caught the attention of the public in Germany and elsewhere in Europe. While not a best-seller, it was surprisingly popular for a book laced with equations that many of its readers could not understand. Throughout his career, Oberth worked diligently and successfully to popularize rocketry and the notion of space travel. He wrote a much more detailed book *(Ways to Space Travel)*, taught, and lectured widely. He even served as technical advisor for one of the first science fiction films, Fritz Lang's 1929 classic *Frau im Mond (The Girl in the Moon)*. (Tsiolkovsky performed a similar service for the first Soviet space film, the 1935 *Kosmicheskoye putechestviye (Space Journey)*.[10]

Like Tsiolkovsky, Oberth believed in the necessity of developing liquid-fueled rockets. He, too, thought about the need to rid large rockets of excess weight by discarding empty propellant tanks and other structures—the staging concept. As a result of his correspondence with Tsiolkovsky, Oberth learned the Russian's ideas pre-dated his own. He promptly gave credit to Tsiolkovsky in his writings, introducing the West to the Soviet scientist.

In 1930, Oberth fired the first test model of his own design for a liquid-fueled rocket engine. Working with him were some students from the Technical University of Berlin. One of them was Wernher von Braun.

Oberth did not know that a rocket using liquid propellants had already been flown in the United States. That launch was accomplished by a lone experimenter, physicist Robert H. Goddard, on March 16, 1926. Goddard, born in 1882, was the father of rocketry in the United States and a pioneer in countless aspects of rocket design. His objective, he wrote, was to turn the rocket into "a dependable scientific tool which could lift recording instruments to a greater height into the atmosphere above the Earth's surface than has been possible by means of balloons or any other device previously developed."[11]

Goddard began his work before the First World War, originally focusing on solid-fuel rockets. In 1914 he received the first American patent for a two-stage rocket design.[12] In the same year, he patented the concept of using a combustion chamber and a nozzle to replace the simple pipe-like container in which the rockets of the day burned their fuel.[13] He was having some success raising the Army's interest in rocket weapons when the Armistice of November 1918 brought the Great War to a halt and ended virtually all American military research and development.

Goddard forged ahead on his own. His historic first launch of a liquid-fueled rocket took place on a farm near Auburn, Massachusetts. The launch tower was based on a windmill frame ordered from a Sears Roebuck catalog.[14] The rocket was 10 feet long and weighed just over 10 pounds. It was powered by gasoline and lox. The altitude reached during the rocket's 2.5-second flight was about 40 feet. Goddard estimated its velocity at 60 miles per hour (mph).[15] At the time, he made no public announcement of the launch.

In a speech commemorating the seventy-fifth anniversary of this flight, Roger Launius, then chief historian of the U.S. National Aeronautics and Space Administration (NASA), reflected on the event's importance. "Many people date the beginning of the space age from the launch of *Sputnik 1* on October 4, 1957," he said. "One could also say that it really began when Robert Goddard successfully launched the first liquid-fueled rocket. Liquid-fueled rockets are what makes it possible to reach the high frontier of space, and Goddard recognized before virtually anyone else that developing that technology was critical to exploring (space)."

In 1926, Goddard was known to the American public in part as an object of derision. His 1919 monograph on rocketry, "A Method of Reaching Extreme Altitudes," came to the attention of the *New York Times,* where it was ridiculed, in an otherwise positive editorial, for claiming rockets could function in a vacuum.[16] The *Times* writer could not have read the paper very carefully, since Goddard described testing his rocket engines successfully in vacuum chambers.[17] In fact, Goddard proved that a properly designed rocket reaches its greatest efficiency under vacuum conditions.

In order to understand the development of rocket propulsion, it is useful to review what is meant by "efficiency." The efficiency of a rocket motor—the thrust produced for a given mass of propellant—is expressed as specific impulse, which is stated in seconds. There is a maximum specific impulse (abbreviated I_{sp}), obtainable from any particular combination of propellants. Engine design, the ratio of fuel to oxidizer, and other factors affect how close to the theoretical maximum efficiency a motor will actually be.

A few examples will illustrate this principle. Germany's famous V-2, fueled by lox and ethyl alcohol, had a maximum (vacuum) I_{sp} of approximately 250 seconds. A rocket motor using kerosene and lox, a favorite combination in the Soviet space program, might approach 360 seconds. The most efficient large rocket motor ever built, the Space Shuttle Main Engine, uses a ratio of six parts lox and one part liquid hydrogen to produce a vacuum I_{sp} of 445 seconds. As for solid fuels, a gunpowder rocket's I_{sp} is limited to 218 seconds, while the Shuttle's solid rocket motors, burning aluminum powder and ammonium perchlorate, are rated at 269 seconds.[18] All these figures are much lower in the dense air at sea level.

Although Goddard became both the focus of absurd hype about moon rockets and the object of unfair characterization as a foolish dreamer, not everyone ridiculed his work. Hermann Oberth wrote him asking for a copy of his paper (Goddard sent one) and later credited Goddard with both inspiring new ideas and validating those he already had worked out on his own.[19]

After the *Times* experience, Goddard published very little.[20] He preferred to work in isolation with a small team of assistants. This limited the impact of his countless innovations. Goddard did, however, exchange some publications with a Russian space enthusiast and writer, Nikolai Rynin of Leningrad, in 1926. In 1927, a technical exhibition, probably the world's first on rockets and space travel, was held in Moscow. Illustrations and models showed not only the concepts of Tsiolkovsky but also those of Oberth and Goddard.[21] According to Korolev's major American biographer, James Harford, Korolev likely attended this event and may have participated in it.[22] Even though Germany's Oberth was the only one of these early enthusiasts who actively publicized his work, the knowledge of rocketry was already seeping across borders and cross-fertilizing future space programs.

Russia was not the only nation in which amateur societies would prove instrumental in early rocket development. In 1933, the British Interplanetary Society (BIS) was formed. While Britain was not destined to develop an independent space program, BIS members produced many influential studies and publications in the pre-satellite era. It was BIS chairman Arthur C. Clarke who, in the magazine *Wireless World* in October 1945, published an article on the utility of placing communications satellites in geosynchronous orbit, some 22,300 miles above the Earth's equator. At this altitude and inclination, he maintained, a satellite would match the planet's rotation, effectively hovering over one spot. The use of the geosynchronous orbit is the founding principle on which today's multi-billion-dollar communications satellite industry is built.

In 1930, the American Interplanetary Society was founded in New York City. Its purpose was the "promotion of interest in and experimentation toward interplanetary expeditions and travel." In 1934, the group was renamed the American Rocket Society (ARS). The reclusive Goddard spurned the Society's request for his assistance, but the organization grew steadily, launching its own experimental rockets in the 1930s and providing a breeding ground for the first generation of American rocket engineers. The Society's *Bulletin* became a pioneering source for the publication and exchange of technical information on rocketry.[23]

Goddard eventually did receive financial support from the Guggenheim

Foundation and the Smithsonian Institution. Aviation hero Charles Lindbergh was an important advocate for the funding of his work. The workshop Goddard established in New Mexico in 1930 produced a wealth of new and improved rocket technology, although dissemination of this knowledge remained very limited.

In 1936, the Smithsonian published a report by Goddard entitled, "Liquid Propellant Rocket Development." Like his earlier work, it received little attention in the United States government or industry. It was more influential abroad, especially in Germany.[24]

The most significant pre-World War II event in U.S. rocketry, aside from Goddard's work, was the birth of a new center of rocket expertise in California. In 1936, Theodore von Kármán, a leading aerodynamicist and director of the Guggenheim Aeronautical Laboratory at the California Institute of Technology (GALCIT), agreed to a proposal from graduate student Frank Malina to develop improved sounding rockets for carrying instruments on suborbital flights. Malina's team was named the Cal Tech Rocket Research Project. After an experimental engine run filled a building on campus with a toxic cloud, the group was nicknamed "The Suicide Squad."[25]

The team worked with both solid and liquid fuels, initially purchasing instruments with the members' own money. Engines were tested in a makeshift proving ground in a canyon called Arroyo Seco, about three miles from the Rose Bowl in Pasadena, where the GALCIT staffers ignited their creations from behind sandbag barricades. Malina's team was aware of Goddard's work, but obtained only limited cooperation from America's leading rocket scientist. Working independently, GALCIT would duplicate and, eventually, surpass much of Goddard's technology.

In July 1939, von Kármán and Malina persuaded the National Academy of Sciences (NAS) to provide $1,000 to the Project for development of Jet-Assisted Take Off (JATO) rockets to help heavily laden aircraft climb off the runway.[26] The program was referred to as "Jet Propulsion Research" because the very word "rocket" still had an outlandish "Buck Rogers" connotation. Caltech leased land from the city of Pasadena and established a permanent home for the Project's experiments.

This contract was the first significant government-funded rocket program in the United States. By 1942, solid- and liquid-fueled JATO units had been tested successfully. The original Project members formed the Aerojet General Corporation, with von Kármán as president, to manufacture the rockets.[27]

Malina and von Kármán also continued their GALCIT work, plunging

Early GALCIT rocket motor experiments in Arroyo Seco. JPL
M-49A. Courtesy NASA/JPL/CalTech

into new types of military rocketry. In November 1943, an analysis of possible German missile performance, written for the Army, carried the name "Jet Propulsion Laboratory" (JPL) for the first time. As the initial trickle of information on German work turned into a river, Army funding to JPL rose dramatically. By 1944, JPL had a long-term contract with Army Ordnance to create Project ORDCIT ("ORD" for Ordnance, "CIT" for California Insti-

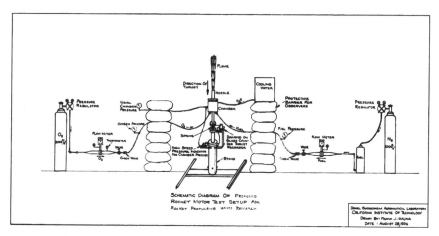

Diagram of GALCIT rocket motor test arrangements. JPL P-9023. Courtesy NASA/JPL/CalTech

tute of Technology) for missile research. From this point, JPL became increasingly independent of Cal Tech and more an Army facility operated by the university.

While the GALCIT project was still in its infancy, Goddard continued to make important advances. In April of 1940, he launched the P-23 rocket, which was 21 feet tall and weighed 500 pounds. It was equipped with turbopumps to force the propellants into the combustion chamber under high pressure. Goddard's first rocket, like many other early liquid-fuel designs, had used pressurized gas for this function. The pressurized gas approach was mechanically simpler. Because each propellant tank was subjected to high pressure, however, the tanks had to be stronger and were thus heavier. Turbopumps allowed for lighter construction, since the propellant was pumped out of the tanks before it was pressurized. The P-23 was the most advanced rocket in the world except for the products of classified military experiments in Germany, which Goddard knew nothing of.

In May 1940, with war raging in Europe and the United States stepping up its military preparedness, Goddard met with representatives of the Navy's Bureau of Aeronautics (BuAer), the Army Air Corps, and the Army Ordnance Department. He offered the government total access to his rocket work, including patents, facilities, and test data. The military's response was an almost total lack of interest.

At the time of Goddard's death in 1945, he held 214 patents concerning rocket technology, including advances in gyroscopic stabilization, gimbal-mounted engines for steering, combustion chamber cooling methods, turbo-pumps, flight controls, clustered rocket engines, and recovery systems.

German rocketeers infringed on several of Goddard's patents, although there was nothing anyone could do about this during a war. In any event, the infringement was largely unintentional. Goddard's patents were unpublished and were not available overseas. While the Germans drew inspiration and some general ideas from Goddard's few published works, they had to develop the specific technology on their own.[28]

When Goddard learned details of the German V-2 in 1944, though, he was stunned by the similarities to his smaller rockets. "I don't think he ever got over the V-2," one colleague said. Goddard was convinced he could have given the United States superior rockets if he'd had the kind of government support that Germans like Wernher von Braun received.[29]

Of all Goddard's innovations, the construction of the first liquid-fuel rocket was probably the most important. Until 1926, all rockets used solid fuel. That in itself was not a constraint: solid-fuel boosters today play important roles in space flight. In the 1920s, however, there were serious limitations on the size and power of solid-fuel charges. Goddard and others also pursued liquid fuels because of another, unrelated advantage: liquids can be controlled. A liquid-fuel rocket can be throttled, stopped, and restarted during flight.

Wernher von Braun was the key figure in developing the full potential of the liquid-fuel rocket. Born in Wirsitz in 1912, von Braun was inspired by the works of Hermann Oberth. Von Braun was a handsome young aristocrat and a natural leader who, at age sixteen, organized volunteers to build an observatory. He earned his bachelor's degree in mechanical engineering in 1932, obtaining his doctorate in physics two years later.

Von Braun was destined to play a pivotal role in transforming into reality Oberth's dream of using rockets for space exploration. In the World War to come, Adolf Hitler's Nazi government would first turn that dream into a nightmare—both for the populations targeted by rocket weapons and the thousands of concentration camp inmates who perished during their manufacture. While von Braun did not make the decision to use inmates as slave labor for rocket production, he did learn about it before the war ended, a fact he avoided disclosing for many years. Questions about the horrors connected with Germany's wartime rocket programs would follow von Braun throughout his life.[30]

Such a future was beyond imagining in 1930, when the eighteen-year-old enthusiast became a member of the *Verein für Raumschiffahrt* (VfR), or

Society for Space Travel. This was Germany's counterpart to GIRD and the ARS. Founded by rocket experimenter Johannes Winkler in 1927, the VfR focused its efforts on developing small liquid-fuel rocket engines. The VfR obtained permission to test its hardware at an inactive Army munitions depot near Berlin, which was rechristened the *Raketenflugplatz* ("rocket flying field").

The German enthusiasts flew their first rocket on May 14, 1931. The VfR's strange-looking design resembled a triangular box kite made of cylindrical tanks for the gasoline and lox propellants, with the engine at the top. It not only worked but also served as a model for the first rockets built by the American Rocket Society, which had no access to Robert Goddard's more advanced technology.

The VfR rocketeers soon received increased attention from the German Army. While some members of the club didn't want anything to do with the military, the pragmatic von Braun decided by 1932 that, "the funds and facilities of the Army would be the only practical approach to space travel."[31] By 1934, the VfR, which had run into financial difficulties, had been effectively absorbed by a branch of the Army Weapons Office *(Heereswaffenamt)* under the direction of then-Captain Walter Dornberger. Von Braun and several other VfR alumni became civilian Army employees.

Some Army officers had begun investigating rockets as early as 1930, excited by the possibility that rockets might supplement the rearming nation's still-weak artillery forces. The German rocket program thus predated the Nazi regime. While it is commonly supposed that Germany turned to rockets to circumvent restrictions on artillery imposed by the 1918 Treaty of Versailles, a review of German records by historian Michael Neufeld has found no evidence this was actually the case.[32]

After three years of work at the Army's Research Station West at Kummersdorf, the growing organization moved to Usedom Island, off Germany's Baltic coast, to establish a new development center and test range near the isolated village of Peenemunde. There von Braun directed development of successively larger and more sophisticated rockets. Oberth, who was more successful as a visionary than as a practical engineer, was seemingly unwanted—although willing to help, he worked at Peenemunde for less than two years and made no significant contributions.[33]

Before World War II erupted in 1939, the Peenemunde rocketeers had successfully flown their A-5 (Aggregate 5) test rocket to an altitude of over six miles. By this time, they had also attracted the attention of the Soviet Union, nominally Germany's ally at that point. Reports made to Soviet intelligence services in 1937 and 1938 show there was a Soviet spy at Peenemunde. Whoever this person was, his cover must have been good, for he remains unidentified to this day.[34]

The culmination of von Braun's work at the rocket development and test center at Peenemunde was the A-4. German propagandists renamed this rocket the *Vergeltungswaffe* ("vengeance weapon") 2, or V-2. (The V-1 was an unrelated jet-propelled cruise missile developed by an Air Force *(Luftwaffe)* organization.)

The V-2 had its first successful test in October 1942 and was first fired operationally in September 1944. Over the next seven months, more than 3,000 V-2s were launched. London and the crucial Belgian port of Antwerp received the brunt of the missile barrage.

The single-stage V-2 stood 46 feet tall and weighed over 28,000 pounds when filled with ethyl alcohol and lox. Propellants were fed into the combustion chamber by turbopumps driven by steam from the decomposition of hydrogen peroxide. An autopilot based on gyroscopes guided the missile and its one-ton warhead to the target. Control was achieved by aerodynamic rudders on the rocket's four fins and by graphite vanes that deflected the engine's exhaust stream.

With a maximum thrust of 58,500 pounds, a burning time of 68 seconds, and a range approaching 200 miles at a top speed of nearly 3,600 miles per hour, the V-2 dwarfed every other rocket in existence. This multifaceted leap in technology was not, of course, achieved overnight. The A-4 was the product of years of test rockets, prototypes, explosions, failures, and frustrations. Every area of rocket design was being pushed into uncertain new realms. Von Braun recalled, "Our main objective for a long time was to make it more dangerous to be in the target area than to be with the launch crew."[35]

Despite the V-2's sophistication, or rather because of it, this advanced rocket actually made no sense as a weapon. Dornberger initially promoted the rocket as a super–long-range artillery piece intended to hit specific targets such as factories and military bases, and that was how the program was sold to Hitler. However, the guidance requirements for such an application could not be met with 1940s technology. Only 44 percent of the V-2 warheads landed within a three-mile radius of the target.[36] Such lack of accuracy restricted the system to striking large targets like cities and harbors. Given the investment required (V-2 development and production cost an estimated $3 billion in 1943 dollars, more than the Manhattan Project to develop America's atomic bomb), the missile was a gigantic waste of Germany's resources.[37]

Arthur C. Clarke recognized this when he wrote in 1944, "No sane

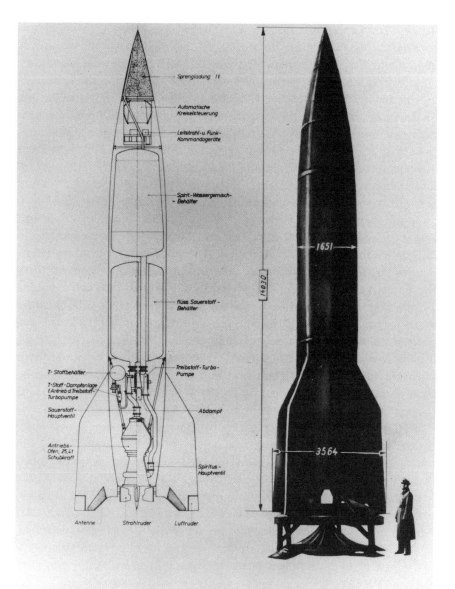

German illustration of V-2 with cutaway depiction. NASA Marshall #7995987.
Courtesy NASA/MSFC Archives

nation would make such a fantastically expensive piece of precision machinery (think of the cost of the turbine engine) to drop a ton of explosives on England. But what a break for astronautics!"[38]

However misguided the military support for the V-2 may have been, it was the reason German rocket development outstripped that of the United States. In the mid-1930s, Robert Goddard's rockets were more advanced than anything in Germany. Yet scaling up rocket technology to build something with the size and performance of the V-2 was impossible without a huge commitment of money and skilled labor. Goddard and his handful of associates could not have hoped to have made the same practical advances that von Braun's organization produced.

While neither the United States nor the Soviet Union devoted major efforts to the advancement of rocket technology during the war, they did not ignore the subject entirely. Russia's *katyusha* rocket artillery was a famous and terrifying instrument of battle. In the United States, ship-to-shore rockets were developed to prepare beaches for amphibious assaults, and air-to-ground rockets were used to blast Japanese troops out of Pacific island caves.

Many of the American rockets, including the famous antitank bazooka, drew on the work of Robert Goddard, despite the failure of Goddard's attempts to interest the Army and Navy in rockets before the war. During the conflict, Goddard worked mainly for the U.S. Navy on improving JATO rocket boosters.

The American and Russian rocket weapons used during the war were simple ballistic rockets, without guidance systems other than stabilizing fins. While Allied combatants experimented with several types of guided missiles (most being glide bombs or converted aircraft) and a few were used in combat, no country built anything approaching the size or sophistication of the V-2. The V-2 program gave Germany experience in large rocket design, production, and launching that was far ahead of the rest of the world.

As the Allies discovered when they examined German papers, the ideas of the Peenemunde engineers went far beyond the V-2. A winged version, the A-4b, had been tested twice. It was intended as a step toward the development of an operational winged missile, the A-9. While the A-9 design was ostensibly meant to extend the A-4's range, there was also a design for a manned version with landing gear and a cockpit. An audacious two-stage concept, the A-9/A-10, was on the drawing boards. (The A-9 would sit atop the A-10, a new and much larger first stage.) There were even sketches made for three-stage intercontinental missiles and orbital launchers, although the technology required for these was far beyond the state of the art.

The second-most important rocket project in Germany was, like the V-2, a precursor to space booster technology. This was an anti-aircraft missile code-named *Wasserfall* (waterfall). The Wasserfall resembled a scaled-down V-2 with an additional set of fins about midway down its body. It was 28.5 feet in height and weighed 7,800 pounds at liftoff. While the Wasserfall reached only the flight test stage, it was an influential design that incorporated two major changes compared to the V-2. The propellants were hypergolic liquids—that is, they ignited on contact. This dispensed with the need for an igniter mechanism, thus improving reliability and simplifying the engine design. The propellant tanks, instead of being separate vessels inside the rocket's fuselage, were integral parts of the structure, with the skin of the missile forming the walls of the tanks. This resulted in significant savings in weight and materials.

Studies concerning space flight were usually produced "on the side" at Peenemunde and were not shown to the military officials who were paying for missile work. Von Braun was even arrested by the Gestapo (secret police) in February 1944. One of the charges leveled at von Braun was that he cared more about spaceflight than Germany's military needs. This, his accusers claimed, meant the missile work had been "sabotaged."

Von Braun's arrest, though, was mainly part of a power play by Heinrich Himmler. Himmler controlled both the Gestapo and the Nazi Party's military arm, the SS. The SS supplied labor for V-2 missile production from its concentration camps, and Himmler wanted to consolidate control over all aspects of the V-2 program in SS hands. Frantic efforts by Walter Dornberger (who was now a brigadier general), assisted by Armaments Minister Albert Speer, succeeded in getting von Braun released and in keeping Peenemunde under the Army's direction.[39]

In January 1945, Himmler struck again, and SS Maj. Gen. Hans Kammler took control of the rocket program. Surprisingly, this turned out to be a fortunate development. Kammler was an ambitious egomaniac with many commands, titles, and responsibilities to occupy him.[40] He devoted little time to overseeing the V-2 , and Dornberger was able to take advantage of the new connection with the still-feared SS to help von Braun get his people and equipment out of Peenemunde before invading Russian troops could occupy the area.

Germany surrendered on May 5, 1945, and Japan less than four months later. The war ended with the world's landscape completely transformed. As the first signs of the new Cold War emerged, the two superpowers that now dominated the planet tried to envision the likelihood of future conflicts and the weapons they might need to wage them. America had the atomic bomb, and Russia was working hard to get it (using espionage to supplement and inform its indigenous research program). Bombs, of course, must be delivered to their targets, and therein lay most of the impetus for the great advances to come in the missile field. Against this backdrop, the V-2, while of negligible military significance, made a huge impact on the thinking of Allied leaders.

Well before the war ended, the U.S. Army initiated efforts to recruit German rocket experts willing to work in the United States. The moving force was Col. Gervais Trichel, head of the Army Ordnance Department's Rocket Development Branch. Inspired by a JPL report on the feasibility of long-range missiles, Trichel sent Capt. Robert Staver to England in February 1945 to begin developing a list of "most wanted" Germans.

Trichel also contacted Col. Holger N. Toftoy, chief of Army Ordnance Technical Intelligence, and asked him to locate 100 V-2s to be shipped to the United States. These were to be studied and launched by the Army and General Electric Company (GE). GE was already looking into ballistic missiles under an Army-sponsored effort called Project Hermes. Toftoy responded by creating his own unit, Special Mission V-2, and intensifying the search for information on German rocket facilities.

A more formal effort to find German rocket engineers and scientists, Operation Overcast, was established in July 1945. (This name was changed in March 1946 to the better-known Operation Paperclip.) The Americans did not know that von Braun was, in effect, already enroute to meet them. On January 31, 1945, Kammler had ordered Peenemunde evacuated. Von Braun and his staff had already decided they wanted to surrender to the Americans, if possible, but neither von Braun nor Dornberger had the authority to decide when or where to move. Kammler unwittingly helped the rocketeers do exactly what they wanted to do.

Heading south through the chaos of a disintegrating Germany to Bavaria, the designated "safe" area, was a harrowing enterprise. The country was in such a dysfunctional state that even Kammler's directive did not guarantee passage. Making the trip with over 500 Peenemunde employees plus families, documents, and equipment required a frantic effort. The trip's success depended on forged orders concerning a nonexistent secret project, an illegally commandeered train, and numerous other improvisations. The rocketeers also had to outmaneuver the SS, since Kammler wanted them kept in "protective" custody in the town of Oberammergau.

Some of the evacuees eventually gathered in Oberjoch, outside of Kammler's area of influence. From there, Wernher von Braun's brother Magnus went to look for Allied troops.

On May 2, 1945, near the village of Schattwald, American Pfc. Frederick Schneikert saw a blond civilian on a bicycle. Speaking in German, he ordered the man to stop and raise his hands. The civilian replied in English, "I am Magnus von Braun. My brother invented the V-2. We want to surrender."[41]

After some initial confusion, enterprising American officers gathered the cream of German rocket experts and technology. The Army eventually brought the top V-2 personnel, including von Braun, to the United States. Some 14 tons of paperwork—designs, reports, production records, and test results—also were retrieved and shipped to America, along with entire trainloads of missile parts and other hardware.

Von Braun and most of his key people entered into an initial six-month contract to work for the U.S. Army. Von Braun received the highest salary under this arrangement: $750 a month. The 115 Germans deemed most valuable were prepared for transit to the United States.[42] Their families could not accompany them immediately, but a compound was established in Germany where family members could live under U.S. protection.

After the Paperclip exodus, other Germans came to the United States to take posts in military or commercial aerospace programs. The U.S. Air Force, following its "birth" in 1947, was instrumental in bringing over additional German experts. These included Walter Dornberger, who joined Bell Aircraft Corporation. Another latecomer was propulsion engineer Krafft Ehricke, who worked first for the Army and then made major contributions to space flight at Convair. Still others were hired by the governments of Britain and France, contributing to rocket work in those countries.[43]

While Soviet leaders were as impressed by the V-2 as their Western counterparts, the U.S.S.R. was a distant second in the race to acquire German rocketeers and hardware. On April 19, 1945, the State Committee for Defense created the Russian equivalent of Operation Paperclip, directing the formation of TsKB-1 (Central Design Bureau 1) to recover German rocket technology. TsKB-1's work, however, was carried out too slowly. Russian efforts to find German rocketeers netted many technicians but only a few men with significant knowledge, even though the Soviet occupation zone (which became East Germany) included all the important V-2 sites.

The Soviets took over what was left of Peenemunde, where much of the equipment had been blown up by the Germans. They also captured the main V-2 assembly plant (the *Mittelwerk*) in the Harz Mountains, which they discovered had been scavenged by American troops before being turned over to Russia.

Soviet Premier Josef Stalin was incensed about the failure of his forces to capture more of Germany's technological treasures. Stalin was aware Germany had been pursuing a rocket program: indeed, some of the pre-war espionage reports from Peenemunde had been sent directly to him.[44] Although Stalin had not paid particular attention to missile development during the war, he was always interested in improving the technological base of the Soviet military. Now he wanted to find out what Russia could gain from the German work.

While the Americans got first pick of the German rocket engineers, Russia did not come out empty-handed. The Soviets quickly set about re-cruiting all available German rocketeers who had remained in their home-land. By August 1945, reconstruction of the V-2 was underway near the Mittelwerk in the town of Bleicherode.

A German-Russian group called Institut Rabe ("Rabe" is an abbrevia-tion of the German terms for rocket manufacturing and development) was established in a former electric power station in Bleicherode. The Germans were led by V-2 guidance engineer Helmut Grottrup. Grottrup initially lived in the American sector of Germany. He moved to the Soviet zone by his own choice, apparently because of his desire to stay with his family and the opportunity to play a major role in rocket development.

In May of 1946, Stalin signed a U.S.S.R. Council of Ministers decree titled, "Issues of Jet Armament." This officially approved a program to de-velop long-range missiles and to establish the required organizational structure. A classified nine-member special committee, headed by Georgi Malenkov, was to oversee all related work. As Malenkov had no technical expertise in rocketry, the key role was played by one of his deputies, Dim-itri Ustinov, head of the Ministry of Armaments.

Ustinov was a thirty-seven-year-old engineer who had risen quickly through the ranks, his success based in part on his own ability and in part on the fall of so many senior officials to the political purges of the late 1930s. At his initiative, several new research institutes were created to im-plement the 1946 decree. One of these was Scientific Research Institute # 88 (NII-88). This organization was housed in a converted tank plant in Podlipki, outside Moscow. Here Korolev was named chief designer in De-partment 3 of the long-range missile branch. Another new organization was OKB-46, a rocket engine development center in which Glushko was appointed chief designer.

There remains some controversy over how critical the German contri-bution was to the rapid progression of Russian missile development. Russia's first operational missile, the R-1, was a V-2 copy, although no Germans worked on it directly. German design work already done for the larger missiles and more powerful engines intended to follow the V-2 must have been useful to Korolev and Glushko. German manufacturing hardware and electronic technology was perhaps even more significant, since the Soviet Union lagged a decade or more behind Germany in both these areas.

In October 1946, Grottrup and over two hundred of the German rocket engineers and technicians working under him were forcibly relocated to the Soviet Union. They were part of a larger wave of unwilling emigrants from a variety of German industrial sectors, totaling more than five thousand people.

Grottrup's group worked on a variety of rocket projects, initially with their Soviet counterparts but later in isolation on the island of Gorodomlya in Lake Seliger, northwest of Moscow. Some Germans remained in Russia as late as 1954 before they were allowed to return home.

If the Russians had to settle for smaller prizes in the race for German rocket technology, they certainly made the most of what they had. The May 1946 decree set in motion one of the greatest industrial enterprises to emerge from the war-battered Soviet Union. From this effort would eventually come the May 1954 decision to build the world's first intercontinental ballistic missile (ICBM)—which became the first satellite launch vehicle.

The end of the war and the events following Germany's surrender ended that country's role as a world leader in rocketry. In dying out, however, the German rocket program furnished people and technology to the American and Russian efforts. While no one realized it at the time, the starting gun for the race to Earth orbit had been fired.

In an ironic coda to the German rocket story, two discoveries by the Russians showed that Germany's achievements owed at least a small debt to Russia. Soviet searches of the Nazi Air Ministry turned up drawings of one of Mikhail Tikhonravov's early rockets. The drawings had been classified by the Soviet military, and no one knew when or how they had been spirited to Berlin. Then in Peenemunde itself, Soviet troops found a German edition of one of Tsiolkovsky's books on rocketry and space travel. It had been annotated throughout by Wernher von Braun.[45]

■ *Chapter 2*

Origins of the U.S. Satellite Program

In the aftermath of the most devastating war in history, some world leaders, including U.S. President Harry Truman, held out at least a brief hope for lasting global peace. It soon became clear, however, that neither the alliance that had brought victory nor the new United Nations could restrain the growing enmity between the United States and the Soviet Union.

Stalin and his inner circle, motivated by a mixture of ambition, paranoia, desire to secure their homeland against any possibility of future invasions, and belief in the global destiny of Communism, shrouded Eastern Europe behind the menacing wall of secrecy known to the West as the Iron Curtain. While Soviet leaders wanted to avoid an all-out war with the nuclear-armed West, they also wanted to establish and expand their own sphere of influence by any means short of such a war. President Truman responded with the policy of containment, intended to keep Communism from spreading any further. The most complex struggle of the twentieth century—the Cold War—would be the Earthly backdrop for humanity's efforts to reach into the heavens.

In many ways, the Cold War would also drive these efforts, as East and West competed for military advantage, political influence, and technological superiority. It was easy for Americans to believe in their own country's promise. The United States had survived with war with its homeland untouched, and American industry had done a magnificent job in turning out thousands of modern aircraft and in building the most powerful navy in history. The end of the war brought an unparalleled burst of prosperity, as the G.I. Bill made a college education possible for millions of people. Federal housing assistance through the Veterans Administration and the Farm and Home Administration sparked a building boom. The nation's Gross National Product (GNP) shot from around $200 billion before the war to $300 billion in 1950, on its way to topping a half-trillion dollars in 1960. The postwar period did bring some difficulties, including labor unrest and increasing turmoil over racial discrimination, but the country's economic prosperity was the dominant feature in the lives of most Americans.

Meanwhile, the U.S.S.R. was recovering from terrible devastation and mourning a death toll that approached twenty million. Yet, remarkably, Soviet industry had not just survived the war, it had advanced. The nation's vast military power was not, as Americans tended to believe, built entirely on massive production of crude technology. Under the most trying of circumstances, Russian industry had built aircraft comparable to the best Western types, along with the T-34/85 medium tank, generally considered the best such vehicle in the world.

What Russia did not have was the broad base of manufacturing technology and managerial expertise that permeated every industry in the United States. In Russia, technical excellence in a given field could be achieved only by a focused, intensive effort. In the country's centrally planned economy, the future of Soviet rocketry depended on the opinions of the national leaders who made the decisions about how to concentrate their resources to provide the greatest effect on actual and perceived Soviet strength. Thus, Stalin's postwar decision to support rocketry was a crucial act.

None of the combatants overlooked the role that technological advances had played in the war. The importance of technology was illustrated most vividly by the V-2 and by the American nuclear weapons that had ended the conflict with Japan—even though both long-range rockets and atomic bombs were in their infancy. By war's end, the use of scientists (both in uniform and out) as advisors and contributors to the militaries of all the combatants had reached unprecedented levels of importance.

One side effect of this phenomenon was the change in the pattern of U.S. science and technology research. Before the war, science had been the province of small laboratories, and applied science (in the form of technology) had been created mainly by corporations large and small. The Manhattan Project model, in which massive government resources were thrown at an effort to employ science in the service of national defense, was something new. It was to become permanent—indeed, predominant.[1]

In the Soviet Union, Stalin had declared well before the war that his nation could no longer be endangered by technological "backwardness."[2] After the destruction of the German invaders (who had begun the conflict with superior technology, although the Soviets had since caught up in some areas), Stalin reiterated this viewpoint and put it into practice with a vengeance. In the United States, Gen. Henry "Hap" Arnold of the Army Air Forces (AAF) voiced his belief that, while the First World War had been won by manpower and the Second by logistics, "World War III will be won by brains."[3]

Both American and Russian experts who examined the V-2 realized that Germany had done more than lay the groundwork for a powerful new class of weapons. It had also made important strides toward the technology needed to place an artificial satellite in orbit.

In the United States, the Navy's Bureau of Aeronautics (BuAer) was the first organization to further investigate this possibility. In 1945, BuAer sponsored a research effort to study an Earth Satellite Vehicle (ESV) Program. The study group, led by Comdr. Harvey Hall, concluded that a satellite for scientific research was feasible in the near future. The project went so far as to let design contracts for a launch vehicle to North American Aviation and the Glenn L. Martin Company. North American produced a design for a single-stage High Altitude Test Vehicle (HATV). The HATV was to achieve orbit in its entirety, without deploying a separate satellite vehicle. The cone-shaped configuration included nine engines burning lox and liquid hydrogen.[4]

BuAer officials looked into cooperation from the other services to provide the estimated $5 million the initial research phase of the project would cost. They quickly ran into two roadblocks. The first was money, which was very scarce in the postwar period. The second was the interservice rivalry that often plagued the U.S. military establishment. AAF General Curtis LeMay insisted space was an AAF province in which the Navy had no business.[5] The ESV concept lingered for another two years before being laid to rest in 1948.

Meanwhile, AAF leaders began their own investigation into the feasibility of a satellite. The AAF tasked Douglas Aircraft Company's Project RAND (an acronym for Research and Development), which later spun off as the independent RAND Corporation, to examine the subject. The RAND engineers reported on May 2, 1946, that an orbital launch, using a multistage rocket and a 500-pound satellite, might be feasible in as little as five years.[6]

The RAND report described three main reasons to develop a satellite. First, the authors predicted a satellite would be "one of the most potent scientific tools of the Twentieth Century." Second, a satellite launch "would inflame the imagination of mankind, and would probably produce repercussions . . . comparable to the explosion of the atomic bomb."[7] Finally, the RAND authors noted the potential military importance of satellites. A satellite could observe the weather over enemy territory, assess damage created by friendly airstrikes, and provide a communications relay station. In an accurate prediction of today's Global Positioning System (GPS), the report even suggested satellites could send navigational signals directly to missiles in flight, guiding them accurately to their targets.[8]

Unfortunately, in 1946 the United States was still in the midst of massive efforts to demobilize the war machine and slash the defense budget. Like BuAer's efforts the year before, the RAND findings failed to convince the officials controlling the relevant purse strings. No serious follow-up effort was undertaken. The complete reorganization of the U.S. military establishment under the National Security Act of 1947 further complicated rocket development, as it introduced additional uncertainty about which of the newly co-equal services—Army, Navy, and Air Force—should be in charge of what.[9]

The idea of a satellite did not die out entirely. In 1948, General Hoyt Vandenberg, then Vice Chief of Staff of the now-independent U.S. Air Force, stated his support for further investigation of a satellite program. The policy statement he signed staked out the position that the Air Force "has logical responsibility for the Satellite."[10] In December of that year, Secretary of Defense James Forrestal's annual report to the President mentioned that the ESV concept had been assigned to the interservice Committee on Guided Missiles for coordination. Still, most of the military and civilian leaders in the Pentagon ignored or forgot about the RAND report, and the Committee on Guided Missiles ended up taking no action. Forrestal's report was the last official mention in open literature of an American satellite program until November of 1954.[11]

Despite the absence of any well-funded programs for satellites or long-range missiles, some important rocketry work continued in the late 1940s and early 1950s. The chief sponsor was the Army, although the Navy and Air Force also made contributions. While the scope of American postwar rocket research was dwarfed by the Soviet effort, the flurry of American military rocket activity initiated in 1945 would pay major dividends in the decade to come. Rocket research attracted enough believers to survive the skepticism of Vannever Bush, head of the Pentagon's Research and Development Board. In December 1945, Bush ridiculed the idea of a long-range missile. "In my opinion, such a thing is impossible and will be impossible for many years," he declared.[12]

The Army established the White Sands Proving Ground near Las Cruces, New Mexico, as a rocket test center in July 1945. The service staffed the new installation with the 1st Ordnance Guided Missile Support Battalion, a group made up largely of enlisted personnel with civilian engineering backgrounds. (In 1951, these men proudly dubbed themselves the "Broomstick Scientists," after a captain who envied the promotions given out based on civilian experience said he was no more impressed by them than he would be "by a bunch of broomsticks.")[13]

When White Sands was opened, the Navy was invited to share the new proving ground for its own experiments. BuAer not only accepted the Army's offer to use White Sands, but contracted with JPL for another study on the feasibility of Earth satellites. The first major rocket developed at White Sands was the JPL-directed WAC (Without Attitude Control) Corporal, the result of a project begun in November 1944.[14] This was the first large liquid-fueled rocket funded by any agency of the U.S. government. The WAC was both a sounding rocket and a developmental step toward a planned Army bombardment missile called the Corporal.

On October 11, 1945, a full WAC Corporal, the first rocket to be launched at White Sands, was fired from Army Launch Area #1. The vehicle reached an altitude of 44.5 miles, easily setting an American record. The novel thing about the WAC Corporal, at least for an American design, was its propellant mixture. The fuel was analine (a hydrocarbon used in industrial chemical processes), and the oxidizer was red fuming nitric acid (nitric acid mixed with nitrogen dioxide). These hypergolic propellants could be stored at room temperature, without the cryogenic equipment needed to keep oxygen in liquid form. (Lox evaporates at −297 degrees Fahrenheit.) The 1,500-pound–thrust rocket was normally boosted out of its 100-foot launch tower by a solid-propellant Tiny Tim military rocket motor.

While the WAC Corporal led to the operational Corporal missile, it is best remembered for its scientific achievements. The WAC Corporal was 16 feet long without its Tiny Tim booster and had a body 12 inches in diameter. It weighed 200 pounds empty and 660 pounds at launch. In addition to holding 25 pounds of meteorological instruments, the front section contained a mechanism to release the nose cone, which came down on a parachute.

WAC Corporal being weighed prior to launch. JPL P-293-365. Courtesy
NASA/JPL/CalTech

The WAC Corporal's most famous role was in Project Bumper. The
Bumper rocket was comprised of a WAC Corporal mounted as a second
stage atop a V-2 booster. On February 24, 1949, *Bumper Round 5* reached a
record altitude of 244 miles. This Bumper rocket also reached a speed of
5,510 miles per hour, making it both the highest and fastest machine built
by any nation up to that time.[15]

Project Bumper proved the possibility of staging large rockets and
demonstrated the performance gain that could be achieved by using this
technique. Had a WAC Corporal and a V-2 each been flown separately,
their combined altitude would have been no more than 150 miles.

Even the relatively low level of guided missile activity being pursued
by the U.S. military demonstrated the need for a test range much larger
than the landlocked area of White Sands. The inter-service Committee on
the Long Range Proving Ground was established in October, 1946, to examine possible locations from which missiles could be launched in safety.
A site in northern Washington state proved unsuitable, in part because of
weather; and the initial favorite, near El Centro, California, was ruled out
due to the political difficulties involved in overflying Baja California. That

Bumper Round 8 at Cape Canaveral. On July 24, 1950, this pioneering two-stage design became the first rocket ever launched from the Cape. NASA Marshall #6759315. Courtesy NASA/MSFC Archives

left a 15,000-acre site at Cape Canaveral, just north of the now-surplus Banana River Naval Air Station on the east coast of Florida. The Naval Air Station was handed over to the Air Force in June 1949 and turned into the Joint Long Range Proving Ground Base (later renamed Patrick Air Force Base). On July 24, 1950, *Bumper Round 8* became the first rocket launched from the Air Force's new Long-Range Proving Ground at Cape Canaveral, Florida.

In the late 1940s, Cape Canaveral, the center stage on which the drama of American space exploration would be played out, was famous neither for rocketry nor for anything else. At the time Cape Canaveral was selected, the surrounding area was a sparsely inhabited patchwork of sand, inlets, mangrove swamps, and scrub palmetto forest. This hot, humid zone was inhabited by numerous alligators, occasional American crocodiles, and four species of poisonous snakes. Somewhat offsetting these attributes was the rich variety of marine life and the magnificent bird population, which included numerous species of seabirds and the now-extinct dusky seaside sparrow. Overriding all disadvantages, however, was the fact of the site's nearness to the Equator (28 degrees north) and the thousands of miles of nearly empty ocean to its east.

Following the WAC Corporal came the larger, more capable Aerobee. The Aerobee, which was a pure sounding rocket and not part of a missile program, was originally designed to replace the limited supply of captured V-2s being used for high-altitude research. The Aerojet Engineering Corporation developed the rocket for the Applied Physics Laboratory of Johns Hopkins University (APL) with funding from the Navy Bureau of Ordnance and the Office of Naval Research (ONR). The first launch was on November 14, 1947. The Aerobee used a solid booster (rated at 18,000 pounds thrust) and a liquid-fuel sustainer (4,000 pounds). An advanced version, the Aerobee-Hi, was proposed in 1952 and made its maiden flight in April of 1955.[16] The Aerobee family of rockets became the workhorses of high-altitude research over the following three decades. More than a thousand such rockets were launched.

Another branch of the American space program began its growth just at the end of the war. Members of the Naval Research Laboratory (NRL)'s Communications Security Section, headed by Ernst H. Krause, held a meeting to discuss possible new research projects. NRL engineer Milton W. Rosen suggested the laboratory's wartime experience with missiles had created a good foundation for using rockets to study the upper atmosphere. The NRL's director approved of the idea, and the Rocket Sonde Research Section began operations in December 1945.

The Section's members considered the possibility of using an artificial satellite as a platform for its research. After studying the feasibility of such an endeavor, they decided that, while a satellite could be built, the time and money to do so were not likely to be forthcoming. Accordingly, they refocused their attention on sounding rockets.

NRL researchers were excited to learn the Army would let scientists place experiments in some of the captured V-2s. At an organizing meeting on February 27, 1946, the V-2 Upper Atmosphere Research Panel was formed. Krause was named chairman. Other members included James Van Allen, a physicist with the Applied Physics Laboratory at Johns Hopkins University. Van Allen was working on a Navy missile study called the Bumblebee Project, which contributed to the development of successful ship-to-air weapons.[17] Also in the group were representatives from other scientific organizations, plus the Army Signal Corps. Krause left the next year for other duties, and Van Allen assumed the position of Chairman. Van Allen later wrote, "We had no formal organization, no official authority, and no budget. Nonetheless, we oversaw, in effect, the entire national effort in this field for over a decade."[18]

The agencies participating in the panel gained enormous experience in rocket design and application from the V-2 launches. In 1948, the organization was renamed the Upper Atmosphere Rocket Research Panel. It kept that name until 1957, when it adopted its final designation, the Rocket and Satellite Research Panel.

The panel directed the largest effort mounted to date in probing the upper atmosphere. Cameras, meteorological instruments, cosmic-ray detectors, and other experiments were flown on the sixty-three V-2s launched in the United States between 1946 and 1952. Some of these rockets reached altitudes over 100 miles. Later V-2s carried capsules that could be ejected and would (when they worked) parachute gently to the ground. The Air Force Aeromedical Laboratory even used V-2s to fly monkeys on four missions, making these test subjects the first primates ever to reach the upper atmosphere. Unfortunately, while all the monkeys survived the launch, none was recovered alive. The last monkey launch, in December 1949, is recorded in rather dry fashion in NASA's *Aeronautics and Astronautics Chronology:* "a successful flight indicating no ill effects on monkey until impact of V-2."

Given the situation prevailing during World War II and in the Cold War which followed, it is no surprise that even the rockets that became famous in the service of science were all developed with military support. The Upper Atmosphere Rocket Research Panel had several arguments with military sponsors over the classification of the data it obtained, although the scientists won every time and the information stayed unclassified.

One of the NRL's first contributions to V-2 research, agreed upon in early 1948, was the development of a new fairing to house instrumentation. Not only was the NRL's nose cone lighter and roomier than the original hardware, but it was a necessity: fifty V-2 nose cones had been lost somewhere in transit between Germany and White Sands. The NRL arranged for the U.S. Naval Gun Factory at the Washington Navy Yard to build twenty-five new V-2 fairings costing approximately $1,000 each.[19]

It was also the NRL that provided telemetering equipment, even erecting ground stations on the Army's range at White Sands for receiving and recording signals from the rockets. Thirty-five sets of the telemetering package, which handled ten channels of information and cost $3,000 per set, were ordered.[20]

Starting to fly experiments aboard the V-2s was not a simple matter. Even when the telemetry equipment and the new nose sections became available, the instruments and procedures needed a lot of work. Previous experiments on small rockets and aircraft had not subjected instruments to the high altitudes and rough launch conditions experienced on the V-2. A great deal of improvising was needed to create suitable instrumentation. In one instance, the NRL's Ralph Havens broke the tip off an automobile headlight bulb and converted it to a crude gauge to measure atmospheric pressure.[21]

Almost all U.S. V-2 firings were carried out under the direction of GE engineer Leo "Pappy" White, who led a team of more than thirty engineers and technicians based at White Sands. White was known for his heavy North Carolina accent, and he would drawl "Main stage," as the command to begin an ignition sequence. His first V-2 launching had been an eye-opening experience. No blockhouse had yet been built, so, communicating via a telephone, White directed the launch from the questionable safety afforded by lying underneath a Jeep. As the V-2 rose from the launch pad, it flipped by ninety degrees to the horizontal and flew directly at the Jeep. White bolted from under the vehicle and tore through the sagebrush like a jackrabbit—for about two seconds. He was then jerked off his feet by a yank on his right arm that nearly pulled the limb from its socket. By the time he realized what had happened—and that he was still clutching the telephone handset—the V-2 had passed overhead.[22]

Even as V-2 experiments began, NRL researchers knew they would eventually need a successor to the German vehicle. In 1946, the NRL authorized design of a replacement. Milt Rosen headed the effort. His team set the performance objective for the new rocket at "500 pounds of instruments to 500,000 feet." (The comparable figure for the Aerobee was 150 pounds to 426,000 feet, while a V-2 used as a sounding rocket could lift 2,000 pounds to 525,000 feet.)[23]

Rosen, Krause, and their colleagues designed a single-stage, fully steerable guided rocket weighing about 10,000 pounds fully loaded ("wet"). The Glenn L. Martin Company was selected to build a rocket based on the NRL design. A contract for ten such rockets, first called Neptune and then Viking, was let on August 21, 1946 (an additional four rockets were purchased later). Reaction Motors, Inc. (RMI), a small company founded by longtime ARS enthusiasts, was chosen to develop the engine. The Viking engine, designed by John Shesta, was the most advanced American design of its era. It used turbine-driven pumps and burned alcohol and lox to deliver a thrust of 20,000 pounds.

The Viking is sometimes referred to as an Americanized version of the similarly sized V-2. In fact, it was no such thing. According to Rosen, the

V-2 experience was valuable mainly for providing an example of a successful large rocket—essential for credibility in this still-immature field of technology.[24]

The Viking boasted several advances over the V-2. The NRL rocket had a superior control system, coupled to small rocket thrusters that could orient the vehicle even after the main engine stopped firing. The V-2 had had no need for a system of this type, but such a mechanism was essential for keeping instruments trained on the sun or other scientific targets. Other Viking features included a gimbaled motor that could be swiveled to provide steering, integral propellant tanks, and the use of aluminum as the main structural material.

Wernher von Braun cautioned Rosen that the Viking design might not work. Von Braun doubted the practicality of steering a large rocket with gimbaled engines (a concept tested at Peenemunde but not adopted) and was unsure of aluminum's capability to tolerate the heat built up on the surfaces of high-speed rockets.[25]

As it turned out, the Viking worked very well. There were twelve Viking launch attempts, with eleven successes, between 1949 and 1955. No two Vikings were identical, since improvements were continually made as the series progressed. The first group of seven rockets, called Type I Vikings, had a body diameter of 32 inches. The later Type II Vikings had an increased body diameter of 45 inches, which expanded the propellant capacity. Both models were about 45 feet tall. The Type II could carry over 1,000 pounds of instruments and reached a maximum altitude of 158 miles, easily surpassing the original benchmarks Rosen had set for the Viking.[26] (Von Braun was not too proud to employ technology validated by someone else: his Redstone missile for the Army made extensive use of aluminum, and its successor, the Jupiter, was steered with a gimbaled engine.)

In the end, the Viking proved too expensive to use in large quantities as a sounding rocket. A Viking cost approximately $200,000, over ten times the price of the smaller Aerobee.[27] While the ONR had emphasized from the beginning of the Viking program that its technology would be useful for guided missiles, efforts to promote Viking's conversion into a missile never attracted support.[28] The Viking contributed significantly, however, to our knowledge of the upper atmosphere and even more to the development of rocket boosters.

Since the Viking was pushing the envelope of rocket technology, it was not surprising that some mishaps occurred as well. The program produced one of the most interesting moments in the history of rocketry when *Viking 8* was bolted down to the launch pad at White Sands for a static firing

Viking 3 being readied for launch at White Sands. The launch took place on February 9, 1950, and reached an altitude of 50 miles. NRL Photo 04-03. Courtesy Naval Research Laboratory

of the engine. The rocket tore loose its restraining bolts and rose four miles into the air, dragging part of the test stand with it, before crashing to Earth.[29] Another memorable moment came when *Viking 10* caught fire on the pad. To stop the fire before it induced structural failure, Navy Lt. Joe Pitts fired a rifle bullet into the alcohol tank to vent the fuel.[30] Subsequent Vikings had a target painted over the alcohol tank in case the problem arose again.[31]

In 1954–55, the NRL was already studying the possibility of mating the Viking and Aerobee rockets to produce a vehicle for high-speed reentry system tests. This configuration, the Viking M-15 (for Mach 15) was never built. While NRL engineers had conceived the M-15 only as a test vehicle, not as a satellite launcher, it later became the basis of the launcher used in NRL's historic satellite program, Project Vanguard.[32]

After its development in 1945, the WAC Corporal did not remain the only rocket program sponsored by the Army. Two other important Army projects, both of which made critical contributions to early space efforts, were the Hermes and MX-774 programs. Hermes, while not initiated by the von Braun group, would become a keystone of its endeavors.

After the contractual arrangements involved in Operation Paperclip had been concluded, the German rocket scientists from Peenemunde were moved to the United States in three separate groups. The first batch, including von Braun, arrived on September 19, 1945. The émigrés, who went through seemingly endless rounds of interrogation and paperwork, killed time by devising an enormously complex version of Monopoly that allowed for contracts, holding companies, and other refinements. It was February 1946 before the entire team was reassembled at Fort Bliss, Texas. This was their home for the next few years, although the rocketeers spent much of their time at White Sands.

Initially, the Germans were assigned to translate their earlier work and act as consultants to American rocket projects. None of the rocket work was well-funded, and von Braun and the others often felt that their expertise was being under-utilized when they explained their technology to Americans and helped fire rebuilt V-2s.

Not that the V-2 work was without challenges. A great deal of improvising and remanufacturing was needed to replace missing rocket parts, and the rocket failure rate was high. The V-2 had been designed for a shelf life that was measured in weeks between assembly and launch. Its components were never intended to endure transatlantic shipment to the United States and a cross-country rail journey to New Mexico, followed by months or years of storage. By the time the V-2s were fired, many crucial

Hermes launch in 1945. This program led to crucial advances in engine and guidance technology. NASA Marshall #9401909. Courtesy NASA/MSFC Archives

mechanical elements were severely stressed or broken, resulting in a high mishap rate.

On May 19, 1947, came the most famous and unnerving incident. A V-2 went drastically off course and landed in a cemetery in Juarez, Mexico. No one was injured, but the diplomatic and political furor was considerable. As Earnst A. Steinhoff of the von Braun team told it,

A captured V-2 being readied for use in the research program at White Sands. NRL photo 2-6. Courtesy Naval Research Laboratory

The control system failed after 15 or 20 seconds. It was already supersonic. By the time the American officials arrived at the cemetery, all the Mexicans were collecting and gathering up pieces of the skin. They had several hamburger stands there. They sold 10 or 15 tons of relics even though the entire missile was only 4 tons![33]

Also in 1947, von Braun was allowed to make a brief trip back to Germany to marry Maria von Quistorp, to whom he had proposed by mail. The honeymoon was a bit awkward because the groom had been assigned a twenty-four-hour guard to make sure he would not be kidnapped by the Soviets. This was not mere paranoia: the Soviets had tried to snatch von Braun from American custody before he left Germany the first time, but he was too well guarded.[34]

In October 1948, the Army Ordnance Department designated Redstone Arsenal near Huntsville, Alabama, as the center of research and development activities concerning rockets. A year later, the Secretary of the Army approved the transfer of the Ordnance Research and Development

Division Sub-Office (Rocket) from Fort Bliss to Redstone. By June of 1950, the German rocket scientists and engineers, with 800 military personnel, civil service employees, and contractors,[35] were relocated as part of this organization, which was renamed the Ordnance Guided Missile Center.[36]

The rocketeers' new home was a sprawling compound originally built for manufacturing chemical munitions. It included several areas marked off-limits due to chemical contamination, and it boasted an enormous mosquito population. In spite of these unenticing features, most of the Germans enjoyed their new quarters, and many made Huntsville their permanent residence. The inevitable bad feelings among the local citizens about the presence of former enemies dissolved remarkably quickly, thanks to efforts by Army and local government officials, the enthusiastic way in which the newcomers became active members of the community, and traditional Southern hospitality. The Germans eventually became American citizens and accumulated a long list of accomplishments, including the creation of America's largest space-launch vehicles.

In July 1950, the Redstone engineers began studying the feasibility of a ballistic missile with a range of 500 miles. A year later, the specter of the Korean War and the possibility that it would widen into a conflict between the superpowers resulted in this work being prioritized and accelerated. In order to make the missile smaller, and thus more mobile, and also to speed up its development, the range requirement was cut to 300 miles. In April of 1952, the new rocket design was named Redstone, after the site of its origin.

As the missile project entered the hardware stage, the arsenal's commander, Colonel (later General) Toftoy, proved himself a reliable supporter of the Redstone program. Toftoy, who held the commander's position twice, had been instrumental in bringing V-2 technology to America and in arranging for V-2s to serve as sounding rockets. He thought it vital to maintain a community of scientists and engineers, both military and civilian, with rocket expertise. He believed that the knowledge held in such a community would provide a database of rocket design expertise important to all future missile and space programs.[37]

Toftoy and like-minded officers bent Army procurement regulations to ensure the arsenal was expanded with necessary test stands, workshops, storage areas, and all related facilities.[38] In January 1953, the office charged with the Redstone project was redesignated the Guided Missile Development Division. Von Braun was appointed the Division's chief.

The first test model of the Redstone was launched on August 20, 1953. The Redstone took some design concepts from the A-4 and incorporated additional technology from the Hermes program. (Indeed, the original vehicle concept leading to the Redstone was designated the Hermes C-1.) The Hermes effort included firing test rockets based on the Wasserfall and investigating several more advanced designs with a variety of sizes and propulsion systems. By the time the last rocket carrying the Hermes name was canceled in 1954, the program had made major contributions to rocket motor design and guidance systems.[39]

The A-6 engine used in the operational Redstone was descended from Hermes technology. A Hermes-based engine had already been developed further by the Rocketdyne division of North American Aviation (NAA) for the Navaho, an intercontinental winged cruise missile NAA was building for the Air Force.[40] The A-6 thus had this engine, the XLR-83-NA-1, as its direct ancestor.

The Redstone's liftoff mass was 62,750 pounds, and the thrust at liftoff was 78,000 pounds. The vehicle stood 69 feet tall and was 6 feet in diameter. The missile's integral tanks housed lox and ethyl alcohol. Guidance was provided by an inertial system controlling graphite exhaust vanes and small aerodynamic rudders. The front section, including the warhead and guidance mechanism, separated and reentered without the rocket body. One particular innovation was the use of a flight computer into which a target program could be loaded on tape.[41]

The other major American rocket program of the postwar period was Project MX-774. In 1945, farsighted officers of the Air Technical Service Command of the AAF let a contract for a development program intended to culminate in a guided missile with a range of 5,000 miles. This was a seemingly impossible requirement for the time, but it was undertaken by Consolidated Vultee Aircraft Corporation, better known by its later name of Convair.[42] A team led by Karel J. (Charlie) Bossart was assigned to the task. The company was awarded a contract for $1.9 million, an enormous amount for American postwar rocket research, but insufficient for a full-scale development effort.

Accordingly, a three-step approach was planned. Two series of test vehicles, the MX-774A and MX-774B, would be built before the operational MX-774C. In practice, the only design to reach flight status was the MX-774B. This rocket was nicknamed "Old Fashioned" because it looked so much like a V-2. This was no accident. Using the V-2's well-proven aerodynamic design avoided the time and effort required to develop and test an entirely new shape.

The MX-774B resembled a two-thirds-scale V-2, 31 feet high and 30 inches in diameter. However, very little of the internal structure was comparable to that of the German missile. Independently of the NRL's Viking effort (although there was some discussion between members of the two teams), Bossart used his experience in aircraft design to focus on reducing structural weight by every possible means.[43]

The first technique to reduce structural weight was to use integral tanks. These had become common in airplanes, and the practicality of their use in large rockets had been demonstrated by the Wasserfall. The MX-774B went a daring step further by using an extremely thin-walled aluminum body structure internally stiffened by pressurized nitrogen instead of a metal framework. Pressure-supported rocket bodies had been suggested by Oberth and Tsiolkovsky, but no one had yet built one.

Another innovation employed by Bossart was the use of a warhead that separated from the spent booster before re-entering the dense lower atmosphere. With the V-2, the entire rocket re-entered, creating extra drag, severe aerodynamic heating, and vibrational stress. This added weight, because the whole structure had to stand the stresses of re-entry. Many early V-2s, weakened by these re-entry forces, broke up as they neared their targets.

Finally, the MX-774B used engines that could be gimbaled, or swiveled, by rods activated by the guidance system. Four engines built by RMI, with 2,000 pounds of thrust each, were combined in a propulsion unit called the XLR-11. Given this limited amount of thrust, Bossart's obsession with weight reduction made a great deal of sense.

While the gimbaling system added complexity, it more than compensated by allowing the engines to work more efficiently. Insertion of vanes in the exhaust stream for steering reduced the V-2's effective thrust by as much as seventeen percent. With the MX-774B, the ability to move each nozzle independently allowed full control of the missile's roll, pitch, and yaw axes with a very small thrust penalty.

When Bossart was done, he had achieved impressive advances in design. Despite the MX-774B's size, its empty weight was one-eighth that of the V-2.

The MX-774B rocket had one V-2 feature that was, in retrospect, humorous. Bossart's use of the V-2 shape extended to the fins. The V-2's fins looked like right triangles with the tips cut off. When Rudolf Hermann, a member of the V-2 design team, saw the MX-774B's fin design, he laughed. The odd shape, he explained, had nothing to do with aerodynamics. The tips had been deleted from the fins only to allow the missile to fit through German railway tunnels.[44]

The AAF canceled Project MX-774 in July 1947 in favor of long-range atmospheric cruise missiles. Between 1948 and the initiation of Project MX-1593 (the Atlas) in 1951, the U.S. military had no program for long-range ballistic guided missiles. The concept of intercontinental cruise missiles never panned out, and the United States eventually returned to the ballistic approach. The delay gave the Soviets—who pursued both types of missiles simultaneously in different organizations—time to catch up to and surpass U.S. work on ballistic missiles.

After the MX-774 was canceled, Convair used leftover government funds and some of its own money to conduct three flight tests of the MX-774B at White Sands in 1948. None of the MX-774B flights were completely successful. *MX-774B No. 1*, launched on July 13, terrified the launch crew by losing thrust very early in its flight and making a thirty-foot crater only 600 feet from the blockhouse. Even this hair-raising escapade proved that the gimbaling system worked fine—so well, in fact, that the fins were unnecessary.

Innovations from the MX-774 program found their way into many later rockets, most notably Bossart's design for the Atlas ICBM. The Atlas, which stood alert as an ICBM from 1959 to 1965, gave rise to a family of launch vehicles that would still be in service four decades later.

There was also civilian rocket research going on during this period, although the scale was small. The U.S. government's civilian agency for the advancement of aviation and related technology was the National Advisory Committee on Aeronautics (NACA). Early in 1952, NACA produced a report on proposals for very high altitude flights of both manned and unmanned vehicles. These were reviewed at the June 24, 1952 meeting of the agency's Committee on Aerodynamics. As a result, committee member Robert J. Woods recommended that NACA lead a program of basic research on space flight. NACA established a working group to review the available information on the topic and to develop concepts for future vehicles.[45]

Also in 1952, NACA began a rocket research program at the Pilotless Aircraft Research Division (PARD) of the agency's Langley Laboratory at Wallops Island, Virginia. The experiments conducted by PARD addressed a number of problems, including aerodynamic heating loads placed on rockets and the physics of bodies reentering the atmosphere. In October 1954, Langley researchers flew the first American four-stage rocket. Two years later, they flew the world's first five-stage vehicle.[46] Beginning in 1954, a group of NACA engineers began studying possible reentry vehicles that could bring humans back from space.[47]

Rocketry and space travel got an international boost from the formation of the International Astronautical Federation (IAF). German and French space enthusiast organizations, joined by the British Interplanetary Society, organized the inaugural IAF Congress in Paris in 1950. Delegates from eighteen nations attended. The next year's Congress, in London, featured the first delegation from the United States. Von Braun had submitted a paper, but he was denied permission to travel abroad, so Frederick C. Durant, a Navy officer and member of the ARS board of directors, read it for him.[48]

From the first year onward, the IAF leadership invited the Soviets to participate. They began attending in 1955, when two academicians—members of the Academy of Sciences—showed up. The Commission on Interplanetary Communications of the Academy of Sciences became an IAF member in 1956. The Commission was the only government agency to be an IAF member—all other members were private organizations.[49]

The American support for the IAF had an interesting sponsor: the Central Intelligence Agency (CIA). While the CIA kept its involvement secret, Fred Durant worked for the CIA from 1951 through 1954 and continued to provide assessments to the agency thereafter. As he put it, the CIA, which was desperate for intelligence on Soviet rocketry programs, wanted "Biographical intelligence, assessment of technical capabilities (individuals and organizations), plus ears open for rumors, comments, and discussions of technical papers presented."[50]

While American rocketry was advancing, albeit in fits and starts and punctuated by funding problems and program cancellations, ideas for satellites and far more exotic space vehicles continued to surface. The subject caught the public's attention largely because of von Braun. His visions were expressed in a series of articles published in *Collier's* magazine in eight issues from March 1952 to April 1954. The series was suggested by *Collier's* to science writer Willy Ley, a German-born VfR veteran. Ley contacted von Braun, who had, by 1952, awakened to the fact that getting support for space flight in the United States was a different endeavor than the campaigning he had done in Germany.

Under the Nazis, power and money had flowed largely through the party and the military. Only a few key people had to be convinced to fund a program. In America, von Braun realized, he had to appeal to a broader audience. "I will go public now, because this is where we have to sow our seeds for space exploration!" he declared to an associate.[51] The *Collier's* opportunity was perfect.

An introduction by the magazine's editors opened with an attention-grabbing paragraph:

What you will read is not science fiction. It is serious fact. More-over, it is an urgent warning that the U.S. must immediately em-bark on a long-range development program to secure for the West space superiority. If we do not, somebody else will. That somebody else very probably would be the Soviet Union.[52]

Von Braun, teamed with *Collier's* assistant editor Cornelius Ryan, pro-ceeded to follow this rather alarmist introduction with a description of the wonders awaiting humanity: manned flights (von Braun thought in terms of military men as astronauts), space stations, and trips to the Moon and Mars. Talented artists, most notably Chesley Bonestell, turned von Braun's thoughts into spectacular illustrations of space stations, space shuttles, as-tronauts, and Moon bases.

Bonestell was already known to the American public as a painter of space vistas and space-travel scenes. In 1949, the former architecture stu-dent had collaborated with Ley on a bestselling book, *The Conquest of Space.* In a 1950 review of the book, Arthur C. Clarke commented that Bonestell's meticulous paintings had "been mistaken for actual color photographs by those slightly unacquainted with the present status of interplanetary flight."[53]

After the *Collier's* series, Bonestell's art appeared in many other publi-cations and made a significant contribution to the nation's growing interest in spaceflight. It helped that Bonestell researched his work exhaustively and became an expert on space technology in his own right. Von Braun once recalled providing his own sketches of space technology to help Bone-stell with his work, "only to have them returned to me with penetrating detailed questions or blistering criticism of some inconsistency or over-sight."[54]

The *Collier's* series led to books, more articles, and, in 1955, a series of Walt Disney Productions television specials starring the charismatic von Braun.[55] The first of these, "Man in Space," was telecast on March 9. After airing, it was borrowed for showing in the Pentagon, reportedly at the re-quest of the President.[56]

Naturally, much speculation focused on whether spacefaring machines would be followed by humans, as von Braun predicted. This was an era during which science fiction dealing with people in space was extremely popular. While this theme had been common in American fiction for many years, it picked up speed after World War II and might be said to have gone into orbit in 1950, when producer George Pal and science fiction writer Robert A. Heinlein brought out the film *Destination Moon.* This was a well-researched drama that went as far as possible, given the technology of the day, in depicting weightlessness, spacewalks, and other aspects of human space travel. Pal and a host of imitators began cranking out more space-themed films, and the emerging medium of television followed their lead.[57] Programs such as *Captain Video* and *Space Patrol* became staples of TV networks throughout the 1950s.

The 1950s was also an era of widespread interest in unidentified flying objects (UFOs). The modern UFO phenomenon got its start with pilot Kenneth Arnold's 1947 report of a chain of metallic-looking objects over Washington state and became something of a national obsession over the next few years. Millions of Americans believed UFOs were spaceships carrying intelligent beings studying the Earth—a possibility that, for several years, was given serious consideration by the Air Force and the intelligence community. If other civilizations could voyage through space, then obviously so could we.

The Air Force, in partnership with NACA, began the dramatic and successful X-15 rocket research aircraft program in March 1954. The Air Force also initiated Project 7969, "Manned Ballistic Rocket Research System," in February 1956.[58] The Army, however, lagged behind in suggesting a manned program. Although several early studies had been done, the service's formal proposal for a suborbital manned flight, project ADAM, was not officially submitted to the secretary of defense until August 1958.[59] Even the Navy belatedly got in on the act, proposing a cylindrical spacecraft with deployable wings called Manned Earth Reconnaissance 1 in April 1958. However, all military proposals for manned orbital missions were eventually rejected when President Dwight Eisenhower decided human space flight would be the responsibility of a new civilian agency.

Although the *Collier's* series sparked the American people's preoccupation with space, such interest did not mean immediate government action. The next practical step in satellite development came in 1953, when a new proposal attracted wide attention among both scientists and the military.

In that year, S. Fred Singer of the University of Maryland published plans for his MOUSE—Minimum Orbital Unmanned Satellite of the Earth. Singer was not a novice in space science. He was a former APL colleague of James Van Allen's and had worked on cosmic ray experiments launched from White Sands.[60] Singer believed MOUSE could be built using existing technology and that a suitable launch vehicle would be available within a few years. MOUSE would be a spherical satellite (there was an alternative cylindrical design as well), weighing about 100 pounds and carrying instruments to analyze solar and cosmic radiation.[61] As Van Allen recalled it, nothing in the proposal was ground-breaking to the small space science community—the concept of a satellite was "in the air all over the place"—but Singer was one of the first to lay out a detailed concept in a public forum.[62]

On June 23, 1954, Fred Durant, now president of the IAF, called Lt. Comdr. George Hoover of the Office of Naval Research. Durant knew that Hoover, a naval aviator and a multitalented engineer and inventor, had been thinking about a satellite program.

Hoover's title was Manager, Weapons Systems, Air Branch, ONR. A designer of pioneering automatic navigation systems, Hoover was interested in the problem of gathering data on the outermost reaches of the atmosphere for the high-altitude hypersonic aircraft of the future. A satellite was the logical way to do it. Durant told him Wernher von Braun would be visiting Washington for a few days and suggested the three get together to talk about the subject. Von Braun, at this point, was Director of Development Operations for the Army Ordnance Guided Missile Center. (On February 1, 1956, this organization would receive its more famous name, the Army Ballistic Missile Agency or ABMA.)

The energetic Hoover needed no urging. He arranged a June 25 meeting that included, in addition to Durant and von Braun, Fred Singer and Fred L. Whipple.[63] Whipple was a Smithsonian astronomer who had done pioneering work on optical tracking of meteors, and he was interested in applying that expertise to the challenge of tracking an artificial satellite.

As von Braun recalled it, Hoover opened the Washington meeting by saying, "Everybody talks about satellites, then nobody does anything. So maybe we should put to use the hardware we already have."[64] Von Braun had an immediate answer. The Army rocketeers had spent a lot of time, albeit unofficially, looking at that very topic.

Earlier in 1954, Charles Lundquist, who had an unusual combination of credentials—he was a Ph.D. in mathematics and a private first class in the Army—had begun working on orbital calculations in addition to his duties in the Technical Feasibility Studies Office at Redstone. He received encouragement from his office's director, Ernst Stuhlinger. At about the same time, other offices at Redstone, sparked by inquiries from von Braun, began examining the same area.[65]

When Hoover made his suggestion, von Braun responded by saying the Redstone missile would make a serviceable first stage for a satellite launch vehicle. The group was excited by von Braun's idea, and a follow-on meeting was held in August. Encouraged by the support voiced in these gatherings, von Braun's organization produced the "Minimum Satellite Vehicle" proposal, dated September 15, 1954. The launcher in this concept was the Redstone, with clusters of solid-fuel Loki rockets added to form three upper stages.[66]

Years later, reflecting on the first ONR meeting, von Braun remarked, "At that time it wasn't very fashionable to even think or talk in the Department of Defense about satellites. George Hoover's contribution to get the ball rolling should not be forgotten."[67]

A mere lieutenant commander like Hoover, however enthusiastic, could not simply agree to a major joint program with the Army. The idea was presented to Rear Adm. Frederick R. Furth, chief of Naval Research. Furth was willing to agree to the program if the chief of Army Ordnance, Maj. Gen. Leslie E. Simon, came on board.[68] While Hoover talked to the Navy, von Braun went back to Huntsville, where he quickly secured permission from his superiors to obtain Redstone stages and use Army personnel.[69] The base commander, General Toftoy, in turn talked to Simon, who gave his blessing. If anyone involved knew about the Air Force's 1948 declaration of jurisdiction over satellites, they ignored it, and the Air Force apparently made no protest.[70]

The Redstone, at this point, had been in flight testing for a year. The Loki was also a proven commodity, having been developed by JPL for the Army as an anti-aircraft rocket. The Army never deployed it as a weapon, but, beginning in 1951, it had a long career as a sounding rocket. The first person to use the Loki for this purpose was James Van Allen, who had moved from APL to the University of Iowa (then called the State University of Iowa). Van Allen mounted Lokis on harnesses under balloons to create "rockoons," which were very successful in carrying instruments to extreme altitudes for cosmic-ray research.

Van Allen was to play a major role in American space science. From a childhood filled with crystal radio sets and electric motors (he once terrified his mother with a spectacular discharge from his home-built Tesla coil), he pursued a variety of interests in physics and chemistry, and earned his doctorate in nuclear physics in 1939.[71] In 1954, at forty, he was head of the university's Department of Physics and Astronomy. His career already included service as a naval gunnery officer, a developer of proximity fuses, head of the Upper Atmosphere Rocket Research Panel, and the drafter of specifications for the Aerobee sounding rocket. Along with S. Fred Singer and others, he developed the rockoon concept with ONR support in 1951.[72] The first balloons he used could carry a Deacon sounding rocket to about 70,000 feet. There the motor was ignited and the rocket shot upward through the thin envelope of the balloon.

While not an engineer by training, Van Allen had an excellent grasp of the technology he used in his investigations of physics. He also demonstrated a talent for improvisation. In 1952, he took his rockoons aboard the U.S. Coast Guard icebreaker *Eastwind*. The *Eastwind* was headed for Greenland, which suited Van Allen's interest in studying atmospheric radiation at high latitudes. During the first two launches, the balloons worked well, but the Deacon rockets failed to fire. Suspecting the intense cold was putting the launching timer out of commission, Van Allen heated cans of orange juice and packed them around the mechanism. The next rocket worked perfectly.[73]

On April 5, 1950, Van Allen hosted a gathering of scientists at his home in Silver Spring, Maryland, to discuss international cooperation in scientific research. The guest of honor was one of the world's leading geophysicists, Sidney Chapman of Great Britain. In the course of the discussion, American physicist and engineer Lloyd V. Berkner asked Chapman, "Sydney, isn't it about time we had another International Polar Year?"[74] (International Polar Years, periods devoted to international cooperation in the study of the polar regions, had been organized in 1882–83 and 1932–33.)

Chapman enthusiastically endorsed the suggestion and became its major international promoter. The idea of a Third International Polar Year was later broadened and renamed the International Geophysical Year (IGY). The IGY, which would run from July 1957 to December 1958, would also spur the United States and the Soviet Union to adopt Earth satellite programs. As a 1959 article in *TIME* magazine put it, "The race into space may be said to have started in Van Allen's living room that evening in 1950."[75]

Lloyd Berkner and Sidney Chapman did not originally discuss satellites. As the IGY agenda included the study of the atmosphere, though, it was inevitable that the topic would come up. Those like Van Allen and Singer, who studied the environment high above the surface, including the effects of solar radiation and other extraterrestrial influences, knew all too well the limitations of the tools at hand. Sounding rockets gave only brief glimpses of the upper reaches, while balloons were limited in altitude. As stated by Walter Sullivan of the *New York Times*, "From the ground, our view into space is hardly more enlightening than the view of the heavens obtained by a lobster on the ocean floor."[76]

The IGY proposal was endorsed by the International Council of Scientific Unions, which appointed an IGY oversight committee in 1952. The organization was formally designated the Special Committee for the IGY, referred to as CSAGI from the French initials of its name. CSAGI, which eventually included representatives from sixty-seven nations, was headed by Sidney Chapman. In a meeting on October 4, 1954, a CSAGI resolution was passed urging member countries to consider "the launching of small satellite vehicles" as part of the IGY.[77]

The satellite envisioned by the von Braun group was truly minimal—it would weigh only about 5 pounds and have no instrumentation of any kind. George Hoover recalled, "There was little disagreement about the need for an instrumented satellite, but the cold hard facts were that 5 pounds was the maximum capability that could be orbited . . . without major development."[78]

The inert satellite was the basis of the effort's unofficial nickname, Project Slug. A few months after the proposal came out, it acquired the formal designation Project Orbit. That quickly morphed into Project Orbiter.[79] The Orbiter satellite would be launched from a Navy ship stationed at the equator. The Navy already had a ship for guided-missile experiments, the USS *Norton Sound*, which had shown it could handle large rockets. In May 1950, a Viking had been successfully fired from this vessel in the Pacific Ocean.

The equatorial location was chosen for Orbiter because it would allow for a rocket to be launched in an eastwardly direction, thus gaining the greatest possible boost from the Earth's rotation. In fact, the Redstone-Loki combination envisioned in 1954 could not have orbited a satellite *except* from a launch at the equator. The projected orbital altitude was 200 miles.[80]

Hoover became the project officer for Orbiter. The projected launch date was the summer of 1956 (later revised to August 1957).[81] All this went on even though Secretary of Defense Charles E. Wilson was far from convinced of the utility of satellites. When asked in December 1954 whether the Soviets might orbit a satellite before the United States, he replied, "I wouldn't care if they did."[82]

Before the end of 1954, the ONR had let the first contracts for Project Orbiter. Varo Corporation, which had Fred Whipple on its payroll as a consultant, was hired to study the optical tracking problem. The Alabama Engineering and Tool Company and the Aerophysics Corporation were put on contract to work with the Army on the Loki upper-stage cluster.[83]

It soon became apparent, however, the Army/ONR team wasn't the only U.S. organization making serious plans for a satellite. On the civilian side, a special Space Flight Committee of the American Rocket Society delivered an important report to the National Science Foundation in November 1954. Chaired by Milt Rosen, the committee gathered several prominent experts to write on the practical applications of a satellite.

The resulting report, entitled "On the Utility of an Artificial Unmanned Earth Satellite," took a conservative view of the technology likely to be available in the next few years, and this approach gave the Committee credibility. The scientists and engineers on the Committee reported that a small satellite could make important contributions in astronomy, astrophysics, biology, communication, geodesy, navigation, geophysics, and meteorology, as well as host a variety of useful experiments that could benefit from weightlessness and/or vacuum conditions.

Some of the speculation in this document seems amusing today. For example, one writer suggested illuminating a reflector-covered satellite by assembling a battery of powerful searchlights on the ground. Much of the report, however, was impressively prescient. One paper mentioned the possible use on board satellites of a 1954 invention from Bell Telephone Laboratories: a "solar device, consisting of thin silicon strips with an even thinner covering of boron" that could convert sunlight into electricity. This paper, by Homer Newell of the NRL, predicted new problems that would arise for machinery in space. These included outgassing (the continual release of molecules in gaseous form from all exposed surfaces) and the related slow vaporizing of metal structures, which causes the metal-joining phenomenon now called "cold welding."

While the ARS report focused on science, many of the fields discussed were of interest to the military. The military services were interested in the structure of the upper atmosphere (through which missiles were now traveling), the high-altitude radiation environment, and the possible improvements in geodesy and mapmaking. At that time, latitude and longitude coordinates as measured in the United States and as measured in Europe had differences of hundreds of feet.[84] This was no small matter, as the military wanted to aim missiles accurately over long distances. Observations of a satellite in a known orbit could harmonize location data and improve maps around the world.

While the United States was considering satellite proposals, so was its Cold War archrival. On January 10, 1955, a Radio Moscow broadcast discussed the subject of satellites. According to the experts quoted on this program, an Earth satellite appeared feasible and could be launched by the U.S.S.R. in the near future.

In April, 1955, the U.S.S.R. Academy of Sciences created a Commission for Interplanetary Communication, chaired by Academician Leonid Sedov (one of the two Soviet delegates to the 1955 IAF Congress). The commission's announced goal was the development of an "automatic laboratory" in Earth orbit.[85] U.S. experts had no way of knowing whether the Russian announcements were serious or mere propaganda, but these developments raised the level of American interest in satellites considerably.

Another force influencing satellite development by both superpowers grew out of the IGY. American plans for this 1957–58 endeavor were directed by the U.S. National Committee (USNC), which created a Technical Panel on Rocketry. In January 1955, this panel appointed a subcommittee to study "a long-playing rocket," a unique euphemism for a satellite. William H. Pickering, the New Zealand-born physicist who directed JPL at the time, explained, "this is about the time the long-playing records came out, 33 rpm. We had the long-playing rocket which would go up and round and round and round."[86]

The subcommittee consisted of three experts. One was Pickering, who had earned his Ph.D. at Caltech and then joined JPL, where he managed the Corporal program before becoming director in 1954. The second was NRL's Milt Rosen, and the third was John Townsend, assistant head of NRL's Rocket Sonde Research Section.

The subcommittee members reported that a satellite was technically feasible and scientifically worthwhile. Rosen described three possible launch methods. First, a large rocket like the Redstone could be fitted with upper stages. This was the Army-ONR Project Orbiter plan, with which all three subcommittee members were familiar. The second method involved using a new launch vehicle with two or three stages. This idea was based on the Viking M-15. The third way was to build a new, much more powerful rocket that could carry a large satellite.[87] These were the ideas that, in some form, would clash before the famous Stewart Committee a few months later.

On March 10, 1955, the full Technical Panel recommended to the executive committee of the USNC that a satellite program be included in the IGY. The executive committee endorsed a recommendation calling for five instrumented satellites weighing 30-50 pounds to be orbited within the IGY. Given the state of rocketry at the time, the committee believed that they were likely to get five successful orbiting spacecraft if ten were built and launched. The estimated cost was over $7 million.

The executive committee recommendation went to Detlev Bronk, president of the National Academy of Sciences, and Alan Waterman, head of the National Science Foundation. Both men set about making contact with the Department of State, the Department of Defense, and the White House. Lloyd Berkner, now vice president of CSAGI, joined them in lobbying Executive Branch officials to look favorably on a project that would require government funding and major assistance from several agencies, especially in the DoD.

While Secretary Wilson was unenthusiastic, he did not block the request. By the end of March, the IGY proposal reached Donald Quarles, Assistant Secretary of Defense for Research and Development. Already on Quarles' desk was the Army/ONR Project Orbiter idea. In addition, the NRL had sent Quarles two memos on satellite feasibility: one on tracking requirements, including the first proposal for the system to be called "Mini-track," and one on the potential for building a Viking-based satellite launch vehicle.

As Donald Quarles was perusing the papers on his desk, the momentum toward full-scale, officially sanctioned satellite programs had already reached critical mass in both the United States and the Soviet Union. The pieces of the satellite puzzle, including missile development, advanced rocket engines, and communications technology, were falling into place. The drive for space was fueled by national ambitions and the personal beliefs of spaceflight enthusiasts, who had finally found receptive ears within their governments.

Many historians, led by Walter McDougall (winner of a Pulitzer Prize in 1986 for his groundbreaking history of the Space Age, . . . *the Heavens and the Earth*), have argued that the military co-opted the ambitions of scientists and "space dreamers" to fuel enthusiasm for ever-more-advanced missiles and military space programs. According to this line of thought, the military, especially in the United States, moved behind the scenes to build scientific demand and encouragement for satellites in support of a shadow-agenda of national security.[88] In the Soviet Union, there was less need to recruit broad support outside the military. Despite the public activities of the Academy of Sciences, the scientific community was only marginally involved.

Sociologist William Bainbridge has made the interesting argument that it was actually the other way around—that the space enthusiasts sold the military on costly, complex weapons (liquid-fueled missiles) that were not actually the best solutions for hurling nuclear weapons but were, instead, ideal for space flight.[89] To Bainbridge, the "Spaceflight Movement" of like-minded—if not always connected or organized—men from many nations actually co-opted first the German military and then those of the United States and the U.S.S.R.

Both analyses are oversimplified. Any series of events as complex as the human reach into space has a number of causes, none of which can ever be isolated and compared as though they were ingredients in a formula. History is not chemistry: it is not possible to say with any certainty that "Factor X contributed 46% to the decision and Factor Y 54%." What actually occurred was not a clear case of co-option by one side or the other, but rather, it was a matter of many individuals and organizations pursuing their agendas, seizing on mutual interests when these were present, and trying to co-opt or outmaneuver other actors when they were not. There was not a distinct military community, neither in the United States nor in the U.S.S.R., that was set against a completely separate scientific or space-flight community. Many people believed in the importance of both missiles and exploration. When speaking to military audiences, for example, Wernher von Braun emphasized the importance of national defense and beating the Soviets into space; and when speaking to scientists, he exhibited equal and genuine enthusiasm for the exploration of a new frontier.

George Hoover, speaking in early 1956, made a satellite sound inevitable. While obviously both aware and part of the military interest in space flight, he explained its appeal in scientific terms. "A satellite," he said, "is being established because it is the logical next step in a very normal research program, the results of which will be beneficial to the nation. A satellite is the only upper atmosphere research tool . . . which will provide the required knowledge to permit man to learn about himself, the world, and the planetary system in which he lives."[90]

Along similar lines, Fred Durant has observed that the United States was the world leader in aeronautics in the early 1950s, with military and civilian programs striving to create machines going "higher and faster." For the next step, "Rocket technology was required." As fuel for the technological fire, Durant cites science fiction, speculative scientific articles like the *Collier's* series, presentations on the utility of space technology through the IAF, and the continuing influence of feasibility studies including the 1947 RAND report. By the time of Project Orbiter, Durant explains, "A network of 'believers' in the U.S. and Western nations was growing. The time was right for action."[91]

Whatever the exact mix of driving forces, the tipping point had been reached by the end of 1954. Both superpowers were irrevocably committing themselves to space.

Indeed, in the spring of 1955, Quarles knew something most of the civilian and even the military satellite proponents didn't. While the IGY scientists were making their case, a satellite program was already being discussed at the highest levels of the U.S. government. What even Quarles did not know was how seriously the same agenda was being advanced in the Soviet Union.

Chapter 3

The Dream of Sergey Korolev

While the United States was debating the establishment of an official satellite program, Chief Designer Sergey Korolev, whose identity was a state secret, and his team at Special Design Bureau 1 (OKB-1), a new organization created by NII-88 in 1950, were building long-range missiles much larger than the American Redstone.

From the beginning, Russian designers knew that the R-7 ICBM they were working on would also be capable of launching a satellite. In practice, that was almost all it turned out to be useful for. This complex giant of a rocket wasn't practical to maintain as an operational ICBM, and only a handful were ever deployed in that role. Instead, it became the basic design on which Russian launch vehicles would be based for decades to come.

Sergey Korolev was a complicated, incredibly determined man. Like von Braun, Korolev combined the capabilities of a first-rate engineer with those of an inspirational leader. Korolev was a Russian patriot and remained one, despite suffering six years of unjust imprisonment. When Premier Josef Stalin blessed the missile development program after the war, Korolev and other enthusiasts like Valentin P. Glushko and Mikhail Tikhonravov were ecstatic to be handed the kind of authority and resources they had always wanted.

This freed them neither from the Soviet bureaucracy,

which Korolev battled (skillfully and usually successfully) throughout his career as chief designer, nor from petty politics and competing fiefdoms. Still, it was the kind of opportunity Korolev could not have dared to imagine during his years of imprisonment. He made the most of it.

Korolev did not emerge from a vacuum. Russia had a long tradition in science, aeronautics, and science fiction, including fiction about space travel. In 1908, medical doctor Aleksandr A. Bogdanov published a novel, *Red Star*, about friendly visitors from Mars (who, as it happened, were believers in a Communist-type system). In 1915, physicist Yakov I. Perelman wrote the first popular nonfiction book on space travel, which sold well for twenty years. Translations of the works of imaginative Western authors such as Jules Verne also were very popular in Russia. Despite the turmoil of World War I and the Bolshevik revolution, Russia's intellectual soil was fertile ground for space theorists like Tsiolkovsky and rocket engineers like Korolev.

Russia's first club for space enthusiasts was founded in Moscow in 1924. Two years later, Tsiolkovsky published his most comprehensive work, *Exploration of Space by Reactive Devices.* Between 1928 and 1932, Nikolay Rynin published a nine-volume encyclopedia collecting everything known or theorized about space flight. Korolev's book *Rocket Flight in the Stratosphere* was published in 1934 under the sponsorship of the Ministry of Defense.[1]

Throughout the 1930s and the war years, rocket research received government support, although this was almost entirely devoted to weaponry. In 1933, at Marshal Tukhachevsky's initiative, the Moscow GIRD and Leningrad GDL were merged under military command to create the Reactive Scientific Research Institute (RNII) in Moscow.[2] Ivan Kleimyonov of GDL was placed in command of this organization, with Korolev as his deputy. This organization made some important progress in guidance systems and in both solid- and liquid-fuel propulsion despite internal bickering (Korolev was demoted at one point for insubordination.)[3]

This progress came to a complete standstill due to the massive, irrational purges initiated by Stalin in the late 1930s. This was a time when anyone could be accused of some form of disloyalty and sentenced without even a semblance of a meaningful trial. Millions of Russians were executed or imprisoned, including many of the country's best engineers and scientists. In June 1937, RNII's patron, Marshal Tukhachevsky, was arrested, charged with collaboration with Germany, and executed.

A year later, Korolev was arrested for "subversion in a new field of technology." More precisely, he was charged with having committed a form of sabotage by holding back RNII's progress on rocket weapons. He was also accused of wasting RNII funds. Valentin Glushko had already been arrested, and his coerced "confession" was part of the evidence against Korolev.

Sentenced to ten years' imprisonment, Korolev ended up in the brutal Kolyma gulag in Siberia. Over one fourth of the freezing, underfed, overworked prisoners in this camp died every year. Korolev's stay in the camp led to an array of health problems from which he never completely recovered.

In 1940, Korolev was transferred to a unique Soviet institution known as a *sharaga* or *sharashka*. Sharagas were confined work areas for those prisoners who had abilities needed by the government. Korolev worked in a Moscow sharaga, TsKB-39, an aircraft engineering design bureau inside a prison. The sharaga was headed by Andrei Tupolev, a leading aircraft designer who was himself now a prisoner. Tupolev had once been one of Korolev's academic instructors and was instrumental in having Korolev plucked from the gulag and sent to the sharaga.[4]

Engineers laboring in sharagas designed some of Russia's most important wartime aircraft and munitions. They worked in part because they still believed in Russia and in the importance of winning the war, and in part because they knew the alternative: leaving the relative comfort of the sharaga, where they had heated barracks and adequate food, for misery and probable death in a gulag.

Korolev was moved several times, finally to a sharaga in Kazan where he and fellow prisoner Glushko worked on JATO rockets and jet engines.[5] Neither man was released until 1944, when jurisdiction over the design bureau was transferred from the NKVD (secret police) to a civilian agency. Korolev stayed as a paid employee of this organization for another year. During this period, he designed his first long-range rockets, intended to carry warheads up to forty miles.[6]

When Russian troops closed in on Berlin and the end of the war came in sight, the future of rockets and space vehicles in the U.S.S.R. must have looked uncertain. Many of the engineers and technicians Korolev had worked with at RNII had been arrested or conscripted into the Army. Some had been executed, others had been killed in combat or worked to death in the gulags. Two prominent pre-war space enthusiasts, Nikolay Rynin and Yakov Perelman, died in the epic siege of Leningrad.

Amid this disaster, Korolev somehow kept looking forward. In 1946, he saw his daughter Natasha reading Jules Verne, as he had done so many years before. He told her, "You know, in about 30 years a human will be on the moon." When she protested that such a feat was impossible, he responded very seriously, "Please remember this day. I tell you, man will walk on the moon."[7]

Lunar flight must have seemed like an absurd fantasy in the ruined nation. But Soviet leaders had already decided to seize the opportunity demonstrated by Germany's rocket developments, and an all-out effort was beginning to pull together the remaining expertise in rocketry and reconstitute a major research and development program.

The Russians had been aware of the V-2 at least since the fall of 1944, when British officials asked for help in studying a former V-2 test center in Soviet-occupied Poland. A collection of V-2 parts had been shipped back to Russia and partially reassembled. Russian rocket experts who viewed the reconstructed missile, including Tikhonravov, were stunned at the German advances. "This is what cannot be," one engineer marveled.[8]

The Russians, like the Americans, obtained copies of the plans von Braun and his team had drawn up for future developments. Boris Chertok, one of the first Russians to inspect the Mittelwerk (he took over a house von Braun had occupied briefly during the exodus from Peenemunde), recalled, "What we learned shook our imagination."[9]

Once the go-ahead to exploit German technology was given, rocketry became a high priority in the Soviet military and research communities. By September 1945, Korolev found himself commissioned as an Army colonel and sent to Germany.[10] He helped analyze the German V-2 work, then returned to Russia to duplicate the V-2 for the Soviet Army as the R-1. Glushko, now chief designer of the bureau in which he had been a prisoner, continued his work with rocket engines. Eleven years later, Glushko's engines and Korolev's rockets would make *Sputnik* a reality.

Korolev was not infallible. While he was always interested in liquid-fuel engines, he doubted the practicality of building large ones until the V-2 proved the problems of scaling up liquid-propulsion systems were solvable.[11] In the early 1960s, he carried on a bitter dispute with Mikhail Yangel, who headed a rival missile design bureau. Korolev argued against developing missiles using storable but toxic liquid propellants, such as the oxidizer nitrogen textroxide, even though these were desired by the military to shorten missile reaction time and were used successfully in one American ICBM of that era, the *Titan 2.*

Nor was Korolev always an easy man to work with. On the one hand, he often went out of his way to greet new engineers and make them feel welcome. He nurtured the talents of others in his organization, creating "a galaxy of Academicians."[12] He also did everything he could to help his subordinates with concerns such as housing and medical care. On the other hand, despite Korolev's solicitous nature, the years of imprisonment had understandably changed him. Associates described Korolev as a stern taskmaster who was difficult to befriend. He seemed to take technical failures personally and could never get his work out of his mind. Korolev was always cautious about any discussion of politics, although he did eventually join the Communist Party. He had a nervous habit of eating every crumb of food at each meal, as if he were still a prisoner who did not know when he might next be fed. In 1948, Korolev divorced his first wife, Xenia, who had remained devoted to him during his imprisonment. The next year, he married Nina Ivanovna Kotenkova, a younger woman who translated English periodicals for his design bureau.[13]

Whatever Korolev's shortcomings, they were more than made up for by his sheer determination. Without him, the Soviet Union would have had little chance to be the first nation in space. Lieutenant General Kerim Kerimov, who was a military liaison to OKB-1, summed up Korolev by saying, "He had a relentless determination—almost like a disease."[14]

As it was, Soviet rocketry made steady advances after the war. The R-1 first flew in 1948 and entered military service in 1950. Several variants of the R-1 were used—as America used the V-2s and Vikings—for research. (The U.S.S.R. also used V-2s in scientific work.) R-1s carried biological payloads as well as instruments to study cosmic rays, solar activity, the ionosphere, and meteorology. Another variant, the R-1A, was used to test designs for warheads that would separate from the missile upon re-entry. The R-1, however, was not built in great numbers, because the Russians had great difficulty in manufacturing its components. What the R-1 did accomplish, along with captured V-2s, was to lay important groundwork by giving Russian engineers, technicians, and soldiers experience in the building and handling of large rockets.

In 1947, Helmut Grottrup and his German colleagues had been told to design a new missile with a range of 370 miles. By December 1948, they produced the G-1. The Russians opted not to put this design into production, choosing instead a Korolev product called the R-2. (All Gottrup designs had the "G" designation, whereas other rockets used the "R" designation for *raketa* [rocket vehicle].) Some features of the G-1, however, including the use of integral propellant tanks, were adopted for the R-2 and subsequent missiles. The R-2 kept the V-2's lox-alcohol propellant combination, although Glushko's RD-101 engine raised the thrust to 90,600 pounds.

Well before the R-2 made its first flight, Korolev was already thinking about the design of a missile with a far greater range. In July 1949, Stalin met in the Kremlin with Korolev, Dimitri Ustinov, and Igor Kurchatov, the head of the Soviet nuclear-weapon program. Stalin voiced his opinion that the atomic bombs of the United States and England were threats to the survival of the U.S.S.R. (This was one month before the U.S.S.R. exploded its own atomic bomb.) He added, "But we are not Japan. That is why you, Comrade Kurchatov, and you, Comrade Ustinov, and you [Korolev] as well, must speed things up! Are there any more questions?!"[15]

Stalin had decided where Soviet resources would be concentrated—on nuclear weapons and the means to deliver them. The first thing the Premier wanted "speeded up" was a medium-range missile on which work had already begun in April 1948. This vehicle, known as the R-3, fell well short of the military's requirements and was never deployed operationally. The next step was the R-5M, which could throw a warhead weighing over 3,300 pounds a distance of 760 miles. It was deployed beginning in 1956, becoming the first long-range missile actually placed into service with a nuclear warhead. (The American Redstone missile also reached military units in 1956, but was not deployed to an operational location [Europe] until 1958.)

Research on an intercontinental missile, which would become the R-7, began in December 1950. Some aspects of Soviet policy were altered after Stalin died on March 5, 1953, but Nikolai A. Bulganin continued as defense minister, and the priority given to ICBM projects did not change. While the new premier, Georgi Malenkov, directed a relaxation of Stalin's confrontational foreign policy, it did not last long enough to make any difference in the course of the strategic arms race. (Neither did Malenkov, who held his post less than two years before being forced to yield to Bulganin.)

A decree dated May 20, 1954, gave final authorization for the development of an ICBM. With Korolev concentrating on the this project, development of smaller missiles devolved to a new design bureau in Dnepropetrovsk. Korolev's assistant, Mikhail Yangel, became chief designer at this bureau. Several such design bureaus, some of which would compete with Korolev's, were eventually created to develop various technologies that originated in OKB-1. In 1957, when Korolev's satellite project was behind schedule, Yangel would offer a proposal to use his bureau's R-12 missile as a booster instead of Korolev's hardware.

American space and missile programs were largely dependent on the aviation industry, with most of the major development projects undertaken by aircraft manufacturers. The Redstone program, sponsored by the Army's Ordnance branch, was an exception. Under the Army's arsenal system, development and even limited production of weapons was undertaken at government-owned facilities. By contrast, the Soviet missile industry, and hence the space effort, grew out of the artillery industry under the direction of the Ministry of Armaments.[16]

After 1956, American long-range missiles were assigned to Air Force jurisdiction. In the U.S.S.R., such weapons belonged first to the Army and later to a separate service, the Strategic Rocket Forces.

As Korolev's organization could not undertake all aspects of missile design and development, a Council of Chief Designers was formed. This included Korolev, Glushko, and four other chief designers from bureaus providing supporting equipment, such as communications gear.[17]

For the moment, however, the R-7 was OKB-1's top priority. A missile that could carry Russia's heavy atomic warheads to the United States was the kind of weapon that, in the view of Soviet leaders, would gain the respect of America and the world. It would reorder the struggle between Communism and the West.

One factor influencing the space race over the next decade was the design of nuclear warheads. While both countries soon possessed the hydrogen (or fusion) bomb, the United States was able to miniaturize its weapons. Indeed, serious Air Force interest in ICBMs was sparked by the February 1953 report of the independent Strategic Missiles Evaluation Committee (a.k.a. the Teapot Committee), which predicted that fusion warheads could be made much smaller and lighter than originally thought. In particular, the Air Force increased funding for its Atlas missile program, which had been a relatively low-priority effort since its beginning as a classified program in 1951. On December 16, 1954, the Atlas project was announced to the public. This event lagged only a few months behind the approval of Korolev's equivalent program, of which the Americans had only hints.

The Teapot Committee's prediction proved correct. Thanks to the smaller American warheads, U.S. missiles were simpler than their Soviet counterparts. This had advantages in cost, maintainability, and other important areas. It also meant these missiles, when used as launch vehicles, were less capable of placing objects into orbit.

The Jupiter IRBM, for example, first launched in 1957, carried a W-49 fusion warhead with a yield of 1.45 megatons of TNT. The missile's total payload weight, including the Mark 3 reentry vehicle (RV), was 2,600 pounds. The Atlas missile was designed to carry a fusion warhead of 3.75 megatons and a Mark 2 RV, with a payload weight of 3,500 pounds.[18] Korolev had to build a missile capable of hurling a 3.5-megaton payload weighing over 9,000 pounds between continents.[19]

While the focus of the Soviet effort was on missiles, Korolev and other space enthusiasts never stopped thinking about satellites. As in the United States, a variety of studies and proposals were made throughout the postwar years. In September 1953, Russia's Defense Ministry officially sponsored a new satellite study. In February 1954, Korolev discussed the matter with Ustinov, who agreed to examine further proposals on the topic of satellites. Following up this opening, Mikhail Tikhonravov petitioned the government on May 26 to approve the launch of what he called a "simplest" satellite (weighing 2 to 3 tons)!

Sergey Korolev during his time as chief designer. NASM Photo 84-10319. Courtesy National Air and Space Museum

Tikhonravov had escaped the purges and had spent the war as an officer working on military rockets. When the conflict ended, he was deputy commander of a military rocket bureau, NII-4, under the Ministry of Defense's Chief Artillery Directorate.[20] He directed research into improved liquid-fuel rockets and conceived the "rocket packet" or "parallel staging" concept later used in the R-7. Korolev added a cover letter to Tikhonravov's satellite petition, arguing that beginning a satellite project now was "timely and feasible."[21]

On August 30, 1955, the Soviet Academy of Sciences recommended a satellite program. Exactly five months later, the powerful Council of Ministers approved the idea of letting Korolev's bureau develop and launch a satellite.[22] Korolev's cause was helped further when, during a visit to OKB-1 by the senior Soviet leadership in early 1956, he lobbied Nikita S. Khrushchev, then the first secretary of the Communist Party, to endorse the satellite project. Korolev argued (somewhat misleadingly) that it would be a simple, low-cost undertaking to put a satellite rather than a warhead on a future ICBM test. Khrushchev replied, "If the main task doesn't suffer, do it." The first secretary was sufficiently impressed to grant Korolev permission to bypass several layers of bureaucracy to contact him directly.[23] Tikhonravov was transferred from OKB-385 in the Ural Mountains to Korolev's OKB-1 and served as his right-hand engineer for the project.

The satellite OKB-1 undertook to build was a large one, carrying at least 500 pounds of scientific instruments in a spacecraft weighing over 2,000 pounds. This design, known as Object D, would eventually become *Sputnik 3*. Like the R-7 development effort, the satellite project was classified. Korolev moved engineers and technicians from OKB-1 to a new and remote launch complex on the barren steppes of central Asia. "Remote" is an understatement: the space pioneers lived in boxcars and amused themselves by pitting scorpions against each other in fights to the death. Still, Arkady Ostashev, one of the original group, remembered forty years later, "Those were great days. It was a lot of fun."[24]

Another rocket designer, Sergey Kuyukov, reminisced for a documentary film that, "The conditions at our launch site were terrible. We had a song. It told of bedbugs, long roads to nowhere, awful food—somehow, we enjoyed it."[25]

This complex had its origin in early 1955, when construction began on a new facility to test the ICBMs Korolev was trying to develop. With its vast land area, the U.S.S.R. opted to locate the entire test range within its borders rather than fire its large rockets from a coastal site as the United States did. Korolev turned to Vladimir Barmin, head of the Design Bureau of Special Machine Building in Moscow, to build what would become the world's first spaceport. Barmin's engineers designed the facility in accordance with Korolev's directions, then traveled to the remote steppe to supervise the military construction battalions sent to carve the future from the empty landscape.

While the launch complex eventually came to be called Baikonur for security reasons, it was actually 300 miles from the city of that name. Instead, it was located north of a remote railway town named Tyuratam in Kazakstan. A new rail spur, a concrete pad, fuel-storage tanks and handling systems, a huge building for horizontal assembly of very large rockets, and all the ancillary facilities needed to support missile launches were built within just two years. Party Secretary Khrushchev gave full support to this activity. Khrushchev wanted to cut Soviet conventional forces in order to free up resources for domestic needs, and he saw the long-range missile as a way to compensate for such a reduction by strengthening the nation's nuclear capability.

After a visit to the historic launch site in 1990, American space expert James Oberg wrote,

> The spaceport was built here because it was not populated, for the simple reason that it is a terrible place to live. The summers are

scorching, the winters bitter, there is no water or shade, and it is heartbreakingly far from anywhere. A few decades ago, only the Kazakh nomads ran their sparse herds here, usually on their way somewhere else. If Earth has any human settlement halfway into outer space, this is it.[26]

As happens with most technically challenging enterprises, the Russian satellite designers encountered technical hurdles that forced their launch schedule to slip. Not only was the satellite hardware not being delivered on time, but the engines for the R-7 were proving less efficient than expected. That problem had to be solved before the heavy Object D could be launched.

While the rocket development struggled ahead, the vital matter of a ground control and tracking system was attended to. On September 3, 1956, a government decree, "On Creation of the Command Measurement Complex" authorized the creation of the Soviet satellite tracking system, known by its Russian initials as KIK. Built by NII-4, KIK was based largely on existing equipment created for missile-test tracking and for the country's air defense system. A tracking and data analysis center staffed with 831 military and civilian personnel was built in Moscow to serve as the KIK's hub.[27]

By November 1956, it appeared to the Soviets that the U.S. IGY satellite might well be launched before theirs. While the U.S. program had not inspired the creation of the Russian one—the pivotal memo of May 1954 made no mention of an American satellite—Korolev knew how to play on the aspirations of Soviet leaders and their fears of Western competition.

Korolev had both personal and professional incentives to be first into space. Beating the Americans not only would be a coup for Russia, but would garner support for further space-flight initiatives already taking shape in the chief designer's imagination. As the Object D program slipped, Tikhonravov suggested they look at a stopgap: a smaller satellite that could be built in time to make certain the first artificial moon was a Soviet one. Korolev had been nursing similar thoughts, and he ordered preparations to commence at once.

While there is a difference of opinion concerning Korolev's technical pre-eminence among Soviet engineers, there is no question about his unsurpassed ability to organize and motivate people to get even the most difficult projects accomplished. He approached his work with what can fairly be called fanaticism, often driving himself to exhaustion. Once he was convinced he had a good idea, not even the famously slow-moving, obstructionist Communist bureaucracy could stand in his way. Now he seized on the small-satellite concept, and he plunged into the twin tasks of getting the technical work done and lining up political support for the change of plans.

On January 5, 1957, Korolev wrote to the U.S.S.R. Council of Ministers asking permission to switch work to a satellite in the range of 90 to 110 pounds. He suggested that two such satellites be launched sometime between April and June. Korolev emphasized the threat posed by alleged U.S. efforts to orbit a satellite first and gain superiority in space, although Soviet intelligence sources had the facts a bit muddled. Korolev described the NRL's Project Vanguard satellite launcher, which had been in development since 1955, as a rocket based on the Redstone, and he cited an Army missile test in September 1956 as a failed satellite launch attempt.[28]

Thus was born the true *prosteyshyy* (simplest) *Sputnik,* also known as *PS-1.* A design team led by Mikhail Khomyakov built the satellite with impressive speed. Engineer Gyorgi Grechko recalled, "We made it in one month, with only one reason, to be first in space."[29]

The spacecraft soon to be famous as *Sputnik 1* was a highly polished aluminum sphere, built in two hemispheres and sealed with a metal frame containing a rubber gasket. The 184-pound satellite was built so quickly that only general blueprints, not detailed engineering drawings, were made, a fact that has bedeviled space historians ever since.[30]

The satellite's only noticeable external features were the four spring-loaded antennas. Two of these were 94.5 inches long, the others 114 inches. These were equally spaced around the satellite. The antennas swept back to provide a streamlined profile. The maximum angle between opposing antennae was less than 46 degrees at launch (46 degrees being the angle of the sides of the payload shroud), expanding to 70 degrees after the Sputnik had been deployed.[31] The satellite fitted under a conical cap on top of the larger cone of the shroud, the antennas poking through small fairings and pressed against the outside of the shroud. Thus, the antennas were exposed during launch.[32] The satellite was filled with pressurized nitrogen to minimize internal temperature fluctuations when in orbit.

On the inside, *Sputnik* was more complex than it first appeared. In addition to the two radio transmitters, there were instruments to measure temperature and pressure within the sphere. The results would be telemetered to the ground by varying the radio frequencies.[33]

Unlike any of the early American designs, *Sputnik 1* also had a ventilating fan and air duct for active cooling. This was vital because the transmitters used vacuum tubes rather than the transistors that would appear

Sputnik 1. NASM Photo 7B-30247. Courtesy National Air and
Space Museum

in later satellites. When the internal temperature exceeded 86 degrees
Fahrenheit, the ventilator circulated the heat-absorbing nitrogen
against the rear hemisphere of the casing. This was coated and polished to
radiate more heat than it absorbed. The satellite's structure weighed
30.6 pounds, the equipment 128.7 pounds (of which 112 pounds was
the power pack with its silver-zinc batteries), and the antennae 18.5
pounds.[34]

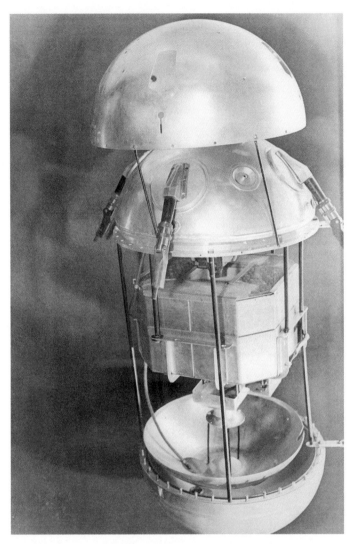

Exploded view of *Sputnik 1*, showing its housing for batteries and instrumentation. NASM Photo 7B-30246. Courtesy National Air and Space Museum

The system for separating the satellite from the booster was also intricate. The *Sputnik* was pushed away by gas pressure, but there was also a backup system using pyrotechnics. A spring system cast off the conical "tip" shroud at the same moment the satellite was separated. The *Sputnik* then emerged from its spot nested in the top of the main shroud, unfolding its antennas to their operational position. Finally, gas jets in the top of the R-7 core stage slowed the rocket body, so it could not overtake and collide with the satellite.[35] (This was a precaution American engineers would later wish they had included in their own designs.)

The chief designer was meticulous about the construction of his satellite. Engineer Konstantin Feoktistov recalled, "Korolev came over to the shop and insisted that both halves of the sputnik's metallic sphere be polished until they shone, that they be spotlessly clean." Korolev even scolded the plant's chief engineer over the surface quality of a *Sputnik* mockup, proclaiming, "This ball will be exhibited in museums!"[36]

Mikhail Khomyakov's deputy, Oleg Ivanovsky, gave an interview in 1993 in which he recalled the challenges of rushing the *PS-1* to completion. The metal of the satellite had to be very highly polished to promote optical tracking, and its two hemispheres had to seal perfectly to hold in the pressurized nitrogen that would assure an even temperature for the instrumentation. "We had to find new techniques of manufacturing the surfaces in order to achieve the necessary optical and thermal qualities," Ivanovsky said. "We had no experience in this work. I recall one episode when we had to persuade the production shop that the satellite was a new item, not a missile."[37]

A conical satellite was considered, but Korolev insisted on the sphere. A sphere not only had practical advantages but was, reportedly, more pleasing to the chief designer's sense of aesthetics. *Sputnik* engineer Mark Gallai called the satellite, "an elegant ball . . . with an antenna thrown back like a galloping horse."[38]

Korolev hoped to launch *PS-1* in March, but the R-7 could not be debugged in time to meet that schedule. A series of R-7 failures even led to a directive from the Kremlin to Korolev to shut down his efforts, but the dogged engineer ignored orders and made an R-7 fly almost perfectly on August 21, 1957. With that achievement, apparently, all was forgiven.[39]

The R-7's flight was announced to the public, although some experts in the West doubted the Soviets had actually succeeded with what the official communiqué called a "super-long-range, intercontinental multistage ballistic missile." In the days before over-the-horizon radar and infrared-detection satellites, the world had to take Russia's word about its achievements, and Soviet claims were often inflated. This one, however, was not.[40] Korolev had achieved a feat not to be duplicated by the United States until the Atlas ICBM completed its first long-range flight in November 1958.

Before the R-7 triumph, Korolev had scored a personal victory. In April, he was notified that he had been "rehabilitated" by the government. His earlier imprisonment was declared unjustified, and the chief designer of Russia's top-priority weapons program was now a trusted citizen again.

The R-7 was easily the largest rocket in the world. The August launch was of a configuration called the R-7 8K71. The test missile stood 92 feet tall and was strikingly squat and broad at the base, due to Tikhonravov's parallel staging concept. Instead of placing the upper stages on top of the first, four strap-on boosters were attached surrounding the core vehicle. Each strap-on had a single RD-107 engine with four combustion chambers and four nozzles. The core had a single RD-108 with the same configuration but a longer burning time. All the engines ignited simultaneously at launch. The RD-107 and RD-108 were Glushko designs fueled by a lox/kerosene mixture.

The engines were not gimbaled: the Russians had yet to solve the mechanical problems involved in such a system. Likewise, the ingenious but complex arrangement in which each turbopump fed four engines was necessitated by the limitations of Russian manufacturing and metallurgy. Glushko, despite his skill as a designer, was unable to construct a single large combustion chamber that would work without developing vibrations strong enough to tear the engine apart.[41] Accordingly, he settled for using four smaller chambers in each booster. This arrangement also provided some redundancy, since a fault in one chamber or nozzle of the R-7 would mean there were still 19 chambers producing thrust. Four small rocket motors for directional control were mounted on the core vehicle, and two more on each of the strap-ons. At liftoff, the entire assembly weighed 591,000 pounds and produced over 870,000 pounds of thrust.

The rocket was transported to the pad, a mile from the assembly building, on a railway car. The R-7 was moved in an assembled, horizontal configuration and then raised to the vertical and enclosed in a metal framework with huge "petals" that opened at launch like a flower to release the missile. The Russians affectionately called this massive beast *Semyorka*—"Old Number 7."[42] When Western intelligence learned of this missile, the R-7 received the North Atlantic Treaty Organization (NATO) designation SS-6 and the name "Sapwood."

The R-7 ICBM had hardly finished its 4,000-mile trajectory before Korolev began talking about the next flight—the satellite launch. He had in mind a special space-launch variant of the R-7, the 8A91, but this could not be readied in time. The missile to be used for the *PS-1* launch was a slightly modified ICBM called the R-7 8K71PS. This variant had a payload adapter, separation system, and nose fairing added in place of the dummy warhead used on the first R-7 launches. To keep the weight and cost down,

The booster that launched *Sputnik 1* was kept secret until 1967. In that year, this R-7 booster was displayed at the Paris Air Show. NASM Photo A-2154-B. Courtesy National Air and Space Museum

about 660 pounds of extra telemetry equipment used on the earlier missile version were removed.

The R-7 program was important enough to be governed by a high-level state committee, and Korolev needed this body's approval to use one of the few available rockets for his satellite. The committee was skeptical about diverting a test article in a critical missile program which, so far, had produced only one successful launch. (It helped when a second success was achieved on September 7.)[43] Korolev, ever the master politician, suggested raising the question of whether the U.S.S.R. should be first in space to the Presidium, the highest body of the Communist Party. Rather than be seen as roadblocks to a potentially important national achievement, the committee members backed down.[44]

In October 1956, an article in the *Moscow News* (translated and published in *Aviation Week*) had publicly discussed the Soviet satellite program, though details of the satellite and launch vehicle remained secret. In 1957, the July and August issues of the Soviet magazine *Radio* described the *PS-1* satellite's basic design, its orbit, and how to build equipment to receive the spacecraft's transmissions. At IGY meetings, Russian scientists openly mentioned their plans, although they refused to provide a launch date.

In November 1956, an analysis by the CIA had pegged November 1957 as the earliest likely date for a Soviet satellite launch. It is ironic that, for all the secrecy enveloping the Soviet program, the CIA's prediction was better than the chief designer's. Indeed, at that point the U.S. government had had a more accurate forecast for the launch date of its adversary's satellite than for its own.

Chapter 4

Turning Point
The Stewart Committee

From the day he entered office in 1952, President Eisenhower was highly concerned about the need for advance warning of a major attack on the United States. As a former general, he was haunted by the idea of a "nuclear Pearl Harbor." The recent U.S. intelligence record did not assuage his concerns. The CIA, founded in 1947, had been unable to predict the Soviets' first atomic bomb test, the invasion of South Korea by North Korea in June of 1950, or the massive Chinese intervention in that war in November, 1950.

The Korean conflict ended in July of 1953, but the Soviet Union almost immediately presented America with a new reason to be concerned about intelligence. On August 12, the first Soviet hydrogen bomb was tested. Once again, President Eisenhower had not been warned.

The explosion of a Soviet fusion device came just two months after Americans Julius and Ethel Rosenberg were executed after being convicted of passing U.S. atomic secrets to the Soviets. Senator Joseph McCarthy's campaign to whip up nationwide fear about Communist traitors was still in progress. Whatever one thought of McCarthy's excesses, it was no fantasy that Eastern bloc spies were still at work in the relatively open society of America, while there was no comparable U.S. capability to penetrate the U.S.S.R. To make matters worse, the hints U.S. intelligence was picking up were foreboding. The Soviets, the CIA reported, were working on missiles much larger and longer-ranged than the V-2.

While the Americans had no specific information about the designs being pursued in Russia, it was commonly assumed the U.S.S.R. was still building on the Peenemunde work. Years before, von Braun had warned that the Soviets could probably have something like his A-9/A-10 design in production by 1949. The threat of long-range missiles armed with hydrogen warheads, combined with the maddening lack of current details about Soviet capabilities, led Eisenhower to establish a top-level study group known as the Killian Panel.

In February 1955, this group, formally named the Technological Capabilities Panel, sent the president a classified report entitled, "Meeting the Threat of Surprise Attack." The Killian Panel recommended accelerating ICBM and intermediate-range ballistic missile (IRBM) development to counter Soviet investment in these areas. This lent urgency to the nation's two IRBM programs, the Air Force's Thor and the joint Army-Navy Jupiter, both of which would play important roles in space. These programs were soon awarded the same top-priority status accorded the Air Force's Atlas ICBM.

Killian Panel members also endorsed developing an advanced spyplane (the now-famous U-2) to gather current information on Soviet capabilities and locate targets for American bombers and missiles. Finally, their report discussed the prospects for developing a reconnaissance satellite. The panel had at its disposal a series of studies on the feasibility of such a device, most conducted by RAND for the Air Force.[1] While not endorsing an all-out program to develop what still seemed like exotic and immature technology, the Killian Panel did advise establishing the principle of freedom of space for future reconnaissance satellites by initially orbiting a scientific satellite.[2]

In 1955, the principle of free transit of space, whether for scientific or military satellites, was not yet a settled issue. It was an ancient dictum that nations exercised sovereignty throughout the airspace above their territories, but how high did this extend? Proposals before the advent of the airplane had included setting an upper bound at the limit to which ground-based artillery could fire, or at the height of the Eiffel Tower![3] Proposals to set legal norms controlling Earth satellites extended as far back as 1932.[4]

The Chicago Convention of 1944 had codified the national ownership of airspace, but the question of an upper limit was not addressed. Did national sovereignty end at some point as the atmosphere thinned out, or did it go on forever? Was space at orbital altitudes equivalent to the open sea, or would orbiting a satellite, especially a military one, above another country's territory be an act of trespass?

The 1954 IGY resolution on launching satellites constituted the first step toward an answer, because the member countries that accepted it knew the resulting scientific satellites, whatever their orbits, would fly over a large number of national territories. Did this translate to freedom for all satellites? Experts had differing opinions, especially concerning the position of a nation as fanatical about secrecy as the Soviet Union.[5] The world's reaction to the first satellite, whoever launched it, would go a long way toward answering this question.

It might be said that in 1955 the American military and scientific communities faced the same problem: their tools were simply inadequate to see what they wanted to see. Whereas scientists were frustrated by the limitations of balloons and sounding rockets, the Department of Defense and the intelligence community were concerned with the limitations of aircraft (which could, at that point, only fly around the periphery of the Soviet bloc) and balloon-borne cameras.

Reconnaissance of the U.S.S.R. by drifting balloons, a program code-named Genetrix, ran for only a month in early 1956. It involved 516 balloon launches, but provided little information.[6] Aircraft reconnaissance was sporadic and highly risky. The Soviets attacked American aircraft (sometimes while they were in international airspace) and protested loudly about the balloons. They had every right to be angry, since there was no question that the United States was violating Soviet airspace.[7]

While Eisenhower reluctantly accepted the risks involved in such trespassing, a broad view from a much safer perch in orbit had obvious advantages. If the military and scientific communities had essentially the same problem, so were they drawn to the same solution.

The Air Force had made its first move in the satellite field well before the Killian report came out. Based on several RAND studies, which were summarized in a report called "Project Feed Back," the Air Force issued a requirement for an imaging satellite under the designation Weapon System 117L (WS-117L) on November 17, 1954.[8] Study contracts to three firms were awarded twelve months later. Despite the 1955 selection of the Navy's Project Vanguard as the nation's scientific satellite program, the Air Force also thought about such a satellite. In 1956, the Air Force started to plan for its own scientific satellite to be launched as a precursor to the reconnaissance spacecraft. This idea bounced around the Air Force and DoD agencies until 1957 before it was dropped.[9]

On May 6, Joseph Kaplan, chair of the U.S. National Committee for the IGY, provided the NSF with a specific budget request for the scientific satellite program. The estimate offered was $7.5 million for ten satellites and a curiously precise $2,234,500 for five ground stations with associated equipment and personnel. Donald Quarles' staff examined these figures and doubled them before adding them to the IGY proposal. Since Congress had appropriated only $13 million for all U.S. IGY activity, it was clear that other departments, most likely the military, had to provide substantial financial help.

Quarles forwarded the civilian satellite proposals to Nelson Rockefeller, then Special Assistant to the President. In a memo dated May 17, Rockefeller strongly endorsed building a scientific satellite as part of the IGY. He argued the United States could score a major political and psychological victory over the Russians if an American satellite were first into space.[10]

On May 20, the National Security Council (NSC) approved the start of a U.S. program to launch a scientific satellite. The decision was published in a classified document designated NSC 5520.

The NSC agreed with Rockefeller that "considerable prestige and psychological benefits will accrue to the nation which first is successful in launching a satellite." The council added "Furthermore, a small scientific satellite will provide a test of the principle of 'Freedom of Space.'" Specifically, NSC 5520 recommended that the United States "launch a small scientific satellite under international auspices, such as the International Geophysical Year, in order to emphasize its peaceful purposes. . . ."[11]

Although the satellite was to be scientific, the program was assigned by NSC 5520 to the Department of Defense. The only restriction stipulated was that the satellite effort must not interfere with military missile programs, which, since the issuance of the Killian report, had been established as the leading military priority in the Eisenhower administration.[12] The council set a goal of launching by 1958.[13]

How to launch a satellite? Which satellite to launch? The NSC left the details to Quarles. In July, Quarles handed the question to the Ad Hoc Committee on Special Capabilities.[14] This eight-member panel was chaired by Homer Stewart of JPL and included representatives nominated by the Army, Navy, and Air Force. In addition to Stewart, the members included Joseph Kaplan, Cal Tech physicist Charles Lauritsen, astronomer Robert McMath, mathematician J. Barkley Rosser, George Clement of RAND, Richard Porter of General Electric's Missile Division, and Clifford Furnas, chancellor of the University of Buffalo. (Which member had been nominated by which service was not disclosed.) Quarles charged the so-called

Stewart Committee with selecting the best approach to putting an American IGY satellite in orbit.

The Stewart Committee members worked quickly and diligently. Before the end of July, they had heard extensive presentations from the Army, Air Force, and NRL, visited the Glenn L. Martin company plant to look at the Viking technology, and developed the first two drafts of their report.

On July 29, while the Stewart Committee was still at work, President Eisenhower announced the U.S. intention to proceed "with the launching of small Earth-circling satellites as a part of U.S. participation in the IGY." Official responsibility was divided: the NAS was in charge of the scientific aspects of the venture, while funding was to be obtained through the NSF. The military was responsible for providing technical and logistic support, including the boosters and launch facilities.

One reason Eisenhower made the satellite project public before the Stewart Committee finished its task was out of fear that the U.S.S.R. might make its own satellite announcement first. Instead, the news reached the Soviets when Fred Durant announced the American initiative at the IAF Congress then under way in Copenhagen. The Soviet delegates did, however, not seem surprised. "All of us were expecting it," Durant explained. "It was just a matter of doing it."[15]

After making contact with Moscow, Leonid Sedov hurriedly announced the Soviet IGY satellite program. Sedov's exact words on this occasion are interesting: "From a technical point of view, it is possible to create a satellite of larger dimensions than that reported in the newspapers which we had the opportunity of scanning today. The realization of the Soviet project can be expected in the comparatively near future. I won't take it upon myself to name the date more precisely."[16]

Actually, Sedov could not have named a planned launch date: in August 1955, there was no plan. He would not likely have known even if there was, since the infant Soviet satellite program was military-controlled and Sedov's commission had little contact with Sergey Korolev's rocket design bureau. Yet, Sedov apparently knew something was in the making since he was saying the U.S.S.R. would launch a satellite fairly soon and that it would be heavier than the American spacecraft. He was right on both counts.

During the Stewart Committee's meetings in July, the committee members considered three options:

1. A proposal from the Naval Research Laboratory, using a 40-pound satellite and a new three-stage launch vehicle based on the Viking;

2. An updated version of Orbiter, put forth by the Army (the Office of Naval Research support for this project was withdrawn at this point, since ONR was the parent office of NRL);
3. An Air Force design launched by the yet-untested Atlas ICBM.

The Air Force concept, sometimes called the "World Series" satellite, was more an exercise in future planning than a serious proposal. The service's submission was a forty-page discussion focusing on the instrumentation that could be carried on a 150-pound satellite. The Air Force was genuinely interested in satellites and was in the process of letting study contracts for the secret Advanced Reconnaissance System (ARS) satellite project. The ARS was then the name for what had been the WS-117L effort, although the WS-117L designation would reappear as the effort went through subsequent restructurings. However, Maj. Gen. Bernard Schriever, the brilliant manager who would steer the service's IRBM and ICBM programs to fruition, was adamantly against delaying the Atlas's development as a missile by requiring it to first serve as a space launcher for a nonessential project.[17]

The $17.7-million Army proposal briefed to the Stewart Committee had been updated considerably from the 1954 Orbiter plan.[18] Most notably, a radio tracking system (using either an Army device under development or the NRL-developed transmitter from the Navy's rival proposal) was added to the satellite's design.[19] The concept, however, remained the same: a 5-pound satellite, orbited by a Redstone-based booster augmented with clusters of small solid-propellant rockets. However, there was also a change in the booster design. The Army recommended the use of scaled-down variants of a more capable rocket, the Sergeant, in place of the earlier Loki.

The Sergeant, like the Loki, was a JPL product for the Army. An inertially-guided surface-to-surface missile, it first flew in 1956 and replaced the Corporal in Army service. At the time William Pickering became the JPL's director in 1954, the Sergeant development project was the lab's top priority.

The 36-foot, 10,000-pound Sergeant missile was far too large for a Redstone upper stage. In the course of the development program, however, a miniature version had been built. This "scaled Sergeant" rocket, about 4 feet long and 6 inches in diameter, produced a maximum of 1,600 pounds of thrust during a burn time of six seconds.[20] When the Orbiter idea was revised, JPL suggested the Loki be replaced by this version of the Sergeant.

JPL engineers had been thinking about satellites long before the Stewart Committee or even the Orbiter design. Ideas for scientific satellites and launch systems had been bandied about the lab for several years. Without Army funding for the idea, though, no hardware had been developed. Now the opportunity arose, and it set JPL on a path into space exploration and away from missile development.

The NRL's plan, titled, "A Scientific Satellite Program," opened with a discussion of a satellite's benefit to geodesy. The proposal was officially designated NRL Memorandum Report No. 487, classified Secret and dated July 5, 1955. In a clever bit of politicking, the geodesy section of the document emphasized the military utility of this "scientific" satellite.

The report went on to cite geophysical and astrophysical research as equally useful applications. Two experiments were described. The first would use photon counters to detect radiation in a range called the Lyman-alpha band. Radiation of this wavelength varies with the distribution of hydrogen in space and the level of solar activity. One photon counter would detect the intensity of Lyman-alpha radiation from interstellar space, while the other would measure that coming from the Sun. The resulting information would help determine the effects of such emissions on magnetic storms, the aurora, and cosmic ray intensity.

The second experiment would use a magnetometer to determine the existence of an electric current, called the ring current, circling the Earth. The hypothesized ring current, circling the planet at the equator at a distance of several Earth radii, was believed to contribute to the same phenomena which were influenced by Lyman-alpha radiation.[21] As the ring current would affect Earth's magnetic fields, it could be detected by measuring the magnetic field encountered by the satellite and comparing the results to those recorded at ground stations.[22]

Two launch vehicle configurations were described. The first, Case A, was a combination of the latest Viking design (called the M-10) with two solid-fuel stages designed by Atlantic Research Corporation. The Martin Company, it was noted, had checked this design and thought it conservative and reliable. The report pointed out that, based on Viking experience, this vehicle could be launched from a ship if desired.

The second option, Case B, was developed from the M-15: it combined the M-10 Viking, an Aerobee-Hi, and a solid-fuel third stage. This launcher could, it was estimated, put a satellite weighing 40 pounds into a circular orbit 303 miles high. The Case A rocket could handle the same payload, but the orbit would be only 216 miles high.[23]

Either vehicle, the NRL reported, could handle a payload of up to 40 pounds for an equatorial orbit and could put a smaller satellite in an inclined or even a polar orbit. The launch schedule would depend on the option chosen: the Case A liquid-solid-solid combination could put a satellite in orbit two years from the program start, while the Case B design would need an additional six months for design and testing of the second-stage control system.[24]

In the body of the report, the impression given was that the Viking M-10 and the Aerobee-Hi could essentially be used in their existing forms. With the exception of the note about designing controls for the Aerobee stage, there was no mention of any need to modify the M-10 or the Aerobee. The requirement for a new third stage, the report said, had already been sent to manufacturers who could provide that hardware.

Appendix D of the proposal added important details on this third-stage point. In either launcher configuration, the first stage would not actually be the off-the-shelf M-10. It would be a modification with a new power-plant (referred to in the report as the Hermes X400), with a spin stabilization mechanism added and the Viking's triangular fins removed. A post-cutoff stabilization system to orient the rocket correctly for dispensing the upper stages was also required.[25]

On August 4, 1956, the direction of the early American space program was determined when the Stewart Committee issued its formal report. The members had voted 5-2 for the Navy proposal.[26] Only Stewart and Furnas apparently supported the Army.[27] (McMath was ill and did not vote.) The decision surprised even Milt Rosen, who had made the Navy's presentation. "I thought they'd win, too. They had a rocket and we didn't," he recalled.[28] Fred Durant found the decision "incredible."[29]

The Army team was startled and infuriated. General Simon protested vociferously. The Army, he argued, had a proven, highly capable rocket, and could also orbit a satellite much earlier—by January 1957. In addition, the Army representatives argued, the Redstone program was far enough along that a satellite project would not interfere with Redstone's scheduled deployment as a weapon. The next missile program in development, the Jupiter, was also going well.

Quarles was impressed enough to ask the Stewart Committee to look at the Army's proposal again. The NRL got wind of this decision, and eventually both services got one more chance present their concepts. The original NRL proposal was hastily tweaked to meet some concerns initially expressed by the committee. Several changes were made to the booster design, and the payload was reduced to 20 pounds. The series of test vehicles planned for launch before the first orbital attempt was expanded.[30] The

NRL launch timetable had been compressed from thirty months to eighteen—almost equal to what the Army promised.[31]

General Simon offered an improvement of his own. He suggested the Redstone could be modified to use a more powerful engine, which was then under development for the Navaho. This would raise the orbital payload to 162 pounds.[32] Before the Stewart Committee re-voted on the matter, Quarles floated a proposal of his own. He suggested the Army could provide the first stage and the Navy the satellite and upper stages, while the Air Force worked on developing its proposal as a backup system.

The Stewart Committee met again on August 23, but nothing was changed. Quarles' interservice compromise was not adopted, and the Committee re-voted on the Army and NRL proposals. Where the first vote had been 5-2 in the Navy's favor, this one was 4-2. (McMath, who had missed the first vote, was also absent for this one. It is not known who else missed the second vote or why.[33]) On September 9, a DoD directive to the Navy authorized the NRL to proceed with the project.[34] The NRL team got its start five and a half months ahead of the comparable milestone in the first Soviet satellite program.[35]

As the Stewart Committee decision has been second-guessed ever since, it is worth examining in some detail why the Committee picked the Navy's program, which (at the suggestion of Milt Rosen's wife, Sally) soon became known as Project Vanguard.

The NRL proposal, without question, offered the most detailed explanation of the satellite's intended benefits to science. In addition, its satellite offered more space for instruments than the smaller Army spacecraft.[36] Von Braun believed the larger payload promised by Vanguard was the most important reason his team lost the decision. He wrote later that he actually thought "very highly" of the Vanguard design and believed it would make important contributions to rocket technology, even though he felt the decision to choose it over the Army's more mature system for this project was incorrect.[37]

In addition to the superiority of the Navy satellite's on-board instrumentation, the Stewart Committee strongly felt the NRL offered a better tracking and telemetry system. This would contribute to the satellite's scientific utility as well.

The booster was another matter. After all, Redstone had been making test flights since August 1953. The NRL offered only one proven stage, the Viking, and its proposal contained very little cost data. Nevertheless, the majority of the Stewart Committee members felt the Navy's three-stage rocket was likely to be cheaper—four times cheaper, in fact—and more reliable than the complex Army booster.[38]

Despite this judgment, the Stewart Committee was well aware the Army's rocket was more mature. Clifford Furnas wrote that, in the deliberations before the first committee vote, the idea that would later be resurrected by Quarles—the use of the Redstone booster and the NRL's instrumentation—came up. However, "We finally decided that breaking the space barrier would be an easier task than breaking the interservice barrier."[39]

In explaining its decision, the committee cited all these reasons, plus the judgment that the Vanguard system offered more potential for growth. In addition, while development of the nearly new Vanguard booster presented considerable technical risk, it would take no resources from the military's missile programs. With both programs promising similar schedules, it wasn't difficult for the committee to opt for the more scientifically capable of the two satellites.

William Pickering believed the fear of interfering with missile programs was the key point in the decision.[40] Stewart later wrote there was also some anti-German feeling among the committee members, although he doubted this was a major influence.[41] The Redstone's design used many features of the V-2, and of course many of the same engineers.

Finally, Milt Rosen believed the planned orbits may have affected the committee's decision.[42] In 1955, guidance systems were in their infancy. Vanguard's orbit was to be a circular path 303 miles in altitude. According to the NRL's proposal, this altitude allowed the satellite to tolerate a significant pointing error—as much as two degrees—and still make a safe orbit with a perigee of 153 miles.[43] The Army's satellite, with an intended altitude of 150 miles, needed to be aimed more accurately. That made Vanguard the safer bet. (In practice, neither program suffered any failures due to insufficient accuracy in orbital injection.)

Some historians have speculated that Vanguard was chosen because it was less obviously a military project. The theory is that the choice was either made by the Stewart Committee or directed by higher authority—perhaps even the President—so Vanguard could serve as a "stalking horse" to establish the principle of unfettered overflight through space above national territories (as discussed in NSC 5520) to ensure that later military satellites would not be challenged.[44]

Len Cormier, then an engineer with the two-man IGY Earth Satellite Office of the NAS, recalls that his understanding at the time was that the decision was driven by the desire to have the IGY satellite launched on a rocket "derived from a research rocket (Viking) rather than from a military ballistic missile (like the Redstone)."[45] If this was the rationale, though, it was apparently never committed to paper. No such reason appeared in the Stewart Committee report or in other records of the time.

Certainly, the Vanguard satellite was not so openly military as its competition. Choosing it fit very well with the purposes of NSC 5520. There is, however, no proof the committee was explicitly charged with picking the "more civilian" satellite. It's worth noting that NSC 5520 recommended a scientific satellite without explicitly saying it had to be non-military.[46] Certainly the NSC members were aware that military participation was unavoidable, since the only programs with experience in large rockets were either entirely military or military-sponsored.

There is an interesting line in the Stewart Committee report's "Conclusions" section. This reads, "If the attainment of the objective of the National Security Council directive is to be ensured, clear and undivided administrative responsibility in the Department of Defense must be promptly defined, assigned and ordered."[47] This indicates an awareness of NSC 5520, but the sentence implies more of a concern with the council's schedule (a launch by 1958) than with the character of the satellite. Stewart himself has stated that overflight had no effect on the Committee's decisions, and in fact was not even discussed.[48]

Indeed, Quarles and others in the Pentagon had serious doubts about the wisdom of the Vanguard choice. If the Army proposal had been ruled out for political reasons, there would have been no reason for the Stewart Committee re-hearing held at the Army's request of a second vote.[49] Given that fact and Stewart's assertion, it is clear that overflight did not play any significant role in the selection of Vanguard.

There is no denying that the satellite program's military aspects were downplayed as much as possible. The original announcement made by President Eisenhower indicated the military would play a supporting role to the government's scientific bodies. Officially, Vanguard was "an IGY project in which the DoD is cooperating, rather than a DoD project."[50]

George Hoover, who had seen his role diminish with the eclipse of Orbiter, dutifully toed this party line. In a February 1956 presentation to an engineers' association, he said, "The project, which is entirely scientific in nature, will be sponsored by the National Academy of Sciences and the National Science Foundation. Technical advice and assistance to the U.S. program will be provided by scientists of the Defense Department. . . ."[51]

Sometimes the effort to portray Vanguard as nonmilitary was slightly comical. On July 1, 1957, the project's director, John Hagen, spoke to Soviet scientists visiting the NAS. When he mentioned the "Naval Research Laboratory satellite," a subordinate interrupted him, saying, "The National Academy's satellite, Dr. Hagen."[52] Major General John B. Medaris, commander of the Army's ballistic missile program and von Braun's immediate superior at Redstone Arsenal, later referred to this attempt to separate military and civilian rocketry as "a costly and ridiculous division of the indivisible."[53]

What about being first into space? Being first was not discussed in the Stewart Committee's report, unless the single sentence referring to the NSC's objectives is counted. There is no evidence the committee was charged with picking the fastest way into space. If it had been, Milt Rosen is convinced the committee would have chosen the Army, regardless of the Navy's promise of a nearly equal development schedule.[54] (While Rosen had endorsed that schedule projection before the Stewart Committee, he privately feared from the start it would prove unrealistic.)[55]

Whatever the reasoning, the decision had been made. The announced objectives of Project Vanguard were fourfold:

1. To develop and procure a satellite-launching vehicle.
2. To place at least one satellite in orbit during the International Geophysical Year.
3. To accomplish at least one scientific experiment.
4. To track the flight to prove the satellite was indeed in orbit.

These were relatively modest goals, and the NRL had no doubt they could be attained. It all sounded easier than it was.

Chapter 5

The Trials of Project Vanguard

Project Vanguard was like a thoroughbred racehorse on a muddy track. It stumbled leaving the starting gate, then had trouble gaining its footing despite the best efforts of all involved. Sometimes it seemed to hit its stride, only to step in another soft spot and be forced to slow down and regroup.

First, the government side of the project had to get organized. NRL was under the authority of ONR, which, until Quarles began the interservice competition, had been working with the Army. Although the ONR had dutifully pulled back and let the Army present the modified Orbiter proposal as its own, Comdr. George Hoover was still incredulous at the Stewart Committee decision.[1] Why, he asked, had the Committee opted for a "blueprint" over the proven Army technology?[2]

Despite the ONR's withdrawal from the Army program, it took until October 6 for the Chief of Naval Research, Rear Adm. Rawson Bennett, to give the NRL formal direction to proceed. For that matter, not all the division chiefs at NRL supported committing to a project that would necessarily overshadow everything else the lab was doing, perhaps taking resources from other programs as well. Captain Sam Tucker, NRL's commander, felt it necessary to make certain everyone at NRL, ONR, and other Navy agencies understood that the Chief of Naval

Operations himself, Adm. Arleigh Burke, expected full support for Vanguard.[3]

The next step was to staff the project. The head of the NRL's Astronomy and Astrophysics Division, John P. Hagen, was appointed project director. Hagen was perhaps best known for two attributes: his calm demeanor and the pipe permanently fixed in his mouth. Homer E. Newell of the NRL became the project's Science Programs Coordinator. He would work with IGY officials and the scientific community to ensure Vanguard's return of knowledge measured up the promises made to the Stewart Committee.

Hagen established a core management group of about fifteen people. In addition to himself, Rosen, and Newell, this included a technical board under Rosen, a team to work on computing the satellite's orbit, and a deputy director, J. Paul Walsh. Assisting this group were representatives from the Army and the Air Force. Some 180 people eventually worked directly for the NRL on Vanguard. Despite the heated competition that had taken place before the Stewart Committee's decision, Hagen never had anything but praise for the support and cooperation extended to Vanguard by the Army Signal Corps, the Army Corps of Engineers, and the test range at Cape Canaveral, now called the Air Force Missile Test Center (AFMTC). The only organization conspicuously absent from this tri-service program was ABMA. In the two and a half years between the Stewart Committee and the eventual success of Project Vanguard, the Vanguard team very rarely sought or accepted any help from the Army's missile experts.[4]

The non-government participation in the project would be led by the Glenn L. Martin Company, builder of the Viking rocket and designated prime contractor for the Vanguard launch vehicle. A communication from Martin, submitted as part of the NRL's proposal to the second Stewart Committee decision meeting, read "whether we are called upon to manage the program or to provide the airframe alone, you can be assured that we will support the program in the aggressive fashion necessary to achieve a satellite at the earliest practical date."[5] The NRL was responsible for the satellite, as well as the guidance system and the Minitrack telemetry and tracking equipment.[6]

Working out this arrangement was not easy. Everyone, including the Stewart Committee, had assumed Martin would be immediately brought on board as prime contractor for the launch vehicle. Martin executives were well aware of their firm's position. They also knew that Vanguard, while not financially lucrative, was going to be a high-profile project with considerable prestige attached.

During two meetings in late August, the company presented a proposal that startled NRL officials. Martin recommended that it would not only provide the launch vehicle but manage the entire Vanguard program. The company would reduce the government's role to that of providing the satellite, arranging logistical support, and performing very limited oversight functions. The endeavor would even be referred to as Martin's satellite project, not the NRL's.[7] Martin executives thought they had proved their worth on the Viking project and that a complex undertaking like Vanguard was best pursued by giving the company broad responsibility. Martin would "carry responsibility for the development, design, manufacture, and test of the complete system."[8] That included ground facilities, telemetry and tracking, and all areas of operations.

John Hagen and his colleagues were anything but receptive. To them, Martin's proposal effectively reduced the government to serving as Martin's support contractor instead of the other way around.[9]

Working out every detail of this problem was a two-year process. Since the NRL and Martin agreed on the urgent nature of the program, they approached the matter by creating a number of agreements instead of trying to settle everything at once. Some decisions (like modifications to the already-planned *Viking Nos. 13* and *14* to test Vanguard hardware and procedures) were handled quickly in separate contracts, while others (like the exact nature of the company's authority to make changes to government-approved plans) were postponed until later in the program. Often, the most contentious issues were not solved until the venture reached a point where postponement was no longer possible.

Not everything was held in abeyance while the initial contract compromises were ironed out. The NRL's telemetry experts, led by Daniel G. Mazur, immediately began working with the Air Force's safety and scheduling officials at Cape Canaveral. Rosen, along with other engineers from both NRL and Martin, began talks with engine manufacturers concerning the new first-stage engine and the still-conceptual third stage. Even the first stages of hardware development required that Martin have some idea of the program's schedule and the funds available. The eighteen-month schedule estimate made to the Stewart Committee was soon dropped, as was the initial cost estimate of $20 million.

Neither the schedule nor the cost estimate had been binding, but moving away from these targets introduced a major element of uncertainty. Any multi-year U.S. Government project was (and is) difficult to budget for. The difficulties would be compounded if there were no fixed schedule and if it were not clear where the funds would be coming from in the first place. The Stewart Committee had made no decision concerning which federal agencies had financial responsibility for Vanguard. Martin offered an initial estimate of $13 million for its own costs, cautioning that this would vary depending on what responsibilities the company was given.

By September 23, an initial contract had been hammered out, although it set aside many issues that would require further negotiations. The contract did not specify an overall cost, but provided for an initial increment of $2 million. Martin did not gain its preferred status as manager of the entire effort, and instead was referred to as "the supplier of the launching vehicle." According to the contract, the launch vehicle needed to place a payload weighing 21.5 pounds in an orbit with a perigee of at least 200 miles. Tracking could be done by optical means and/or by radio. Martin was to provide a firm schedule by January 1956 and deliver a working launch vehicle by the end of 1958. Martin was exempted from having to subject every detail of its design to government review, provided the system performed as required. The launch site would be Cape Canaveral, and the orbital inclination from the equatorial plane was to fall between 30 and 45 degrees.[10]

This agreement did not ensure smooth cooperation between the NRL and Martin. Days after the contract was signed, Martin won the Air Force's much larger contract for the Titan ICBM. Many of the people who were expected to work on Vanguard were switched to the new project. Despite assurances from Martin executives, the NRL managers on the project suspected Vanguard would get the "second string" engineers and support.

The NRL's largest contribution, aside from the satellite itself, was Minitrack. NRL engineers already had experience with phase-comparison radio-tracking systems from Viking. Another source of expertise in this field was Convair, which since 1948 had been developing a tracking system called Azusa to support missile development programs.[11] Although Convair was working for the Army and Air Force, company engineers exchanged ideas with Milt Rosen and other NRL researchers.[12]

Azusa, like the Viking tracking equipment, used the phase difference (caused by the difference in the path length traveled by the radio signals) between satellite-transmitted signals received at different antennas on the ground. The measurement of the difference between signals allowed tracking system operators to calculate the angles between the ground stations and the satellite, thus providing the spacecraft's location. The Navy's development of Minitrack, which got its first workout locating *Sputnik 1*, was the origin of the Naval Space Surveillance System, still in use in 2004.

The task of devising a radio-tracking system for Vanguard fell to John T.

Mengel of the NRL's Tracking and Guidance Branch. Mengel and his colleagues, most notably Roger L. Easton and Martin Votaw, drew on technology from the Atlas and Viking tracking systems and related work done by another branch of the NRL, which had a system using sonar instead of radio waves, for undersea applications. The best ideas from all these efforts were synthesized to produce what was, for the time, a very advanced and sensitive system. Minitrack could locate a satellite in three dimensions and provide three vectors of velocity to describe its motion.

The Navy engineers had a lot of trouble at first building a reliable miniature transmitter for the IGY frequency of 108 MHz.[13] Part of the solution was to jettison the vacuum tube technology they were used to and adopt a relatively new invention: the transistor. The transistor had been invented by Bell Labs in 1948, and it was one of the breakthrough technologies that permitted satellites of manageable size and high reliability.[14]

The NRL eventually deployed fourteen Minitrack stations. Twelve were in the Western Hemisphere, forming a "fence" from Blossom Point, Maryland, south to Santiago, Chile. The others were in South Africa and Australia. The radio system was originally intended as a secondary means of tracking. The primary system was to be an optical tracking network, designed by Fred Whipple and his colleague J. Allen Hynek, which relied on development of advanced Baker-Nunn telescopic cameras and the enlistment of groups of amateur astronomers in a program called Project Moonwatch.

As it turned out, the Baker-Nunn cameras took longer to develop than expected and never did make a major contribution to Vanguard, although they were very helpful to later satellite programs. Moonwatch, on the other hand, was organized very quickly. Over 250 Moonwatch teams—half of them in the United States, the other half spread across many nations—provided countless observations of Vanguard and other satellites.[15]

Work on the scientific aspects of the satellite program had begun very quickly. On October 2, 1955, the NAS established a Technical Panel on the Earth Satellite Program (TPESP), chaired by Richard Porter, a veteran of both the Stewart Committee and the Hermes rocket project, which he had directed.[16] The Technical Panel created two working groups. The Working Group on Internal Instrumentation (WGII), chaired by James Van Allen, was to review proposals for experiments to be installed in the Vanguard satellites. The Working Group on External Instrumentation (WGEI), chaired by William Pickering, would establish the plan for tracking and telemetry.

In the wake of the official announcement by the IGY Earth Satellite

Program, interest in the scientific potential of satellites had risen dramatically. The satellite became not merely a theoretical possibility but a looming reality, and astronomers, physicists, and others pondered what instruments might be placed on such an orbiting vehicle. In January 1956, the Upper Atmosphere Rocket Research Panel held a meeting devoted entirely to satellite-borne experiments. Out of this meeting came proposals covering all areas, many of which would emerge as hardware for the Vanguard and other early American satellite programs. Thirty-three unclassified papers from this symposium were published as a book titled *The Scientific Uses of Earth Satellites*, and this helped excite the scientific community even further.[17]

In order to deal with the resulting flood of ideas, Van Allen's group established four criteria by which experiments could be ranked. These were scientific importance, technical feasibility, competence (the demonstrated ability of the people and institutions involved to follow through on their proposals), and importance of a satellite vehicle to the proposed work (that is, how essential it was that the research be accomplished using a satellite instead of balloons, rockets, or other means).[18]

Of the twenty-five experiments submitted, four were assigned "Flight Priority A," meaning they would be put on the first four satellites available. These received full funding from the National Science Foundation and other IGY sources. Seven experiments were assigned "Flight Priority B." These were allotted some developmental funds and could be considered once the Priority A experiments had been accommodated.[19]

The four Priority A experiments were:

"Satellite Environmental Measurements" (studies of temperature, pressure, and micrometeorite impacts). Proposed by Hermann E. LaGow of the NRL.

"Solar Lyman-Alpha Intensity" (detecting variations in solar emissions in the narrow band called Lyman-alpha radiation). Proposed by Herbert Friedman of the Electron Optics Branch of NRL's Optics Division.

"Cosmic Ray Observations in Earth Satellites" (mapping of fluctuations in cosmic ray intensity and correlation with the Earth's magnetic field). Proposed by James Van Allen.

"Measurement of Interplanetary Matter from the Earth Satellite" (more sensitive micrometeorite detection and reporting). Proposed by Maurice Dubin of the Geophysics Research Directorate at the Air Force Cambridge Research Center.[20]

Since the NRL was planning for six satellites, there was room for some Priority B experiments and even some latecomers to be added to the list. Late in 1956, the WGII endorsed an experiment, proposed by the NRL's James Heppner, titled "Geomagnetic Measurements." This was a descendant of the magnetometer experiment discussed in the original NRL paper presented to the Stewart Committee. To gauge the intensity of the Earth's magnetic field and to perform related measurements, the satellite would carry a magnetometer that projected out from the body of the spacecraft. This would obviously complicate the satellite's design, but the scientific return was judged to be worth the trouble.[21]

Other possible candidates were:

A cloud-cover measuring experiment using photocells, proposed by William G. Stroud of the Signal Corps Engineering Laboratories.

A 30-inch inflatable sphere NACA scientists wanted ejected to study atmospheric density and drag.

A study of the Earth's radiation balance (using four small sensors to analyze how much radiation the Earth received from the Sun and other sources and how much it reflected back into space), suggested by Verner E. Suomi of the University of Wisconsin.[22]

The satellite and its instrumentation provided the scientific rationale for the program, but satellite development was meaningless without a suitable booster. As Rosen had feared, the original development schedule was overly optimistic. No one had ever built a large three-stage rocket, and it took months just to decide on such basic specifications as the weight allotment for each stage.

Throughout the Vanguard program, there was never a consistent funding mechanism or a reliable budget projection. Vanguard funding was doled out in small portions from a variety of sources. Direct Congressional appropriations, IGY funds, NAS money, and several sources within DoD were called on at various times.

At one point in 1957, even the CIA kicked in $2.5 million. At the time, the agency had no official role in space, other than the collection of intelligence on the Soviet program. (The agency was not given charge of a space project until February 1958, when the President assigned it the lead role in the CORONA reconnaissance satellite program.) The CIA may have been looking ahead to future space endeavors. As Fred Durant put it, it "seems quite logical that some elements of the Agency would want a 'seat at the table.'"[23]

The up-and-down funding profile contributed to further delays, which resulted in higher costs. Launch facilities, test equipment, and the innovative Minitrack system all required more effort and money than originally projected. Finally, the costs of the instrumentation on the satellites had not been included in the early estimates. The $20 million figure was soon doubled, then doubled again, and Project Vanguard officials struggled to keep their projections current as demands for additional funds came in from all areas of the program.

In selling its proposal, the NRL had acknowledged the relative immaturity of its rocket design, but it had assured the Stewart Committee the challenge was manageable. The first stage of Vanguard would be developed from the proven Viking, and the second stage would come from the Aerobee-Hi sounding rocket. Only the third stage would be entirely new.

In practice, the obstacles proved to be considerable. The entire launch vehicle design depended on the size and weight of the payload. The contract specified a payload of 21.5 pounds, but did not specify the shape. Martin initially assumed the cone shape displayed in the NRL presentation to the Stewart Committee would be used, and the rocket design effort went forward on that basis. By the middle of October 1955, though, scientists on the TPESP were pressing for a change to a spherical satellite.[24] A sphere would allow more room for instruments and, as a symmetrical shape, would provide much better information about the extent and character of the upper atmosphere as it was tracked.

Hagen knew this decision's effects would ripple through the entire launch vehicle design process, but he approved it.[25] Using a sphere instead of a cone added requirements for a protective shroud and a more complex release mechanism. More importantly, it meant the third stage would have to be redesigned with a larger diameter.

On November 1, NRL notified Martin of the change. The new plan called for a sphere 30 inches in diameter, a major change from the 20-inch cone Martin was accommodating in its design. To keep the changes to the launch vehicle to a reasonable minimum, Martin engineers proposed a 20-inch sphere instead. They persuaded Hagen that the 30-inch sphere was impossible unless the entire launch vehicle was to be redesigned. The 20-inch sphere was agreed upon only after James Van Allen's suggestion, that some of the satellites be made cylindrical in order to save weight and reduce complexity, was considered and rejected. With only six launch attempts authorized, NRL officials were in no mood to complicate things by having two satellite designs.[26]

Some members of the NRL team, especially scientists, were excited by the possibility of using photovoltaic, or solar, cells to provide power on board the satellite. Where batteries would last days or perhaps weeks, solar cells could theoretically keep a satellite transmitting data for years. Others were wary of using this technology, which one conservative engineer labeled "unconventional and not fully established," on the satellite. Lobbying by the pro-solar crowd, encouraged by Army photovoltaics expert Hans Zeigler, eventually overcame the resistance. Vanguard would have both batteries and solar cells.[27]

While this and other technical issues were being discussed, the matter of who was in control of the program resurfaced. The NRL and Martin had different ideas about radio equipment for telemetering both satellite and launch vehicle information. The NRL intended to specify its newest Minitrack equipment as the solution, and Martin resisted having that type of detail dictated by the government. While this issue was eventually resolved in NRL's favor—with outstanding results—the dispute resurrected some bad feelings.

At the end of November 1955, the Martin official who managed the Vanguard contract wrote to the Navy that the "original concept of an overall Martin responsibility for the design, construction, testing, ground support and launching procedures . . . dictates that the specifications be limited in coverage to general requirements." Matters did not improve when, in December, a Martin vice president asserted that his company had always expected to have full responsibility for design and operation of the entire system, tracking included.[28]

Another round of sometimes-heated discussion ensued. The contractor-government relationship was not well defined until the final contract, incorporating thirty-one pages of design specifications and three technical appendices, was signed on April 30, 1956. Minor skirmishes would continue almost until the end of the program.

The question about the size of the satellite, while pivotal, was not the only impetus for design changes. Countless improvements were needed to both the first and second stages of the booster to adapt the existing designs to their new functions.

The most obvious change was a major redesign of the first stage. The Viking-based first stage ended up being not so much a modification of the Viking M-10 as an evolution into a very distinct rocket. As the NRL's Jim Bridger put it "We did indeed bring Viking experience to the Vanguard program . . . but for all practical purposes the Vanguard vehicle was new, new from stem to stern."[29]

While the first stage had to lose the Viking fins and gain new control systems, all other challenges paled next to the need to select, develop, and install a new engine. This was the GE X-405, an outgrowth of engine technology developed in the Hermes program. The engine of the Viking only had to lift a maximum of 15,000 pounds gross weight from the launch pad, while the Vanguard stack was projected to be at least 5,000 pounds heavier. Even more challenging was the required increase in velocity. The Viking never exceeded 5,000 feet per second (fps). Vanguard needed to reach 25,000 fps to establish its preferred orbit. To provide a margin for error, a target of 26,420 fps was established.

Replacing the engine in the first stage may have seemed only moderately difficult to those members of the Stewart Committee who lacked rocket-design experience, but it effectively meant using only the original outer casing for the stage and redesigning everything else. The use of a new engine meant an increase in the vehicle's gross weight, a shift in weight distribution and the center of gravity, changes in the vibrational and acoustic environments for the entire launch vehicle, and other effects on the design.

An agreement with General Electric on the new engine was quickly reached. A purchase order from Martin, signed on October 1, 1955, specified the engine was to be ready by October 1956. It had to deliver 27,000 pounds of thrust with a sea-level I_{sp} of 254. The stage eventually had a gross weight of 16,850 pounds and a thrust of just over 30,000 pounds.

Shortly after the first-stage paperwork was finalized, Aerojet General, builder of the Aerobee, was given a contract for the second stage. While GE was the only source seriously considered for the first-stage engine, Aerojet had to fend off a proposal from Bell Aircraft Corporation. Aerojet had the Aerobee experience on its side and put in the lowest bid. Bell thought the project would cost $2.675 million: Aerojet bid just over $1 million. (The work would eventually cost $4 million.)[30]

As with the first stage, developing the redesigned second stage turned out to be no simple task. With time, more and more functions were added to this stage. In addition to the engine and propellant tanks, it housed the guidance system for both the first and the second stages; the mechanism to initiate the jettison of the nose cone covering the satellite; a system to spin the vehicle before the third stage, which had no guidance control, was released; a destruct system; and a radar beacon. All this increased the original weight estimate considerably.

Martin and Aerojet kept the second-stage diameter the same as originally estimated, 32 inches, but lengthened it to increase the propellant capacity. The 32-inch diameter was not fixed due to any technical reason, but because, as explained by Martin's William G. Purdy, the engineers had chosen "the widest piece of standard rolled aluminum sheet we could find."[31]

The propellants were to be unsymmetrical dimethyl hydrazine (UDMH) and white fuming nitric acid. These hypergolic propellants were selected because they reduced the uncertainty involved in igniting a rocket stage at high altitudes (34 miles) and speeds. The stage's gross weight was finally fixed at 4,770 pounds, of which 3,240 pounds was propellant. The thrust was 7,500 pounds.[32]

Selecting a third-stage design and contractor was also difficult. Thiokol Chemical Company, one of the leaders in solid-fuel propulsion, was the first company approached. However, a Thiokol representative informed Martin in September that the notional requirements concerning power, weight, allowable maximum burning time, and casing size added up to a combination that was simply impossible to provide. Further discussions produced no resolution: Thiokol experts did not believe a rocket fitting Martin's performance requirements could be powered by a rocket motor limited, as Vanguard designers wanted, to a gross weight of 365 pounds and a casing diameter of only 11 inches.[33]

Eventually, the NRL and Martin looked elsewhere. To ameliorate the perceived risk involved in the innovative third stage, two contracts for completely different motor designs were let. One was to the Grand Central Rocket Company of Redlands, California, the other to the West Virginia–based Allegany Ballistics Laboratory (ABL). The ABL design used a fiberglass casing, another first for a large rocket, and an advanced double-base propellant. A double-base solid propellant combines two compounds, such as nitrocellulose and nitroglycerin, which could also be used alone as single-base propellants (or monopropellants). Most earlier solid rockets used monopropellants, with nitrocellulose being the most common choice.

The apprehension concerning the use of an unproven solid-fuel third stage turned out to be unfounded. The Grand Central stage performed well on Vanguard's early flights, including the first two that reached orbit. ABL's X-248 (also called the Altair), used on the last Vanguard launch, allowed the booster to more than double its payload and was adopted or modified for use on several other launch vehicles.

Partly as a result of the challenges involved in turning a sounding rocket into a space launcher, Vanguard produced a series of important design innovations. Increased use of aluminum and fiberglass resulted in an impressive mass ratio (ratio of the mass of the propellant to the total mass of the fully loaded rocket) of 0.86, compared to a maximum of 0.80 for

Viking.[34] This improvement was quite a feat, considering Vanguard needed additional structural weight for staging, a destruct system, and other functions that did not apply to Viking. (The comparable figure for the A-4 was 0.67, and for the much smaller Aerobee 0.55.)[35] Another example of the inventiveness of Vanguard designers was the use of a "free" power source— exhaust from the turbopumps—to power jets on the first stage used to control the roll of the vehicle.

Once the 20-inch spherical satellite design was decided upon, the TPESP had to inform prospective experimenters on the characteristics of the Vanguard satellite. In November, Newell explained to the panel that the satellite could contain about two pounds of instruments, not counting the batteries and telemetry equipment. Experiments would have to operate in temperature ranges from 41 to 122 degrees Fahrenheit and could be subject to spin rates as high as 400 rpm.[36]

The basic Vanguard satellite design looked simple: a metallic sphere with four antennas which, when unfolded, projected at 90 degrees from the surface rather than being angled back as in *Sputnik 1*. The sphere would actually be comprised of two concentric spheres. The outer sphere provided the load-carrying structure and protected the inner sphere, which contained the instrumentation. Both would be filled with pressurized helium.

By April 1957 the design had changed. Instead of an inner sphere, NRL engineers opted for a cylindrical instrument container attached to the outer sphere by a framework of slender metal tubes. The outer shell was made by a contractor, Brooks and Perkins of Detroit, which took flat sheets of magnesium and spun them into hemispheres. NRL technicians took these components and riveted them into a sphere holding the "pot" of instruments, along with telemetry equipment and other electronics built mainly at NRL. The NRL's Whitney Matthews developed a space-saving design that stacked the electronics on circular cards inside the cylinder.

Nine pounds of the allowable weight on each satellite would be consumed by the batteries and the transistorized Minitrack transmitter. The transmitter was connected to the four deployable antennas. These would be folded against the outer surface of the satellite and extended using hardware designed by Robert C. Baumann, who headed the NRL team responsible for the structural aspects of the satellite.[37] Vanguard's magnesium shell had a coating of gold, atop which were deposited four more layers: one layer of chromium, one of silicon monoxide, one of aluminum (highly reflective for visibility) and, finally, a heavier coat of silicon monoxide.

At the beginning of the Vanguard program, it was determined that the Air Force facilities at Cape Canaveral provided the only site equipped to host the launch operation. The Navy quickly began negotiations with Major General Donald M. Yates of the AFMTC for facilities.

Despite a sometimes acerbic relationship between Yates and his Navy counterparts, the general got the job done, arranging for a new pad and blockhouse to be added to the existing construction contract for Thor IRBM test facilities at Launch Complex 18. The new pad for Vanguard was designated 18A. A storage and assembly building, Hangar S, was also constructed, and an NRL-Martin team called the Vanguard Operations Group (VOG) took up residence. While Hangar S was under construction, the VOG set up a temporary assembly facility in an existing building, Hangar C. By October 1956, fifty people worked at Hangar C. The VOG staff would eventually grow to 150.

While Vanguard booster assembly was to take place at Martin's plant in Middle River, Maryland, the company had no facilities for static testing such a large vehicle. A static test stand was built at Cape Canaveral, and the Viking launch gantry at White Sands was disassembled and shipped east to be installed on pad 18A.[38]

The April 1956 agreement between NRL and Martin laid out the sequence of launches. The first six launches would be designated Test Vehicles (TVs). TV-0 and TV-1 would actually be the last two Viking rockets. TV-3 would be the first rocket with all three stages live. TV-4 and TV-5 would carry satellites, but they would not be part of the planned schedule of six operational launches. Those rockets, which lacked some of the instrumentation required for testing and thus had greater payload capacity, would be designated Space Launch Vehicles (SLVs).

The same month this agreement was reached, the Army again approached the Stewart Committee, which had remained in existence to advise DoD on the satellite program. Army leaders suggested there should be a backup to the Vanguard program, using their Redstone-based launcher. In May, the committee rejected the proposal on the grounds Vanguard was making satisfactory progress and no backup was required.[39]

The Vanguard TV-0 flight, on December 8, 1956, seemed to reinforce the committee's confidence. The rocket, *Viking 13*, rose to an altitude of 126 miles. At 50 miles, a Minitrack radio transmitter was ejected to simulate a satellite. The transmitter's beacon was tracked successfully.

TV-1 was not launched until May 1, 1957. Both Martin and its subcontractors had difficulty meeting schedules, and a series of nagging problems slowed work at the Cape. When the flight took place, however, it was another success. The launch was intended to flight-test all aspects of the Vanguard third stage's operation while continuing to refine the working of the guidance and telemetry systems. All objectives were met, and the Grand Central third stage, launched as the second stage on this configuration, performed well. The maximum altitude reached was 121 miles.

Just after this success came the most serious eruption of Vanguard's chronic financial crisis. In January of 1957, a new cost estimate for the project, $83.6 million, had been approved. On April 30, Percival Brundage, director of the Bureau of the Budget, sent President Eisenhower an ominous memo. Brundage warned that, while $70 million had been arranged for Vanguard, this left a serious gap. Not only was the money available well short of the $83.6 million estimate, but that estimate was falling by the wayside. The new estimate was closer to $110 million. Brundage noted that funding to cover the increase was difficult to identify. "Apparently, both the Department of Defense and the National Science Foundation are very reluctant to finance this project to completion. But each is quite prepared to have the other do so."[40]

The President was not pleased. At a National Security Council meeting on May 10, 1957, Eisenhower expressed his personal annoyance at the program's spiraling costs and agreed with Brundage that no agency was taking the responsibility for funding Vanguard. He reminded Vanguard officials that one of the program's goals, national prestige, could be met by getting just one satellite with some valid experiment in orbit. Eisenhower directed that every effort be made to contain the program's costs and avoid "gold-plating."[41] The President did add there seemed no way the United States could back out of the project entirely after its public commitment.[42] So Vanguard went ahead, albeit under greater scrutiny than ever.

Unfortunately, it turned out to be many months before the third Vanguard test launch could be attempted. After the success of TV-1, a June launch date was planned. TV-2 had the complete three-stage configuration, although only the first stage was live. Getting this first all-new Vanguard vehicle into the field, however, turned out to be a nightmare. The pressurization and roll-control systems needed extensive rework and partial redesign. So that Navy engineers could at least perform some inspections, Martin ended up shipping the rocket to the Cape with crucial systems missing. Work normally done in the factory then had to be accomplished in the field.

When inspectors looked at the partially-completed TV-2, they found debris in the propellant tanks and dirt in the first-stage engine. This resulted in the engine being taken out and shipped back to General Electric. Other gremlins seemed to pop up daily. Hagen branded Martin's performance "unacceptable," in part because of the prime contractor's responsibility to inspect the GE engine before installing it. When a new engine was finally installed, it took seven static tests to get the system working properly. The firing date slid into August, then September, and finally October.

These events did not go unnoticed. The July issue of the magazine *Missiles and Rockets* lamented, "Project Vanguard wallows in fantastic bureaucratic mire." The magazine's staff complained that countless hurdles had been set up to prevent the press from getting current information on the supposedly unclassified Vanguard, presumably to protect whoever was responsible for the mounting delays. The magazine fingered GE's first-stage engine as the rumored culprit.[43]

As the schedule for TV-2 kept slipping, the NRL came up with an idea to make sure Project Vanguard placed at least one satellite in orbit during the IGY. In July of 1957, the NRL changed the plan specified in the April 1956 agreement, informing Martin that TV-3 should be capable of orbiting the miniature satellite originally slated for TV-4.

The test satellite was a tiny sphere, less than 6.5 inches in diameter and weighing under 4 pounds. It was designed by NRL engineers and scientists led by Roger Easton. In a 1996 interview, Easton described it this way:

> It had seven mercury batteries about AA size, I guess. Above the batteries it had this little transmitter. We had a transmitter on the skin with a quartz crystal, cut so it would change frequency with temperature. I think the one in the middle would also change frequency with temperature, so we would get a crude idea of the temperature. The transmitter on the skin was a little different frequency than the one in the middle. It had six antenna elements. Four of them were circularly polarized, and the other two were dipole. The battery power supply had a plug you could take out and look at. The reason we did that was that we had so many delays in the launch that the batteries would run down. So, we would go up and plug it in just before they were supposed to launch it.[44]

When the TV-2 test finally took place, it went very well. On October 23, 1957, the rocket reached an altitude of 109 miles and flew 335 miles downrange. The effect on morale in Project Vanguard, however, was not as great as it might have been. Nineteen days before the flight of TV-2, the world had changed.

■ *Chapter 6*

Russia Triumphant

Given Russia's public pronouncements, the launch of the world's first satellite should not have been a surprise. Reflecting the claims and hints provided by the Soviets themselves, the July 1957 issue of *Missiles and Rockets* read, "Reports point to a Russian try within 10 weeks."[1] A July 5 assessment by the CIA chief, Allen W. Dulles, speculated that the Soviets might try as early as September 17. That date would be the 100th anniversary of Tsiolkovsky's birth, and, Dulles noted, "the Russians like to be dramatic."[2]

In August came the Soviet claim to have launched an ICBM. At the end of September, William Pickering got a very strong hint of things to come. On September 30, he was in Washington for a six-day IGY conference on rocket and satellite research. At one session, Pickering listened as a Soviet delegate, Sergey M. Poloskov, spoke in his native language. According to a translator, Poloskov made the benign comment that a satellite would be launched in the near future. An American scientist who spoke Russian whispered to Pickering "That's not what he said—he said 'imminent.'"[3] Two days later, another Soviet delegate was more cautious. He answered a question from Len Cormier about the schedule with the phrase *na kanune*—"on the eve," an ambiguous term which could have meant anything from the next day to months in the future.[4]

Despite all of this, it seemed as if no one in the United

States government expected what happened at Tyuratam on the night of Friday, October 4, 1957. The satellite and launch vehicle had been on the pad for two days when Sergey Korolev gave the order to fire. The complex "petal" structure surrounding the rocket opened perfectly, its long stabilizing arms swung up and back by counterweights. Engineers and technicians streamed from the pad as various tasks were done, until the rocket stood alone in the cold night. The oxidizer tanks were topped off. Five minutes before liftoff, a warning light reported a malfunction in the oxidizer loading system. After a hasty conference, Korolev ordered the warning overridden.[5] At 10:28 p.m. Moscow time, the R-7 thundered into the sky.

The Soviet space program did not have tracking stations outside the Eurasian continent. After the station in Kamchatka, at the northeastern-most extreme of the U.S.S.R., reported in, the tracking crews settled in for a long wait.

Surprisingly, the wait was shorter than expected. Due to unusual atmospheric conditions, a signal reached the station in Murmansk while the satellite was over South Africa. Engineers on the ground were unsure whether to believe this was actually from *Sputnik 1* until a second tracking station received it as well. Wrote Vladimir D. Yastrebov, head of the ballistics team computing the orbit, "We were overwhelmed by an indescribable feeling of triumph and elation. . . . Then it was back to work."[6]

Colonel Mikhail Rebrov recalled the events at Tyuratam:

The small room where the radio receivers were was overcrowded. Time dragged on slowly. Waiting built up the stress. Everyone stopped talking. There was absolute silence. All that could be heard was the breathing of the people and the quiet static in the loudspeaker. . . . And then from very far-off there appeared, at first very quietly and then louder and louder, those "bleep-bleeps" which confirmed that it was in orbit and in operation.

Once again everyone rejoiced. There were kisses, hugs and cries of "Hurrah!" The austere men, who were greeted out of space by the messenger they had made, had tears in their eyes.[7]

Korolev told his hardy band of engineers, "Congratulations, the road to the stars is now open."

Sputnik 1 created a sensation reaching far beyond the Russian space community. (The Russians did not formally name this satellite as such: the Russian term for an artificial satellite was *Sputnik zemli*, or "companion of the Earth."[8]) The satellite orbited every ninety-six minutes, steadily transmitting its famous beep. As *LIFE* magazine put it: "An eerie, intermittent croak—it sounded like a cricket with a cold—was picked up by radio receivers around the world last week. It came from beyond the stratosphere and signaled an epochal breakthrough into the new age of space exploration."[9]

Western radio operators, both hams and professionals, rushed to tune in the signals while countless other people looked for the satellite. Picking up the beeps was no problem, thanks to the Russian decision to use frequencies most hams could pick up. American scientists complained this ignored a 1956 CSAGI resolution that all IGY spacecraft would use a frequency of 108 MHz.

While the Soviets generally provided minimal information through IGY channels, they had actually made an exception here. Academician I. P. Bardin, a Soviet representative to CSAGI, had written to Lloyd Berkner in August specifying the frequencies planned for Soviet satellites. This message, however, seems to have gone astray.[10] From a public-relations point of view, the lower frequency was better: picking up broadcasts on 108 MHz required large antennas that were not widely available. As it was, radios all over the world soon resounded with the call from *Sputnik.*[11]

The night *Sputnik* was launched, the Soviets were hosting a party at their embassy in Washington to close out the week's IGY meetings. Walter Sullivan of the *New York Times* joined the group and asked William Pickering what the Soviets had said about their satellite. Pickering, surprised, assured him the Soviets had said nothing. The party proceeded without any mention of *Sputnik* until Sullivan informed Lloyd Berkner, who interrupted the gathering to make an announcement. He offered a toast to the Russian achievement.[12]

James R. Killian, who shortly after *Sputnik* was appointed the first Special assistant to the President for Science and Technology, wrote in his memoirs, "The real significance of the news for me lay in two key words: 'Russian' and '184-pound.'" The event "did violence to a belief so fundamental that it was almost heresy to question it: a belief I shared that the United States was so far advanced in its technological capacity that it had in fact no serious rival."[13]

Sputnik brought a surprising reaction from Vannever Bush, now president of the Massachusetts Institute of Technology, who had been so negative about the prospects of long-range rocketry a decade before. Bush seemed to have forgotten his earlier belief when he commented, "If it wakes us up, I'm damn glad the Russians shot their satellite. We are altogether too smug in this country."[14]

If the little sphere caused consternation among Western governments, it also excited scientists who knew that the Earth satellite concept, long a theoretical possibility, had at last been proven feasible. Daniel Goldin, NASA's Administrator from 1992 to 2001, recalled:

> I was 17 at the time and taking a physics class in college. My professor, Dr. Donald Cotton, wrote the following words on the blackboard: 'Sputnik is watching you.' At the end of class, he explained what it meant. We couldn't believe what we were hearing. Going home, I started thinking that, more than ever, I wanted to work on the space program.[15]

Arthur C. Clarke was in Barcelona for an IAF meeting when a reporter for a British newspaper woke him up with a phone call. "It was a complete shock," he said. "I had not anticipated it in the least. But I knew it would change the modern world."[16]

The Soviet government had not made any public pronouncements about viewing the satellite competition as a race. Despite the top-level interest in missiles and satellites (evidenced by the fact Korolev needed approval from the Council of Ministers to change satellite designs), no one expected the kind of impact *Sputnik* had on people around the world. On October 5, *Pravda* gave the story a minor front-page location, headlined "Tass Report," and beginning:

> In the course of the last years in the Soviet Union scientific research and experimental construction work on the creation of artificial satellites of the Earth has been going on.
>
> As the result of a large, dedicated effort by scientific-research institutes and construction bureaus the world's first artificial satellite of the Earth has been created. On 4 October, 1957, in the U.S.S.R. the first successful satellite launch has been achieved. According to preliminary data, the rocket launcher carried the satellite to the necessary orbital speed of about 8,000 meters per second. At the present time the satellite is moving in an elliptical trajectory around the Earth and its flight can be observed in the rays of the eastern and western Sun with the help of simple optical instruments (binoculars, spyglasses, etc.).

The article closed by hailing *Sputnik* as an example of how "the freed and conscientious labor of the people of the new socialist society makes the most daring dreams of mankind a reality."[17]

Actually, the satellite could not be seen with "simple optical instruments." However, the R-7's core stage, 90 feet long, had followed *Sputnik 1* into orbit. This is what people were observing when they "saw *Sputnik*." Radar stations could also see the booster: Korolev's engineers had added an angle reflector to the rocket to facilitate tracking.[18]

By the next morning, *Pravda* writers were beginning to understand what was going on. The headline for October 6 read, "World's First Artificial Satellite of Earth Created in Soviet Nation." On October 8, *Pravda* printed congratulations from governments around the world, grouped under the banner headline, "Russians Won the Competition."

Even members of Korolev's team were impressed by the publicity accompanying their feat. Boris Chertok, who had become Korolev's deputy for the R-7 project, said, "We thought the satellite was just a simple thing: what mattered to us was to test the rocket again to gather statistics on how its systems were functioning. And suddenly the whole world was abuzz. It was only later that we understood what we had done."[19]

The security-minded Soviets went to great lengths to obscure any details of the rocket itself. Misleading claims that *Sputnik* had been launched by a three-stage rocket—essentially, a larger Vanguard—seemed logical to Western experts and were repeated without question in the news media.[20]

In the book *Sputnik into Space* (1958), a Soviet writer named M. Vassilev included alleged photographs of a futuristic and highly impractical-looking aircraft with a twin fuselage launching a two-stage rocket. The rocket had long triangular fins like the vanes of an arrow. This, the author informed readers, was the *Sputnik* launcher.[21] In fact, it was a still from a Soviet animated movie titled, *After Sputnik—The Moon.*[22]

The R-7 remained a secret, at least to the Western public, until the Soviets displayed what they called the "Vostok rocket" in 1967. Even then, the only reference was to *Vostok* (the first Soviet manned spacecraft, launched in 1961), and no information was given to indicate this rocket had launched *Sputnik 1.*

Sputnik 1's main contribution to science was the information gained about the Earth's ionosphere by studying the radio beeps. Examining the orbit of the satellite and the highly visible R-7 stage also brought new knowledge of the planet's gravity and the upper reaches of the atmosphere. The satellite's inclination to the equator was 65.1 degrees, with a perigee of 141 miles and an apogee (highest point) of 587 miles.

At an IGY meeting in Spain a few days after the launch, Sedov told Ernst Stuhlinger, "We prepared our first satellite only for optical and radio tracking. Even in this simple form, it will give us invaluable scientific information. We did not want to complicate the first launching unnecessarily."[23] The Soviets for many years maintained the fiction they had always intended to launch the small satellite first and the larger *Sputnik*s later. At the same meeting, Sedov expressed astonishment that the United States had pursued the "very marginal" Vanguard design instead of using the proven Redstone and the services of von Braun. "You could have beaten us so easily," he said.[24] He also ducked questions on the military origin of *Sputnik,* insisting it was simply "a Soviet satellite."

Sputnik burst in on an America that was, at the time, largely content. In November 1956, President Eisenhower had won re-election easily on the slogan, "Peace, Progress, and Prosperity." The economy had been growing steadily since a mild recession ended in 1955, and the growth of the middle class had continued. After 1955 the nation had more white-collar than blue-collar workers. While the 1950s is often thought of as a time of complacency and conformity, the nation was witnessing the emergence of new forms of expression, such as "rock and roll" music, and a fascination with new technology, which would both improve everyday life and change the world. Magazines such as *Science Digest* were prophesying a future of unlimited energy from nuclear power plants, personal flying machines, and sophisticated robots.

There had been no war since 1953, when the Korean war was brought to end by, among other factors, Eisenhower's expressed willingness to consider using nuclear weapons. The year 1956 had brought overseas crises—the Suez Crisis in the Middle East and the brutal Soviet suppression of the anti-Communist revolt in Hungary—but neither of these had put Americans into combat, and both were now past.

The major domestic story in the fall of 1957 concerned desegregation. The President and Congress had enacted the 1957 Civil Rights Act, creating the Civil Rights Commission. Among other tasks the Commission had before it was the enforcement of the Supreme Court's 1954 decision in *Brown v. Board of Education.* Its implementation was not going smoothly. At the time *Sputnik* was launched, the nation was following the tense confrontation at Central High School in Little Rock, Arkansas. Arkansas Governor Orval Faubus had refused to allow desegregation of the all-white school. The President, angered by Faubus's challenge to Federal authority, had sent troops to enforce the mandate.

It has become accepted that *Sputnik* generated widespread panic among the American people. In fact, there is no evidence this took place. Aside from a few well-publicized incidents, the American people, while surprised and somewhat concerned by Russia's achievement, did not consider *Sputnik* a calamity. One *Newsweek* reporter in Denver summed up the local mood: "There is a vague feeling that we have stepped into a new era, but people aren't discussing it the way they are football and the Asiatic flu." The magazine's reporter in Boston went to far as to describe the reaction as "massive indifference."[25] Only half the people responding to a Gallup poll agreed *Sputnik* was "a serious blow to U.S. prestige."

If the American public was not panicked by *Sputnik*, it was impressed about the reach into space and what it portended. A Gallup poll in that epochal month of October found forty-one percent of the American people believed humans would reach the moon by 1972. A similar poll in 1949 had found only fifteen percent believing humanity would make it by 1999.[26]

The U.S. military had more immediate concerns. American missile experts correctly assumed that, whatever the launch vehicle's configuration, it was a modification of the Soviets' ICBM. Knowing the size and orbit of the satellite, they could work backwards to figure out how large and powerful the missile involved must be. Estimates of a vehicle with 500,000 pounds of thrust were discomforting when no American missile or space launcher then in operational service could generate even 90,000 pounds. The Atlas missile, with a thrust of 360,000 lbs, had been flight tested twice at this point. It had failed both times.

Worried analysts in and out of the military noted that the U.S. Strategic Air Command (SAC), while superior to its Soviet counterpart, had its bombers concentrated at forty-four bases in the United States and overseas. In the absence of adequate information on Soviet ICBM and IRBM production and deployment, it was easy to picture a surprise attack destroying America's power to retaliate.

Military nerves were not eased when the Soviets dropped hints the *Sputnik* was equipped to scan the Earth below it.[27] This seemed unlikely, given the satellite's size (American reconnaissance satellite designs were for spacecraft weighing 500 pounds or more). Still, it was hard to be sure of anything when the balance of power had, at least psychologically, been cast into doubt.

Privately, the U.S. government's concern over *Sputnik* went beyond the immediate military uses of space. A then-secret assessment by the CIA, written four weeks after *Sputnik 1*'s launch, stated, "the successful Soviet launching and orbiting of a satellite of this size, taken together with two probable tests of an ICBM flight vehicle, has considerable military significance. It shows a high order of Soviet technical capability, especially in propulsion. These events . . . have resulted in an immediate increase in Soviet scientific and military prestige in the eyes of many peoples and a number of governments."[28]

The American media was not so sanguine as the nation's public. Several major newspapers and news magazines, notably *Aviation Week* and *U.S. News and World Report,* began a drumbeat of criticism aimed at the Eisenhower administration for letting the Communists launch before the United States. As might be expected, the opposition party—in this case, Democrats, the most prominent being Senators Lyndon Johnson and Stuart Symington—also took the stage to issue negative assessments of the President's leadership. Not surprisingly, all this had an impact on the American people. Over the next few months, according to polls, the initially calm public reaction evolved into a state of concern, if not outright alarm.

The President, while startled by the launch, saw no reason to panic. He was genuinely puzzled when the outcry in the press continued despite his efforts to spread calm.[29] Eisenhower told Americans "our satellite program has never been conducted as a race with other nations" and insisted that *Sputnik* did not raise his apprehensions about America's security "one iota."[30] In private, he told aides "I can't understand why the American people have got so worked up over this thing. It's certainly not going to drop on their heads."[31]

Colonel (later General) Andrew J. Goodpaster, President Eisenhower's staff secretary, recalled in 1998:

> We weren't surprised by *Sputnik.* We knew the capabilities that we were developing, and the capabilities that the Russians were developing. We knew a satellite of that kind could be put up [in orbit]. This was a place where Eisenhower went wrong for about 36 hours. And his expression was this was nothing that we didn't foresee or know about, but the American people until that moment had not realized the vulnerability that had now developed. That they could be reached by long range rockets, which could be nuclear armed. And our country, for the first time, was exposed to that kind of danger. And so where he brushed it off as something that we had foreseen, it really created great anxiety, almost panic within the United States.[32]

Eisenhower could not tell the American people all the reassuring information he knew, since much of it concerned military secrets he chose to keep concealed. These included the U-2 flights, which had been monitoring the U.S.S.R. since July 1956, as well as the work being done toward reconnaissance satellites. The President also stayed silent concerning the details of American progress toward IRBMs and ICBMs. All this fueled the myth of the "missile gap," which was to dominate debate over American defense policy for the next five years. Eisenhower did display a test version of a Jupiter missile nose cone, recovered after being flown on a modified Redstone by von Braun's team, on television as an example of American technology.

Eisenhower refused demands from Congress for an all-out crash program to expand and accelerate missile and space work. He did eventually ask for a $1 billion supplemental defense appropriation, mainly to field America's Thor and Jupiter IRBMs more quickly.[33] He privately acknowledged some of this funding was driven by the need to reestablish public confidence, not the immediacy of the Soviet threat.[34] Despite the harsh rhetoric flowing from the Democratic leaders who controlled Capitol Hill, these men were perhaps not quite as worried as they seemed, for Congress added only moderately to the Eisenhower administration's post-*Sputnik* defense budgets. [35]

Secretary of State John Foster Dulles tried to "spin" the news in another direction, claiming the Russian achievement was due to the use of German experts and technology.[36] Several lesser officials and news outlets expanded on this theme and claimed the Soviets were first because "their Germans are better than our Germans," even though the idea was absurd and the government, especially the Army Ballistic Missile Agency, knew it.

Inside the White House, Donald Quarles, now Deputy Secretary of Defense, was called to account. President Eisenhower, despite the calm he displayed to the public, expressed surprise at the turn of events and wanted an explanation. Quarles confirmed that a Redstone-based launcher could probably have beaten *Sputnik*, but pointed out the U.S. program had never been given a timeline more urgent than simply launching during the IGY.[37] The President agreed on that point. Quarles also noted "the Russians have done us a good turn, unintentionally, in establishing the concept of freedom of international space."

In fact, not a single government formally protested the overflight of *Sputnik.*[38] In July 1959, the acceptance of *Sputnik* and the IGY satellites that followed it was cited as a key precedent by the new United Nations Ad Hoc Committee on the Peaceful Uses of Outer Space (COPUOS), which published a report endorsing "freedom of space" without making a distinction between types or missions of spacecraft.[39] The U.S.S.R. would later argue that a distinction between peaceful satellites and those engaged in "illegal espionage" should be made. That case, however, had already been lost.[40]

Quarles' observation and the wording of NSC 5520 have occasionally been cited as evidence the President actually wanted the Russians to launch first and made sure the American program lagged behind.[41] This idea has not been supported by any of the participants in the decision-making process, or by any declassified documents concerning the satellite effort. Eisenhower would have had to have been a psychic to have predicted in 1955 when the Russians would launch, and that Vanguard would be a more complex undertaking than was believed at the time. The theory that "we let the Russians beat us" stands on no ground whatsoever. Indeed, it is disproved by Eisenhower's grilling of Quarles, since of necessity, both these men would have had to have been in on the scheme.

There was no question America had not moved as quickly as it could have in this field after World War II. As von Braun put it: "The six years between 1945–51 are irretrievably lost. The Russians are turning out more scientists than we are, and good ones too. We could have done what they did if we had started in 1946 to integrate the space flight and missile programs. Our lot has been one crash program after another."[42]

A few months later, with two American satellites in orbit, von Braun took a broader view. "I was disappointed, and a little bitter, that we hadn't been able to do it before they did. . . . Looking back now, I'm not sure that I was right. The Russian Communists may well have done themselves an ill turn by humbling us in the space race. Unwittingly, they made the sleeping American giant awaken."[43]

Looking back thirty-two years later, William Pickering agreed. "I must say, if I think about it from the viewpoint of history, I suspect that the whole space program is better because the Russians went up first. It shook up the complacency of the West . . . it was a challenge for us to do better than they were. The result was that the space programs got a lot of support from this country. . . . In fact, the whole formation of NASA might not have happened if we had gone first."[44]

As part of the *Sputnik* debate, some in Congress and the media second-guessed the Stewart Committee's decision. The Eisenhower administration defended the process, saying the committee was correctly motivated by the desire for maximum scientific payoffs and the necessity of avoiding conflict with missile programs. Quarles told the Senate Armed Services Committee that allowing the ABMA to launch the first satellite would have delayed the Jupiter missile's development by three months, although

Medaris and von Braun had been insistent in 1955 that there would be no delays involved.[45]

At the IGY meeting then going on in Washington, Russian delegates from the U.S.S.R. Academy of Sciences offered explanations of their own. However, the Academy of Sciences was only nominally in charge of Soviet IGY efforts, and in fact had little connection with the military-directed *Sputnik* program beyond making recommendations about scientific research and providing public relations.

A common Soviet statement was that scientists and engineers were held in higher esteem in Russia than in America, and consequently were more motivated. When an American commented that *Sputnik* was stealing headlines from the World Series, Academician Anatoli A. Blagonravov, showing his apparent lack of interest in whatever the World Series was, replied, "In Russia, scientists are not compared with football players." Curiously, Blagonravov then went on to claim that he was in charge of a project to rocket a man into space.[46] This was completely false, but, in the atmosphere of the post-*Sputnik* days, the statement apparently went unchallenged. So did hints by the Soviets that *Sputnik 1* carried reconnaissance apparatus, probably a camera.[47]

Many Americans agreed in principle with Blagonravov. Von Braun commented, "I believe something drastic must be done to raise the status of scientists in the public eye in this country. In Europe a professor is considered quite a man. But here, whenever a scientist achieves some eminence they throw rocks at him."

Blagonravov's colleague, A. W. Kasatkin, had a different explanation. "In America, several companies are working on this project. There is friction between them, because they compete with each other. In my country, all the efforts are coordinated under our government. Therefore, we came through before the U.S." He added, "Don't make any mistake. We are also ahead in engineering and in science."[48] The Soviet program was not the monolithic, smoothly-functioning machine Kasatkin made it out to be, but few outside the U.S.S.R. had any clue to that fact.

America's consumer culture also came in for criticism—both from American politicians and the Soviets. One Russian put the difference between societies this way: "Americans design better automobile tailfins but we design the best intercontinental ballistic missiles and earth satellites."[49]

Russian delegates at the United Nations could not resist adding jabs of their own. One asked whether the United States would be interested in applying for assistance under Russia's program to aid undeveloped nations.[50] In a speech on November 6, Khrushchev needled, "It appears the name

Vanguard reflected the confidence of the Americans that their satellite would be the first in the world. But . . . it was the Soviet satellites which proved to be ahead, to be in the vanguard."

The reaction of Americans working with rockets and satellites was mixed. A few initially suspected the Russian announcement was a hoax, but that theory was demolished by October 5, when the NRL announced the Earth's new companion had already been tracked crossing the United States four times.[51] The first visual observation of the launch vehicle from American soil was made on October 10. In late November, scientists in New Mexico studying meteors with specialized telescopic cameras photographed *Sputnik 1* itself.[52]

Joseph Kaplan described the *Sputnik*'s weight as "fantastic," a point all the experts agreed on. This was doubly true because the satellite had not been launched, as Vanguard would be, from a low-latitude site offering a major boost from the Earth's rotation.

Rear Admiral Bennett backed up Administration officials by arguing the United States had never viewed the satellite program as a race. He questioned the announced weight of 184 pounds and dismissed *Sputnik* as "a hunk of iron almost anybody could launch." He insisted there was no need to accelerate Vanguard in response.[53] Indeed, a *New York Times* article published on October 5 quoted "American scientists" working on Vanguard as saying with relief, "The pressure is off. Now we can concentrate on doing a good job."[54] Another scientist offered a prescient comment: "Maybe the Russian-American competition hasn't been so bad on the satellite if it encourages us into beating them to the moon."[55]

William Holaday, Special Assistant to the Secretary of Defense for Guided Missiles, suggested the Soviets had gone all-out in a race to put the first object in space, while the American program was an IGY science project and had proceeded in the open at the proper pace. Holaday claimed *Sputnik 1*'s launch did not mean the Soviets were ahead in missile technology.[56]

Publicly, the United States played the diplomat. American political and scientific officials congratulated their Soviet counterparts, and the administration began working on ideas to control possible military activity in space. On January 12, 1958, President Eisenhower wrote to Premier Bulganin, suggesting a pact to reserve space for peaceful purposes. Ten days later, Nikita Khrushchev, the Communist Party chief (who was soon to replace Bulganin by assuming the Premier's job as well), publicly turned the Americans down. Khrushchev reiterated the long-held Soviet position that all arms-control matters were linked, and that space must be discussed in the context of a broad agreement to ban nuclear weapons, close some American overseas military bases, and achieve many other goals.

James Van Allen was launching rockoons from a ship in the Antarctic when he heard the *Sputnik* news. The ship's radio room managed to tune in the signal from the Soviet satellite. Van Allen jotted in his field notebook, "Brilliant achievement . . . Tremendous propaganda coup for the U.S.S.R. . . . Confirms my disgust with the Stewart Committee's decision to favor NRL over the Redstone proposal. . . ." He calculated the Russian vehicle, if it had the same efficiency as Vanguard, must have a gross weight at launch of about 100 tons (an underestimate by a factor of almost three).[57]

Not surprisingly, *Sputnik* led to a flurry of changes in government organization, accompanied by calls for much larger changes. Ten days after *Sputnik*'s launch, the ARS sent the White House a proposal for organizing future American space efforts. The Society suggested establishing an Astronautical Research and Development Agency (ARDA) along the lines of NACA. ARDA would not include military space projects, but would direct all scientific and other civilian endeavors. The estimated budget needed for the new agency was $100 million per year.[58]

In November, the Rocket and Satellite Research Panel recommended the creation of a civilian-led National Space Establishment to conduct an ambitious space research program. The cost: $1 billion a year over the first 10 years.[59] Also in November, the NACA established a Special Committee on Space Technology, chaired by H. Guyford Stever of the Massachusetts Institute of Technology.[60]

These proposals and others were discussed amidst a backdrop of continuing review and investigation of America's rocket and satellite programs. The DoD quickly had studies of its own underway, as did the individual services. The Preparedness Investigating Subcommittee of the Senate Armed Services Committee began hearings on November 25, 1957, that would stretch until late January 1958. In February 1958, the Senate created a Special Committee on Space and Aeronautics to draft legislation concerning the nation's space programs. The next month, the House created the similar Select Committee on Astronautics and Space Exploration.

On December 5, the DoD announced a plan to create the Advanced Research Projects Agency (ARPA) to manage all military space efforts. Five days later, the Air Force created a Directorate of Astronautics to direct work on satellites, anti-missile systems, and other space concepts. This action was quickly rescinded by the Secretary of the Air Force as premature.[61]

Sputnik had another effect on American space progress that was certainly unintended but had long-lasting repercussions. Bill Guier and George

Weiffenbach of Johns Hopkins APL noticed the measurable degree to which the pitch of *Sputnik 1*'s beeps changed as the satellite moved, a result of the well-known phenomenon called the Doppler shift. Since Guier and Weiffenback were working from a known, fixed position on the ground, they could use this data to calculate the satellite's orbit. Their boss, Frank McClure, took the next theoretical step in 1958. McClure suggested that, if they could calculate the orbit of a satellite from a known point, they could turn the procedure around and calculate the position of a point on Earth from a satellite in a known orbit. The satellite needed to transmit two continuous signals, which could be compared with each other to correct for ionospheric interference. This was the genesis of the Navy's Transit satellite-navigation system, the predecessor to the modern GPS.

Sputnik 1 reentered the atmosphere in January 1958, before the United States would even launch its first satellite. In fact, before the United States put anything in space, the Soviet Union would launch a much larger satellite: *Sputnik 2,* with the 8K71PS upper stage attached, put approximately 7,000 pounds into orbit on November 3, 1957. The satellite alone weighed over 1,100 pounds. The orbit ranged in altitude from 131 miles to 1,030. The inclination, 65.3 degrees, was almost identical to *Sputnik 1*'s.

Sputnik 2 was another rush job, in many ways a more impressive one than *Sputnik 1*. The first satellite had been up only a few days when Premier Khrushchev told Korolev, "We never thought that you would launch a *Sputnik* before the Americans. But you did it. Now please launch something new in space for the next anniversary of our revolution."

Khrushchev had reasons for supporting the *Sputnik*s that went beyond national pride. The Soviet Union had achieved impressive industrial growth during the 1950s, but neither the perennially backward agricultural sector nor the average Soviet citizen had reaped much benefit. Khrushchev, as mentioned earlier, wanted to reduce the size of Soviet conventional forces in order to redirect investment into other areas. This would be much easier if potential enemies were cowed by the threat of Soviet missiles, and the most spectacular way to convince the world about such missiles would be to launch satellites.

Building a much larger, more complex satellite in a matter of weeks would have been considered an impossible job by most engineers. But Grechko said of Korolev, "It was, I think, the happiest month of his life." Korolev was in his element, directing a crash program to move ahead in space, with the stakes high, the resources unlimited, and the eyes of the Soviet leadership and the world on his results.

He succeeded, celebrating the November 6 revolution and once again capturing the world's attention. It was not just the size of the satellite that earned fame, but the passenger: *Sputnik 2* carried an 11-pound female dog named Laika ("barker"). People everywhere followed news of the first living creature in Earth orbit. In the Soviet Union, her likeness and name even appeared on a brand of cigarettes.[62] Laika could not be recovered, but she performed her mission well, functioning normally in weightlessness, providing a bounty of new scientific data, and serving as a canine ambassador for Korolev and the entire Soviet Union.

Sputnik 2 also carried instruments for studying solar radiation and cosmic rays. These were mounted on the outside of the satellite. The spacecraft was protected during launch by a shroud, which was eventually discarded.

Laika was in a chamber that, in miniature, resembled those in which cosmonauts and astronauts would someday ride. The pressure, oxygen supply, and temperature were regulated, and instruments monitored her pulse, respiration, heart function, and blood pressure. An array of temperature gauges measured conditions inside and outside Laika's chamber, as well as on various other parts of the satellite.

Sputnik 2's transmitters functioned for a week, and the satellite remained in orbit 162 days. Laika died shortly into the mission when the cabin overheated, but, from a scientific point of view, the experiment had already succeeded.[63] There was now no doubt that human life could exist in space. As the editors of *Collier's* had put it just five years earlier, science fiction was indeed now "serious fact."

■ *Chapter 7*

Heartbreak and Triumph
The Path to *Explorer 1*

While Project Vanguard slogged forward and Korolev struggled to make his R-7 work, the ABMA was not forgetting about space. While banned from overt satellite work, the organization had many other tasks, and some of them—coincidentally or otherwise—continued the development of satellite-related technology.

By 1957, ABMA was a major organization, with 3,500 personnel working on a variety of rocket, missile, and technology programs. The agency took on the hands-on, can-do personality of the hard-charging Medaris and the equally dedicated von Braun.

Von Braun insisted it was vital for a manager to get away from drawings and mathematics and make regular visits to the fabrication laboratory, test stands, and other operational areas to get the "look and feel" of the hardware. "Missile building is much like interior decorating," he said once.

> Once you decide to refurnish the living room you go shopping. But when you put it all together you may see in a flash it's a mistake—the draperies don't go with the slip covers. The same is true of missiles. Sometimes you can take one look and see something obviously wrong—not accessible perhaps, or too flimsy. The people who are working

with it all day are too close to see it. That's why I go to the fabricating shop—I want to know what my baby will look like.[1]

When the Stewart Committee decision was finalized, ABMA engineers
had not abandoned their launch vehicle design. Instead, they applied it to
a different problem.

One of the challenges facing developers of long-range missiles was the
need to develop RVs that could stand the heat of coming back through the
atmosphere at very high speeds. Von Braun had been working on this
since the days of the V-2, which suffered structural failures upon reentry
despite having a short range and low speed compared with the missiles of
the mid-50s. It was the lack of a separate RV that made the problem much
more difficult to solve with the V-2. Developing the RV reduced the problem to a more manageable size, since only a much smaller surface area had
to be protected.

In 1955, the ABMA was developing the Jupiter IRBM, a major advance
over the Redstone. The Navy was involved in this program, since a sea-
going version of Jupiter was planned for use on surface ships and, eventually, on submarines. Jupiter, with a range of 1,750 miles, would subject its
RV to velocities and temperatures far beyond those encountered by previous missiles.

There were two approaches pursued to solve the RV heating problem,
which was seen as the most imposing barrier to IRBM and ICBM development. One, being investigated by the Air Force, was a "heat sink" design in
which the payload was surrounded by enough heavy metal shielding to
absorb the heat. The other, preferred by the Army and under investigation
for the Jupiter program, was called "ablative shielding." On an ablative nose
cone, the outer layers of insulation heated until they burned off, keeping
the payload acceptably cool. While NACA researchers had done considerable work on this concept, it was vital to test such a design under realistic
conditions before the Jupiter was flown.[2]

Von Braun's satellite launcher was perfect for this task, since the upper
stages allowed an RV to be tested at greater ranges and speeds than the basic Redstone rocket could provide. To fit on the small upper stage, a scaled-
down version of the Jupiter RV was developed. Von Braun's colleague,
Ernst Stuhlinger, later wrote,

It is not known which of the two concepts emerged first in von
Braun's thinking: Redstone as a reentry test vehicle, or Redstone as
a satellite launcher. Both applications of a launch vehicle had been

obvious to him for years. When the opportunity arose, he was prepared. Either application would have enabled the other one.[3]

The twelve Redstones set aside and modified for this program received
the new designation Jupiter C.[4] They were not, in fact, Jupiters of any kind,
but applying that name gave these rockets the appearance of being part of
the high-priority Jupiter program. This moved them up in the queue for
launch dates at Cape Canaveral. JPL worked with the ABMA on this project to perfect the upper stages and the telemetry equipment.

The second stage was a ring of eleven Sergeant rockets, and the third
stage was a cluster of three Sergeants in the center of the second-stage ring.
The single Sergeant serving as the fourth stage sat atop the center of the
third stage. The Sergeants were held in position by bulkheads and rings
and were surrounded by a cylindrical outer "washtub" of aluminum. The
base plate of the tub was attached to a shaft mounted on the first-stage instrument section. Two electric motors would spin the tub.

To turn a Redstone into the first stage of a Jupiter C, the Redstone was
lengthened by sixty-five inches to increase the propellant capacity. The upper section of the fuselage was strengthened to support the additional
stages, and an attitude control system, which could orient the upper stages
for firing after release from the first stage, was added.[5]

The Redstone engine was modified, too. The A-6 was upgraded to a
configuration called the A-7. Instead of alcohol, the A-7 used a new fuel,
hydyne. Hydyne was an exotic (and, at the time, secret) blend of UDMH
and diethyltrianine. The Jupiter C was the only rocket ever to use this fuel,
which had a higher I_{sp} than alcohol but was highly toxic and corrosive. For
that matter, the Redstone's A-6 was the last large rocket motor to use alcohol. Kerosene, which has a greater density and is easier to handle and
store, has become the non-cryogenic liquid fuel of choice for space applications. The A-7 had a thrust of 83,000 pounds.

Von Braun observed, "We did *not* point out that, with minor modifications, they (the Jupiter Cs) could also serve as satellite launch vehicles."[6]
Following up the early work by Lundquist, ABMA's Josef Boehm had already designed a satellite to fit atop a Sergeant stage.[7] In May 1956, Medaris
emphasized to his staff, "We must make it perfectly clear to Defense that
we did not carry forward a program which we had been denied . . . that the
work which was done was done first to make a presentation on a satellite,
later the work was carried on because that was the best way to make a reentry missile and the two happened to fit together."[8]

While the Army kept its satellite ambitions low-key, the Air Force continued to prepare (albeit in secret) for a future in which satellites would be used. A month after Medaris' message of caution, Lockheed Missile Systems Division won the contract to develop the Air Force's Advanced Reconnaissance System satellite.

On September 20, 1956, the first Jupiter C flew over 3,300 miles downrange. This was the launch Korolev mistakenly believed was an orbital attempt. He had some reason to think so. This vehicle, designated *Missile 27* by the Army, carried the entire upperworks proposed for the satellite vehicle. Since this launch was intended to validate the vehicle design, the Jupiter C carried a radio transmitter and was not fitted with the 300-pound test RV. This flight also demonstrated the effectiveness of the JPL-designed telemetry and tracking system, called Microlock. *Missile 27* did so well, in fact, that *Missile 29*, its twin and backup, was put back into storage.

The rocket that would launch the first American satellite had just been flight-proven, although neither the Americans nor the Soviets knew it. It would be eleven months before the first Soviet launch vehicle had a similarly successful test.

On direct orders from the Pentagon, General Medaris verified the fourth-stage rocket on *Missile 27* was inert.[9] As William Pickering later explained, "If you put that one rocket in, the damn thing would go into orbit." Things were not quite that simple—the missile lacked some guidance and control equipment needed for a satellite version—but it had nevertheless occurred to someone in the Army hierarchy that von Braun might try to pull off an "accidental" satellite that would upstage Vanguard. In fact, no such action was contemplated. Ernst Stuhlinger recalled that, while von Braun was bitterly disappointed about the Stewart Committee decision, "There was no chance (of an unauthorized attempt) . . . we had our orders, and von Braun was very strict about following orders."[10]

The Army team did not, however, abandon its dreams of satellites. After the Stewart Committee decision, von Braun wrote, "We bootlegged work on the satellite. Night after night, men like Ernst D. Geissler, our ace aerodynamicist, put in endless hours on their own." He added, "Homer Joe (Stewart) was very concerned over the Vanguard schedule and he urged us to find ways to keep our project going as a back-up for Vanguard." William Pickering helped by using some funding provided to JPL under its Army contracts to improve the upper-stage systems.[11]

While actual work on a satellite had to be kept quiet, Medaris did not passively accept the idea that his agency would have no role in the country's nascent space program. On April 23, 1956, he informed Secretary Wilson's office that the Army could provide a backup—or an alternative—

to the Vanguard program and could launch a satellite by early 1957. All he got for his pains was a refusal of the offer, followed by a directive that essentially said, "Don't even think about satellites." In the following months, Medaris and his allies tried to circumvent this prohibition with appeals to other executive branch officials, including Colonel Goodpaster in the White House. As Medaris put it, "In various languages, our fingers were slapped, and we were told to mind our own business."[12]

Medaris was not just engaging in interservice rivalry. He agreed with von Braun that, whether the Secretary of Defense understood it or not, the United States was in a high-stakes, must-not-lose race with the Soviet Union to orbit a satellite. This view, however, was not sanctioned by those who could have granted the Army's petitions.

In November 1956, the National Security Council Planning Board even concluded that "the U.S.S.R. can be expected to launch its satellite before ours" and that the Soviet satellite would be larger than the first American one. The board noted that "prestige and psychological set-backs" would result, but that these would be "at least partially offset by a more effective and complete scientific program by the United States."[13]

This viewpoint was, in hindsight, stunning in both its accurate prediction of the likely events and its complete misunderstanding of their effects. Almost a year before *Sputnik 1*, the NSC Planning Board forecast that the Soviets would launch the first satellite, then went on to say it did not matter because a better U.S. scientific program would be the more important and prestigious accomplishment. All this came two months after the *Missile 27* success, so the board was aware the United States had at least some chance of accelerating its satellite program and beating the Soviets into orbit.

In any event, the United States held its course. The Army had to be content with launching its reentry test vehicles. The Jupiter Cs launched after *Missile 27* had the fourth stage removed and the test RV installed, so they could not have made orbit. It took only two more flights to validate the RV design, however. On the last flight, on August 8, 1957, the test RV was recovered from the target area in the Atlantic Ocean. This made it the first man-made object ever brought back from space. It also established the validity of the ablative shielding concept. Ablative shielding was used on every American RV from that period onward. It was also used on the *Mercury, Gemini,* and *Apollo* spacecraft.

In November 1956, the ABMA's future became cloudy when Secretary of Defense Wilson issued a memorandum giving control over long-range land-based missiles exclusively to the Air Force. While the ABMA would continue to develop the Jupiter, the missile would be turned over to the

Air Force for operational service. In December, the Navy withdrew from the Jupiter program. Nervous about storing liquid-fueled missiles in tight quarters, and encouraged by development in advanced solid fuels and miniaturized warheads, Navy officials opted to pursue the solid-fuel Polaris missile instead. It is a tribute to the leadership of Medaris and von Braun that this double blow did not demoralize the ABMA staff or dampen ABMA's drive toward other accomplishments.[14]

Von Braun had a habit of publicizing his missiles' success which irritated the upper levels of the Defense Department, especially during periods when Vanguard was perceived to be struggling. A paper by Ernst Stuhlinger, presented to the Army Science Symposium at the U.S. Military Academy on July 28, 1957, contributed to the heartburn in the Pentagon. Stuhlinger told his audience almost everything needed to launch a satellite was already in place at ABMA. He even mentioned there was Jupiter C hardware left from the RV test program that might be used for this mission.[15] The Secretary of Defense responded with a directive the very next day that forbid anyone in the military (including civilian employees like von Braun and Stuhlinger), except those connected with Project Vanguard, from discussing anything concerning space with the press.[16]

When *Sputnik 1* was launched, von Braun and Medaris happened to be in the Officers' Club at Redstone Arsenal. They were attending a social gathering welcoming Wilbur Brucker, Secretary of the Army, and Neil McElroy, incoming Secretary of Defense. Von Braun immediately asked—in fact, begged—for permission to put a satellite in orbit.

"We knew they were going to do it. Vanguard will never make it!" he insisted. "We have the hardware on the shelf. For God's sake, turn us loose and let us do something! We can put up a satellite in sixty days, Mr. McElroy. Just give us a green light and sixty days!"[17]

Medaris cautioned, "Ninety days, Wernher."

McElroy did not commit to anything on the spot. When he returned to Washington, the ABMA quickly sent him a satellite plan called Project 416. This option would launch four satellites at a total cost of $16.2 million. Secretary Brucker sent a memo to McElroy on October 7 urging the Army be given the go-ahead. He emphasized the maturity of the ABMA's technology, although he cautiously stretched von Braun's timetable out to four months.[18] The Stewart Committee reconvened on October 25 and unanimously endorsed Project 416.[19]

Medaris was one member of the American rocketry community who had been surprised by *Sputnik.* At the end of September, von Braun and

Stuhlinger, unnerved by the flurry of signals indicating a forthcoming Soviet launch, had pressed him to once again seek permission to launch a satellite in time to ensure beating the Russians. Despite Medaris' earlier efforts to secure permission for an Army launch, this time he replied, "You know how complicated it is to launch a satellite. Those people (the Soviets) will never do it." When "those people" did it anyway, the only comment Medaris could muster was, "Those damn bastards."[20] Now he threw himself and his organization into an all-out effort to catch up.

In the meantime, there was an American space "first" to note, although it had very little public or political impact. On October 15, an Air Force-sponsored Aerobee rocket launched the first objects ever to escape Earth's gravity. At an altitude of 54 miles, an explosive charge in the sounding rocket's nose was detonated. The blast hurled metal pellets upward with an estimated velocity of 33,000 miles per hour, 8,000 miles per hour greater than escape velocity. There was no way to track such tiny projectiles, so the Air Force experimenters had to be content with knowing they had *probably* been the first to propel matter away from the Earth toward deep space.[21]

Project Vanguard, of course, was not standing still in the aftermath of the Soviet feat. According to Milt Rosen, while the Vanguard team was never told it had to beat the Soviets, the project staff felt the public believed a race was underway. It was an unequal contest, Rosen pointed out, because "the Russians always knew where we were, and we didn't know where they were." Given that Vanguard relied on the creation of new, highly efficient rocket motors, "There was no way we could have beaten them if we'd tried."[22]

NRL engineer Martin Votaw remembered seeing a memo two days before *Sputnik* saying there would be no more paid overtime on the Vanguard project. The memo said, in effect, "We're not in a competition." When *Sputnik* did go up, Votaw was called during dinner and told to come back in. He and his colleagues worked seventy-two hours straight to build 40-MHz antennas to track *Sputnik.* The no-overtime rule was never implemented.[23] All efforts were bent toward getting the next vehicle launched as quickly as possible.

On December 6, 1957, TV-3 made the first Vanguard orbital attempt. The program's directors tried to make it clear this was indeed a test: this was the first launch of the full three-stage Vanguard booster configuration, and the second stage had never been flown at all. The decision, made in July, to launch a satellite on TV-3 was reaffirmed in the aftermath of *Sputnik 1.*

When Milt Rosen was later asked whose idea that had been, he replied, "Everyone's." After *Sputnik,* he said, "If we were going to launch any rocket, it was going to have a satellite on it."[24]

The microsatellite was built in-house at NRL. In and on the aluminum "grapefruit," engineers jammed six solar-cell assemblies, a battery pack, two transmitters, three antenna-phasing boards, and six antennas.

As the miniature spacecraft was loaded on the launch vehicle, the tension level became extremely high. The Vanguard program's directors tried to emphasize that actually getting a satellite into orbit would just be a bonus and was not the major objective of the test. Unfortunately, the desire to keep TV-3 low-key was doomed by the enormous political and media pressure to match *Sputnik.*

That pressure had been building ever since presidential press secretary James Hagerty announced in early October that "small satellite spheres would be launched as test vehicles during 1957" on Vanguard. That was a perfectly accurate statement, but its interpretation had spun completely out of control.[25]

The situation became even more tense during three days of delays, when the status of TV-3 was the lead story on every front page and every news broadcast. It is no exaggeration to say the entire world was watching on the cold morning of December 6 as the needlelike space vehicle, glistening in the Florida sunshine and the glare of publicity, was prepared for launch. A large sand dune south of the Cape, called "Bird Watch Hill" by the media, was packed with reporters. An array of long-range telephoto lenses, like a battery of artillery, was focused on the launch pad.

Propulsion engineer Kurt Stehling recalled, "The silvery rocket stood outside looking unkempt, as if it had been hurried out of bed. It was only partly painted, frost covered its middle, and strips of black rubber wind 'spoilers' dangled dispiritedly here and there around the top half like moss festoons."[26]

J. Paul Walsh, Hagen's deputy, was the senior program official in Florida. Trying to keep expectations reasonable, he told one reporter, "We'll be pleased if it goes into orbit. We'll not be despondent if it does not."

The moment of ignition came. In Stehling's colorful words, the first-stage motor came alive with a "heart-rending, hoarse, whining moan like that of some antediluvian beast in birth pain."[27] Two seconds after launch, the seventy-two-foot rocket burst into a spectacular fireball.

Paul Walsh, on the telephone to Hagen, said simply, "Explosion!" Hagen had an equally brief response: "Nuts."

Dan Mazur, the NRL's field manager, reacted with amazing calmness.

His first words to the launch crew were, "O.K., clean up; let's get the next rocket ready."

To punctuate the disaster in a most ironic fashion, the satellite was blown clear and fell to the ground intact, its radio transmitters cheerfully sending signals as if it were in orbit. Even the solar cells were working, although covered with soot.[28]

The third stage was also intact and loaded with potentially dangerous solid propellant. Roger Easton recollected, "They [the military] had some crazy guys fly into the Cape. I guess they snagged onto the thing and took it out and dumped it."[29]

One reporter wrote, "Down Highway A1A, the staffs of the luxury motels—places with indicative names, such as the Sea Missile, the Starlite, and the Vanguard—stopped smiling. It was as if the region's pride had been deflated by the disaster."[30]

Immediately after the failure, efforts were underway to identify the cause. Investigators from Martin blamed an "improper engine start" due to low fuel-tank pressure. Their counterparts from GE believed a fuel line connection had come loose. When it became clear the matter was not going to be resolved quickly—indeed, it was never resolved to everyone's satisfaction—Hagen ordered everyone to press ahead while taking steps to preclude either possibility in future launches.[31]

When the Army began its renewed campaign for permission to back up Vanguard, NRL engineers briefly floated a plan to combine the two programs. The idea was to put the Vanguard third stage atop the first stage of the Army's planned satellite launcher, the Jupiter C. While von Braun agreed the concept appeared feasible, it was not clear this would actually result in a satellite sooner than could be obtained by the ABMA plan alone. As Rosen later reflected, it looked good on paper, but combining stages not designed to be compatible would likely involve unforeseen complications. The idea was allowed to languish and was eventually forgotten.[32]

On November 8, McElroy yielded to continuing entreaties from Redstone Arsenal and the Army staff in the Pentagon and told the ABMA to prepare for two launches in case a backup to Vanguard was needed. Approval for the actual launch was not yet given. Almost a month before this, however, the intrepid General Medaris had risked his career by ordering the preparation of one of the Jupiter Cs that "just happened" to be left over from the reentry vehicle test program. Medaris was saved from having to explain his actions when an initial sum of $3.5 million was provided to the Army to prepare for a possible satellite launch. The target date was January 1958.

Even when publicly announcing the November 8 decision, McElroy emphasized the Army capability was a backup. The DoD press release on the occasion said, "There is every reason to believe Vanguard will meet its schedule to launch later this year a fully instrumented scientific satellite."[33]

In the aftermath of the "Flopnik," as Vanguard TV-3 was dubbed by the press, the Army's orders were changed. Instead of just preparing a backup to Vanguard, von Braun was to launch his satellite as quickly as possible, with permission to launch a second spacecraft in March 1958. Medaris and von Braun had been expecting such directives ever since the November 8 announcement, and Army work had been proceeding on that basis.

The ABMA experts also found time to propose future space efforts. First, the Army began briefing Pentagon officials on a concept for a television-equipped reconnaissance satellite called Janus. The Janus design, produced by Radio Corporation of America (RCA) based on the company's studies for the Air Force WS-117L project, was shot down by DoD on the grounds the Army had no charter in the reconnaissance satellite business.[34]

On a broader scale, Medaris told von Braun to lay out a long-term plan for an ambitious but practical American space program. Von Braun responded with a schedule that included development of new boosters and other hardware needed to put humans in space in 1962, establish a large space station in 1965, land on the moon in 1967, and put a fifty-person outpost on the moon in 1971. The cost was estimated at $21 billion. This plan, while never carried out, was largely adopted as the civilian national space agenda by the NACA Special Committee on Space Technology in 1958.[35]

While the Army proposed developing new military boosters which also had civilian uses, John Hagen suggested the military should look at Vanguard as an IRBM. He estimated the rocket could deliver a 1,000-pound warhead 1,500 miles. This idea, though, was never taken seriously by either the Air Force or Army.[36] Vanguard was a thoroughbred, designed to push the limits of performance. Military missiles must be plow horses, always dependable and needing a minimum of care.

Missile 29, one of the Jupiter Cs prepared but not used for the RV tests, was readied for the first orbital attempt. Von Braun expected his team would also build the satellite, but Medaris agreed with Pickering that JPL should do most of the satellite work. A team lead by Jack E. Froelich began hastily finalizing the design and assembly of a cylindrical satellite that would fit atop the fourth stage of the Jupiter C. This work was based on the design produced by Josef Boehm at ABMA. The only major change was the use of a steel outer casing, rather than fiberglass as Boehm had pro-

JPL engineers inspect a mockup of their satellite. Closest to the satellite are Jack Foehlich *(left)* and Al Hibbs *(right)*. JPL P-918A. Courtesy NASA/JPL/CalTech

posed.[37] JPL referred to the satellite as *Payload RTV-7* (Reentry Test Vehicle 7) or *Deal 1* (as in, "the Russians dealt the first hand, now it's our first deal"), but it would become famous as *Explorer 1.*

Before any American satellite was launched, the Vanguard and Explorer designers effectively swapped configurations. The first Vanguard proposal depicted a conical satellite. This was soon dropped, at the IGY committee's request, in favor of the sphere. Conversely, JPL engineers briefly examined using a small sphere instead of the cylindrical design suggested by Boehm. A sphere, though, would have required a protective nose fairing, and the booster didn't have the capacity to handle the extra weight. The design team went back to the original concept, building their satellites into the extended casing and nose cone of the fourth stage Sergeant.

Building the satellite into the casing made it simpler to construct, but greatly restricted the space available for payload. The satellite portion of the stage was only thirty-three inches long and six inches in diameter. This section was made of an alloy called 410 stainless steel and lined with fiber-

Launch facility at Pad 26A being inspected by ABMA personnel prior to the launch of *Explorer 1*. From left to right are Robert Gorman, Andrew Pickett, Albert Zeiler, Hans Gruene, and Kurt Debus. NASA (NIX) Photo P-05475. Courtesy NASA

glass. Its sandblasted gray surface was marked with white stripes of aluminum oxide. The narrow stripes increased the reflectivity to the sun's rays enough to maintain the satellite's internal temperature.

Museum models today usually depict *Explorer 1* as being longitudinally striped in black and white. This error apparently arose because JPL built several mockups and test articles with varying color patterns, looking for the design that would provide optimal temperature control.[38] At the post-launch press conference, the model available was black-and-white striped, and apparently no one explained to the press that the flight article had a different appearance.

General Medaris wanted all satellite preparations to be kept under wraps. The upcoming shot was referred to only by the missile number. The general made it clear his wishes concerning secrecy were to be strictly ob-

Explorer 1 satellite being mated to its booster. This photograph clearly depicts the actual appearance of the satellite. Note the white striping on bare sandblasted stainless steel. JPL 293-3322B. Courtesy NASA/JPL/CalTech

served. "I desire it well understood that the individual who violates these instructions will be handled severely," he ordered.

On December 20, 1957, an Air Force C-124 cargo plane delivered the first stage of the Jupiter C to Cape Canaveral. While the rocket was checked out in secret, the JPL satellite and the ABMA-built washtub were flown in and tested. The vehicle and payload were erected on Pad 26A at night under blacked-out conditions on January 24.[39]

At William Pickering's suggestion, the satellite-launch variant of the Jupiter C was given the more civilian-sounding name of Juno 1. Juno, in

Roman mythology, was both wife and sister to the ruling god Jupiter. While the Juno designation was thus a fitting one, it was never widely used.

By whatever name, the launch vehicle was a strange-looking contraption. The washtub holding the multi-rocket second and third stages was set spinning before launch for stability. The fourth stage sat on top of this cylinder. The satellite's four trailing wire antennas were exposed, hanging down like a cat's whiskers. The entire stack was seventy-one feet, three inches tall and weighed 64,000 pounds. The satellite weighed 13.9 pounds on its own and 30.8 pounds if the attached fourth stage was counted.

The AFMTC commander, Major General Yates, was in full agreement with Medaris about secrecy. There was to be no repeat of the Vanguard TV-3 media circus. He made a deal with the news media representatives, who continually staked out Bird Watch Hill and other viewing spots outside the Air Force's jurisdiction. In return for keeping quiet about the launch plans, the reporters received advance briefings, launch schedule information, and better vantage points.

The ABMA had promised it could put a satellite up in ninety days. In fact, only eighty-four days passed from the November 8 directive to the launch attempt. Von Braun believed, "We could have done it within sixty days if it hadn't been for the requirement Washington laid down, that the satellite must carry scientific instruments for the IGY program. . . . Actually, we didn't have much to do at ABMA in those eighty-four days. Our Jupiter Cs were practically ready to go. The big job. . . was out in Pasadena at the JPL."[40]

The Army was ready for a launch on January 29, but high-altitude wind conditions were unacceptable. Vanguard was scheduled to make another try as early as possible. If the Army couldn't launch in January, it would have to scrub the mission and turn the range and tracking equipment back over to the Navy team. Two increasingly tense days went by, while Air Force meteorologists peppered the sky with weather balloons and ABMA engineers debated how strong the jet-stream winds could be without putting unacceptable stress on the launch vehicle.

Finally, the winds abated. On Friday, January 31, the Army made its attempt. Kurt Debus and Hans Gruene of ABMA, along with General Medaris and Jack Froelich, were there to oversee the operation. Von Braun, to his chagrin, had been ordered to Washington, to wait with Pickering and Van Allen and to be available to the press after the launch.

Fueling of the first stage began at 8:30 P.M. Eastern time. The destruct system was armed, the platforms around the missile removed, and the gantry rolled back on its tracks. Medaris watched through the green-tinted

Jupiter C with *Explorer 1* satellite on Pad 26A at Cape Canaveral being prepared for launch. NASA (NIX) Photo P-05480C. Courtesy NASA

bulletproof glass of a blockhouse 100 yards away, where he was one of fifty-seven people jammed in to direct the launch.[41] He later wrote, "Flood-lights were turned on and the missile stood like a great finger pointing to Heaven—stark, white, and alone on its launching pad."[42]

A planned 10:30 P.M. ignition time was postponed when technicians

Explorer 1 launch personnel manning control panels prior to the launch on January 31, 1958. NASA (NIX) Photo P-05476. Courtesy NASA

spotted what appeared to be a leak at the base of the booster. An incredibly brave soul ran out to the pad, stuck his head under the rocket, and found this was only a spill left over from loading the hydrogen peroxide used to drive the turbopumps.[43] The countdown was allowed to proceed to "X minus zero." At 10:48, the head of the launch crew, Robert Moser, said, "Firing command," and one of his subordinates pulled out a metal ring on the console and twisted it to begin the firing sequence.[44]

Thirteen seconds later, the first-stage engine ignited. For three very long seconds, the launch crew watched from the blockhouse as the booster built up enough thrust to lift from the pad. When it finally rose, it did so perfectly, accelerating with a roar and a "tremendous golden jet" of flame as it vanished into the night. The United States had finally sent its own satellite on the long climb toward orbit.

There was an anguished moment when the radio receiver in the blockhouse stopped registering telemetry signals from the Jupiter C. Fearing the worst, Medaris grabbed a phone line connected to Hangar D, a larger building three miles away where most of the tracking and support staff was working. "I've lost my signal!" he barked. An agonizing forty seconds later, the general learned AFMTC's central data recording station still had contact with the booster.

Ernst Stuhlinger had perhaps the most critical job that night. The telemetry from an onboard accelerometer, along with radar-tracking data and Doppler shift information (obtained by a system called DOVAP), was fed to his post in Hangar D to indicate when he was to fire the second stage. The data was far from perfect, and Stuhlinger called into play his own knowledge of the rocket's performance and data from a special analog computer, the "apex predictor," which he had developed to help him make the determination.[45]

The first stage burned out 157 seconds into the flight; the rocket was at an angle 40 degrees from the horizontal.[46] A system combining explosive bolts and springs separated the upper section containing the guidance compartment from the first stage. Five-pound-thrust air jets located at the base of the instrument compartment then nudged the upper section to a horizontal position.[47]

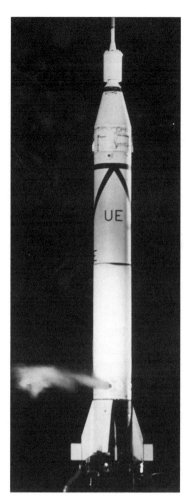

Jupiter C with *Explorer 1* just prior to launch. NASA Marshall #9801800. Courtesy NASA/ MSFC Archives

When Stuhlinger calculated the rocket had reached this point, 260 seconds after burnout, he sent the signal to fire the first group of Sergeants.[48] The upper section then roared away from the rocket, leaving the protective tub and all guidance equipment behind. The third and fourth stages were subsequently fired by timers.

In the blockhouse, General Medaris hovered over JPL mathematician Al Hibbs, who was making calculations based on the telemetry from the launch vehicle and the DOVAP measurements. Half an hour after the launch, Hibbs reported that he could conclude "with 95 percent confidence" there was a 60 percent probability the satellite was in orbit.

Medaris snapped, "Don't give me that crap, Hibbs. Is it up?"

Hibbs replied, "It's up."[49]

The data received thus far indicated that the velocity was adequate and the insertion altitude and angle were good. But the engineers of ABMA and JPL knew they had to wait for probably another hour and a half before the satellite made its way around the Earth and confirmed whether Hibbs was right.

General Medaris sent a teletype message to JPL suggesting their staff have a cigarette and relax. With stereotypical California humor, JPL engineers replied they were "being nonchalant and lighting up a marijuana."[50]

No one was nonchalant in Washington. Von Braun expected to hear news of a signal about half past midnight. Pickering was holding a telephone line open to JPL's tracking stations. Nothing happened at the appointed time, or for several minutes thereafter. Von Braun wrote, "We were miserable. Obviously, we'd been mistaken. The *Explorer* had never really gone into orbit."[51]

Then, 117 minutes after launch, the signal came.

There is a bit of a mystery concerning this event. General Medaris, in his memoir *Countdown for Decision*, recorded that his aide handed him a note reading, "Goldstone has the bird." This quote has been included in most histories of the launch, but it appears to be incorrect. There was no receiving or tracking equipment located at Goldstone Dry Lake in California in January 1958. The first tracking station at Goldstone was set up months later to support the Pioneer lunar probes. JPL had erected a temporary Microlock station for the *Explorer 1* launch at Borrego Springs, 150 miles southwest of Goldstone. The only other station in California was one established by an amateur radio group and located in Temple City.[52] Henry Magill, the aide involved, is certain the note he handed Medaris said nothing about Goldstone. Thus it seems likely Medaris inadvertently ascribed an occurrence from a later launch to the *Explorer 1* event.[53]

Wherever the news came from, it was a major boost to the nation's morale. In Washington, von Braun and the other key participants had been waiting at the Pentagon. Confirmation of the satellite's success, coming at the end of a long string of tension-filled late nights, all-out effort, and a diet heavy on coffee and cigarettes, galvanized the entire building. A jubilant von Braun declared, "We have firmly established our foothold in space. We will never give it up again."[54] At a 2 A.M. press conference at the NAS build-

At the press conference after the *Explorer 1* launch, William Pickering, James Van Allen, and Wernher von Braun display a model of the satellite with the fourth-stage Sergeant attached. This photograph is presumably the source of the erroneous belief that the satellite then in space was painted black and white. NASA Marshall #5663627. Courtesy NASA/MSFC Archives

ing, Pickering, von Braun, and Van Allen raised a model of the satellite over their heads. The resulting picture made newspapers all over the world.

President Eisenhower was cautious when informed the launch appeared successful. He remarked, "Let's not make too great a hullabaloo about this." Later, when it was confirmed the satellite was in orbit, he added, "That's wonderful. I sure feel a lot better now."[55]

Von Braun was diplomatic about the Army success compared with the Navy's perceived impotence. He explained, "It's not that we're geniuses, it is just that we have been working on these things so long we have already made more mistakes than the other people have."[56]

To General Medaris, the only flaw in an otherwise triumphant night was the text of the President's announcement concerning the satellite. Not

The *Huntsville Times* on the morning after the *Explorer 1* launch. NASA Marshall #9248170. Courtesy NASA/MSFC Archives

a word was mentioned about the ABMA or any of its people. While von Braun was center stage at the press conference, it seemed to Medaris that official Washington was going to great lengths, not only to avoid giving the Army credit, but to pretend *Explorer* was not a military endeavor at all.[57] An interesting parallel can be drawn here to the initial *Pravda* story on *Sputnik 1*, which also made no mention of its military involvement.

People in Huntsville, Alabama, knew better. The whole community was fiercely proud of its Army missile center, having long since adopted the Germans as fellow citizens. An all-night party kicked off, which seemed to involve everyone in town. Sirens wailed, bells pealed, and people paraded with signs proclaiming Huntsville the "Space Capitol of the Universe."[58] Some people even burned an effigy of former Defense Secretary Wilson, widely blamed for restricting the Army's rocket programs.[59]

On the next morning's television news programs, Republican congressmen appeared in film clips lauding the launching of "Satellite USA." In the age before satellite television and videotape, this feat of logistics was only possible because the clips had been filmed in advance. Unfortunately, the political wizards had assumed Vanguard would be the first American satellite, so both pictures and narration described a round satellite and a three-stage launch vehicle.[60]

Curiously, the satellite's name had not been selected before launch. After the craft made orbit, several names were suggested. One of these, offered by Richard Hirsch of the National Security Council's Ad Hoc Committee on Outer Space, was "Explorer." Army Secretary Brucker approved it, rejecting his own service's suggestion of "Topkick." In Army parlance, the topkick is the highest-ranking sergeant in an organization. It was a clever name, since the satellite was indeed launched by the "top Sergeant," but Topkick was reportedly deemed "too military."[61] The spacecraft was duly christened *Explorer 1*.

Explorer 1 ended up in a higher orbit than the first Russian satellite. *Explorer*'s perigee was 225 miles, its apogee 1,594 miles, and its orbital period an hour and fifty-five minutes.[62] The higher orbit was sometimes pointed out in the media as if it canceled out the greater weight of *Sputnik 1*. Von Braun's acquaintances at Disney, though, drew their inspiration from *Sputnik 2:* following *Explorer 1*'s launch, von Braun received a cartoon showing a rocket being launched with a fire hydrant on top, as if the Americans were sending a gift to Laika.[63]

Despite being dwarfed by the *Sputnik*s, *Explorer 1* accomplished a more significant feat of space research. JPL engineers had packed a Geiger-Mueller radiation counter into the little cylinder. This was the instrument already given a Flight Priority A designation on the list of experiments for Project Vanguard.

In 1954, Stuhlinger, the only physicist on the von Braun team, had visited Van Allen and apprised him of the Army's progress toward an Earth satellite. Van Allen explained his efforts to map the distribution of "cosmic rays" (high-energy subatomic particles) in near-Earth space. Van Allen had been studying this topic for years, but available methods such as rockoons gave him only glimpses of the radiation's strength and distribution. When Stuhlinger described the severe constraints on power, weight, and volume likely to exist on the first satellites, Van Allen responded that a cosmic ray detector should be compatible with such limits.[64] Stuhlinger, who had worked on V-2 experiments with Van Allen at White Sands, took an interest in the subject, and a crucial partnership emerged.

After his experiment had been selected for Vanguard, Van Allen continued to stay in touch with the Army and JPL staffs, mainly through Stuhlinger. Van Allen's project received $169,225 in funding from the TPESP, and his team built a device using a single Geiger-Mueller tube as a radiation detector. The circuitry would use transistors. While such devices were in their infancy, Van Allen's group discovered, as the NRL engineers designing the Vanguard transmitters had, that transistors offered such advantages over vacuum tubes in size, ruggedness, and power requirements that their use was a necessity.[65]

Back in November 1956, after the success of *Missile 27* had proved the ABMA-JPL launch vehicle concept, Stuhlinger had telephoned Van Allen and asked for a specific design around which an Army satellite could be configured. He also expressed his belief that Vanguard could not make its original schedule, and that there was some chance the Army would succeed in its campaign to build a satellite as a backstop for the Navy project.

Van Allen described to Stuhlinger the concept he had had in mind and set to work defining the details. In April 1957, Stuhlinger, along with ABMA satellite designers Lundquist, Boehm, and Arthur Thompson, came to Van Allen's office to exchange details of the prospective satellite and the cosmic-ray detector.[66] Van Allen's indispensable graduate assistant, George Ludwig, had designed the instrument so it could fit either a Vanguard satellite or the prospective Army spacecraft.

After the Army satellite project was approved in the hectic days following *Sputnik 1*, Pickering and the engineers at JPL, along with von Braun and the USNC, discussed what payloads should be carried. *Explorer 1* imposed hellish conditions on its instrumentation. There was no shroud over the satellite, so any surface-mounted components would be exposed to environmental effects, including significant aerodynamic heating. The maximum acceleration imposed by the final solid-fuel stage was a staggering seventy times the force of gravity (70 G). Finally, the instruments, along with the entire satellite and upper-stage package, would be spinning at up to 750 revolutions per minute during the flight.

There were a number of reasons for the high spin rate of the washtub. First, spinning stabilized the upper stages, which had no guidance system, and kept them on the proper trajectory. Second, in a cluster of rockets, no two ever have precisely the same thrust, and even tiny differences could throw a space vehicle off course. Spinning the entire system helped even out the inconsistencies. Finally, if one rocket failed to ignite, a rapid spin could also counter the imbalance resulting from this situation. The spin rate increased after liftoff, reaching 750 rpm at 115 seconds into the flight. As Kurt Debus explained, this change in spin rate was "to prevent resonance between spin frequency of the high-speed stages and the bending frequency of the Redstone booster, which became lighter as propellant was consumed."[67]

The high spin rate used in launching *Explorer* was only possible because the upper section had been deliberately over-designed. According to Walter Downhower, *Explorer 1*'s payload engineer, the reentry vehicle test program required a maximum spin rate of only 450 rpm for sufficient accuracy. JPL and ABMA engineers, hoping that someday their design would be used for a satellite and knowing that a higher rate would be needed to provide the accuracy for orbital injection, built and tested the contraption for spin rates of up to one thousand. Without this over-design, *Explorer 1* might not have been able to achieve a stable orbit.[68]

Pickering informed his colleagues that Van Allen's experiment, while designed for Vanguard, could also be installed in the Army satellite. Von Braun, who had long been aware of the Stuhlinger–Van Allen collaboration, feigned surprise, saying, "Isn't that interesting?"[69] On October 23, a JPL delegation visited Ludwig to look over the instrument and make final recommendations about fitting it into their satellite.

Van Allen, at this point, was aboard the USS *Glacier* in the Antarctic. He had resumed his study of the upper atmosphere and space using rockoons. Pickering sent Van Allen a radiogram asking permission to install his experiment on the satellite. Pickering had already talked to Richard Porter, and the two men had agreed that Van Allen's experiment had top priority for the Army spacecraft. Ranked in second place was a package of instruments from NRL that were designed to analyze the satellite's environment. This was a modification of another Vanguard experiment. Third was a NACA proposal, also originally presented for Vanguard, to deploy an inflatable sphere, which could be tracked in order to study the structure and density of the upper fringes of the atmosphere.[70]

Naturally, Van Allen enthusiastically approved the use of his instrument. By November 20, George Ludwig was in residence "for the duration" at JPL and was working with Froelich and his California team to put the final touches on Van Allen's instrument and fit it into the satellite.

Ludwig's original design for the instrument package included a tape recorder to capture data when the system was out of touch with Earth stations. He now decided this device might not work under the stress imposed by the payload's spin rate. Accordingly, he removed the recorder and worked on modifying it for later flights. Two months later, Ludwig went to Cape Canaveral to assist with the final checkout when the payload was installed atop its booster.

In flight, the instrument worked perfectly. Preliminary results, announced by Pickering, indicated that the cosmic-ray environment in space was lower than expected and would pose no danger to future space travelers.[71]

There was one curious occurrence, though. There were brief periods when the counter stopped showing a radiation level entirely. This posed a conundrum for scientists on Earth. There was no imaginable reason why the particle count should drop to zero, and the fragmentary nature of the *Explorer* data exacerbated the problem of analyzing this puzzle. First, the data was receivable only when the satellite was within range of Earth stations. The NRL team assembled for Vanguard was a major help here, both in receiving data via Minitrack and in reducing it for analysis.[72] Second, the satellite did not seem to be transmitting continually even during these periods: the transmissions "blinked" on and off. Project engineers soon deduced the cause.

Explorer was supposed to be spinning around its long axis, with the wire antennas forming a rotating circle as the satellite spun. However, the spacecraft was more complex than the engineers had assumed when modeling its behavior. The rotational energy dissipated by the four flexible antennas, aided slightly by the flexing of the vehicle body imparted by the stresses of launch, was enough to begin a transition into a slow, flat spin around the satellite's transverse axis. The resulting non-spherical pattern of the antennas introduced an unexpected modulation of the radio signals. Van Allen called this "an impressive and humiliating lesson in the elementary mechanics of a somewhat nonrigid body."[73]

The Geiger-Mueller tube on *Explorer 1*, while the best device available for the flight, did have important limitations. It could not classify the types of particles that struck its detector. It also had a low upper limit on its counting rate: 128 particles per second.

Despite the interruptions and the limitations of the equipment, a pattern could be deduced concerning the zero-count phenomenon. The count dropped (after a sharp rise) only when *Explorer 1* climbed about 600 miles above the Earth.[74] The precise altitude at which the phenomenon began varied with the spacecraft's latitude. The "blackouts" lasted for periods as long as two minutes.

The explanation of this phenomenon had to wait until late March, when the next radiation counter reached orbit on *Explorer 3*. When that satellite showed a similar pattern, Van Allen began to suspect the counter was not reading zero at all. Instead, it was being overloaded by radiation levels far higher than expected. Lab tests showed that, when this type of Geiger-Mueller tube was hit with very high levels of radiation (over 25,000 counts per second), it did indeed show zero. The result of the analysis was the confirmation of high-radiation zones around the Earth, which would become famous as the Van Allen belts.

Explorer 1 also carried thermistors and two thermometers to study the temperatures in orbit, plus a micrometeorite-impact detection apparatus, which incorporated a microphone on the inside of the satellite shell and a grid of twelve fine wires mounted on the outside. The microphone was intended to pick up the vibrations of an impact, while any micrometeorite that broke one of the wires would trigger an electrical signal.

With these instruments and two four-channel radio transmitters on board, *Explorer 1* was, for its era, a truly impressive example of miniaturization.[75] *Explorer* had a 60-milliwatt transmitter set at 108.03 megacycles and a 10-milliwatt transmitter operating on 108.00 megacycles. Each transmitted four channels of telemetry. The high-power transmitter's amplitude-modulated signals could be received on the Navy-Vanguard Minitrack receivers and those built for JPL's own system, Microlock. The low-power transmitter's phase-modulated signal was designed for Microlock only.[76] There were two fiberglass slot antennas built into the satellite body, plus the four whip antennas.

Two wires in the micrometeorite detection grid broke when the fourth stage was fired. No more were broken during the satellite's working life. The microphone reported several small impacts.[77] The evidence from this experiment indicated that near-Earth space was not, as some scientists had feared, so heavily saturated with meteoric debris that space travel would be unacceptably hazardous.

Explorer 1's telemetry confirmed another welcome fact, one originally indicated by the *Sputnik*s: that a spacecraft's internal temperature could be maintained within acceptable limits. The temperature measured on the surface varied from 14 to 167 degrees Fahrenheit, but the internal temperature stayed between 32 and 104 degrees, even without the active cooling systems the Soviets had used.[78]

The world now had two space powers. America's first satellite functioned until May 23, 1958, when its nickel-cadmium batteries expired. It remained in orbit until 1970. The challenge of *Sputnik* had been answered, and the next stage of the race—the development of more capable, more advanced satellites, and even probes to the moon and planets—awaited.

■ *Chapter 8*

NOTSNIK
The Secret Competitor

As far as the American people knew, the United States in early 1958 had two satellite programs: Vanguard and Explorer. There was, however, a third American team in the race. Like Vanguard, it was a Navy-run project, but the Vanguard directors were not even aware of its existence.[1]

In a classified effort called Project Pilot, the Navy's weapons development center in China Lake, California, was fabricating tiny satellites and putting them into air-launched five-stage rockets. The launch system went by the bizarre acronym NOTSNIK. (NOTS stood for Naval Ordnance Test Station: "nik" was borrowed from *Sputnik*.) NOTS specialized in developing rockets, bombs, and missiles for the Navy. At the time, its top-priority project was the Sidewinder air-to-air missile, a design so successful that variants of it are still in production today.

Project Pilot was initiated by a group of China Lake physicists shortly after *Sputnik 1* had been launched. While this particular team was working on the Sidewinder project, the men took more than a passing interest in the flurry of satellite activity. The inspiration came when several of the Navy scientists gathered one night to watch the *Sputnik* booster track across the heavens.

As recalled by Frank Cartwright, his colleague Howard Wilcox, head of NOTS's Weapons Development

Department, said simply, "We ought to be able to do that." One team member, Leo Jagiello, suggested a more direct military response: "We ought to go shoot the damn thing down."[2]

The NOTS scientists did more than speculate: they set to work. A satellite study was initiated with internal funds, and design work was underway by November, 1957. In the same month, the first suggestions for a NOTS satellite program were briefed to the Navy's Bureau of Aerospace (BuAer) and Bureau of Ordnance (BuOrd) in Washington.

The original plan was to use Sergeant rocket motors—that is, motors from the operational Sergeant missile, not the scaled versions used on the Jupiter C—to build an all–solid-fuel, ground-launched rocket with four stages. The Army, however, rebuffed a request for the Sergeants. After examining several alternatives, including catapult-launched and mountaintop-launched vehicles, the satellite team, which still had only quasi-official status at this point, settled on a rocket dropped from a fighter jet.[3]

A formal proposal describing the air-launched approach was produced in February 1958. John Nicolaides, who directed space programs for BuOrd, approved $300,000 in startup funds.

In search of the money needed to move from studies to building hardware, NOTS officials went back to Washington in May, 1958. By this point, the United States had already responded to *Sputnik*. Thanks to *Vanguard 1*, NOTSNIK would not even be the first U.S. Navy satellite. Still, the capability offered by the air-launch technique remained intriguing. The men from China Lake promised Navy leaders that they could put up satellites in time to serve a useful function as well as to demonstrate the principles and hardware involved. It was agreed the NOTS satellites would be designed to study the radiation produced by Project Argus, a series of high-atmosphere nuclear test explosions set to begin in August.

Emphasizing its potential military functions won the project approval to spend NOTS funds, eventually totaling over $4 million, on a more official basis. Unfortunately, it also gave rise to a schedule that appeared impossible to keep. The NOTSNIK staff had to finish the design work, then fabricate, assemble, and fly the entire system—satellite, instrumentation, and booster—in a few months. NOTSNIK would essentially be tested by its launch into orbit.

The NOTSNIK satellite was a minuscule doughnut-shaped design, 8 inches across and weighing only 2.3 pounds. It perched on the nose of a five-stage booster, whose stages were either built in the NOTS workshops or adapted from existing rocket and missile motors. NOTS was a full-service organization, capable of doing everything from lab designs to fabrication to

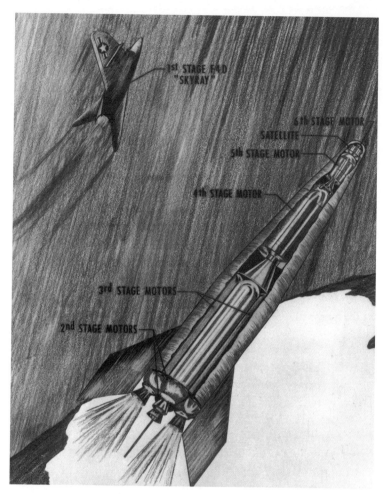

Illustration of the NOTSNIK project, with cutaway diagram of the launch vehicle. In this picture, the first two HOTROC motors are burning. NOTS L036494. Courtesy Official U.S. Navy Photograph/China Lake Photographic Archive

flight testing, and all the station's abilities were employed to do this end-to-end program in record time.

The launch aircraft was to be an F4D-1 Skyray, a transonic delta-wing fighter. NOTS had a special version of this aircraft, stripped down and modified for a variety of high-speed test work. A standard bomb rack under the aircraft's port wing carried the launch vehicle, while a heavy fuel tank was loaded on the starboard wing for balance.

Six satellites were built. The first three carried only basic diagnostic instruments and a radio transmitter. A radiation counter built by NOTS's Rod McClung was added for the Project Argus flights.[4] Telemetry was received using the JPL-developed Microlock system that was also used for *Explorer*.

In the wake of an early proposal to put an infrared television scanner in the satellite, the NOTS spacecraft acquired the alternate moniker "Naval Observational Television Satellite." This particular instrument was designed but was apparently never flown on NOTSNIK. Some NOTS participants recall the payload had been nixed by the State Department for legal reasons, although documentation is inconsistent on this point.[5] The scanner payload would have been used for observing weather fronts, cloud formations, snow cover, etc., and would have provided a resolution of about one mile from an altitude of 1,000 miles.[6]

The NOTS satellite looked more like a "breadboard" design model than an operational spacecraft. The shell was made of fiberglass and filled with a foam potting compound. Holes were cut in the foam to allow for the insertion of components and wires. The satellite was sealed and the rocket motor mounted in the "donut hole." About half the satellite's weight was allocated for a battery that could power the single-watt, 108 Mhz transmitter for about a week. The satellite was mounted to the vehicle with the fifth-stage nozzle facing backward—that is, opposite to the direction of launch.

The launch vehicle looked like nothing flown before or since. As one participant put it, "We used a Tinker Toy approach—bolting things together to see if they'd work."[7]

The first two stages were pairs of HOTROC motors. The HOTROC was the NOTS-designed motor for the Navy's ASROC (Anti-Submarine Rocket), modified with a thinner-walled casing to save as much weight as possible. Each HOTROC was 71 inches long, 11.65 inches in diameter, and carried 300 pounds of propellant. Each rocket burned for less than five seconds, producing a maximum thrust of 14,200 pounds.

There were four HOTROCs bundled in a cluster, and diagonally opposing pairs were fired for the first and second stages. On top of the HOTROCs went the only major component not built at NOTS—an Allegany Ballistics Laboratory X-241 rocket motor, an early version of the X-248 used as the third stage for Vanguard. It produced 2,270 pounds of thrust. Next came a smaller motor built at NOTS exclusively for this program. It was eight inches in diameter and burned for six seconds, producing 1,155 pounds of thrust. Finally, there was a still smaller fifth-stage motor, a sphere three inches in diameter and weighing only about a pound. Its thrust was 172 pounds, produced for one second.

The entire vehicle was 172.5 inches long. It had a maximum fuselage diameter of 30 inches, with a span of 65 inches across the fins. A lightweight aerodynamic shell was fitted over the upper three stages.

The fifth stage was not fired until the satellite was halfway around the world. The spin-stabilized craft maintained the same orientation in an absolute sense, so its orientation with respect to the Earth changed continually. After half an orbit, the nozzle that had been backwards at launch would now be pointing opposite to the direction of travel. The fifth stage would give the satellite the final boost to circularize its orbit and prevent the satellite's premature reentry. This marked the first time a circularization burn, dubbed by William Pickering a "kick in the apogee," was tried on a satellite. It would later become a common maneuver.

There were no moving parts in the vehicle. Once the airplane launched it from 41,000 feet at Mach 0.9 on a lofted trajectory, the rocket would continue guided only by gravity and the spin imparted by the canted fins on the lower section. After the first two stages had burned out, the vehicle would coast until an infrared telescope built into the third stage detected the horizon, telling the rocket it was at the right angle for the third stage to fire. This was expected to happen at an altitude of about forty-nine miles. The third-stage X-241 then burned for thirty-five seconds. Its ignition kicked off a timer that fired the fourth stage almost immediately.

When the fourth stage burned out, the rocket was technically in orbit, but the perigee would be only forty miles—far too low to survive. That was where the fifth stage, timed to ignite about fifty-three minutes into the flight, was to boost the orbit. The final perigee of the polar orbit was expected to be 1,400 miles.

NOTS engineers did everything they could think of to make the vehicle simple and reliable. The 2,100 pound NOTSNIK booster remains the smallest satellite launch vehicle ever designed. It was also the first all-solid-fuel orbital launch vehicle, predating by two years the NASA Scout rocket usually awarded this distinction.[8]

While their inspiration was to put up a response to *Sputnik,* Wilcox and his comrades soon developed a long-range goal as well. They wanted to prove the value of their unusual launch system and help it evolve into a permanent Navy capability. The idea was to move from the highly experimental first-generation booster to more capable rockets that would loft ten-pound satellites and be available throughout the Navy as "munitions-quality rounds." To translate the military-speak, that meant future versions of the NOTS launcher would be made on an assembly line, the way bombs and missiles were, and be designed to sit in storage on a base or aircraft carrier for years. When a rapid look at a scientific phenomenon or

Navy personnel load a NOTSNIK round onto the F4D-1 launch aircraft, July 19, 1958. NOTS LHL L037600. Courtesy Official U.S. Navy Photograph/China Lake Photographic Archive

a military event was needed, a launcher could be taken from storage, mated quickly to the appropriate satellite, slung under a fighter plane, and launched into orbit.

It was an audacious concept, but the people of NOTS were used to audacity. The station nourished a maverick image, often improvising equipment and conducting less-than-official projects. NOTS' Technical Director, Bill MacLean, shepherded the revolutionary Sidewinder into service despite direct orders from his superiors in Washington to drop the effort.

Despite the schedule, morale on the NOTSNIK project was high, and Navy personnel worked 130-hour weeks to prepare for a first launch by July, 1958. There was time only for a few tests on a rocket sled plus two test-attempts from ground launch rails. The first ground-launched vehicle blew up a second after leaving the rail. The second exploded eight seconds before the countdown expired. The intrepid engineers (and a courageous pilot, Commander William West, who assured the NOTS designers the vehicle wouldn't blow up when he was carrying it) pressed on with the actual launch attempts.[9]

At that point, satellite launches were still such a rare and potentially momentous event that NOTS officials were required to notify a White House official in advance. Notice had to be given two hours before each launch attempt, and a report of results made as soon as possible.

The first vehicle to attempt orbit was launched was on July 25, 1958. The rocket was thought to have exploded, although there was some ambiguity because tracking was halted too quickly. The second vehicle thumbed its aluminum nose at Commander West's confidence by blowing up at ignition, only seconds after clearing the aircraft.

The most tantalizing results came on the third attempt, August 22, 1958. Accompanied by a second fighter acting as chase plane, West flew his Skyray to the drop zone over the Santa Barbara Channel. He accelerated to Mach 0.9 and entered a 2-G climb at 58 degrees.[10] At 41,000 feet, an automatic system released the booster. As West's plane continued past the vertical and entered a planned stall, the first two HOTROCs ignited. The launch control center at Point Arguello reported what looked like a good launch, and the rocket disappeared over the western horizon.[11] The NOTSNIK team was ecstatic when a radio signal that may have been from the satellite's transmitter was picked up in Christchurch, New Zealand. But there were no further signals. If the satellite was in orbit, its radio or battery must have failed earlier than expected.

The last three launches were made on August 25, 26, and 28. The entire NOTSNIK launch program thus fit between the sixth and seventh orbital attempts made under the Navy's unclassified satellite program, Vanguard. All of the these final efforts failed: one vehicle exploded, one failed to ignite, and one broke up in flight.

A post-mortem assessment, written by NOTS engineer Frank Knemeyer in 1960, stated that, overall, five of the six launches failed due to a variety of booster malfunctions.

Robert G. S. Sewell, head of the Long Range Missile Branch at NOTS, did not find the project's record surprising. He offered his impression that, "This is a prime example of how not to run a program." He cited insufficient resources, unrealistic schedules, uncoordinated activity, and "panic at all times" as just some of the reasons why NOTSNIK achieved results that were, at best, "unknown." He did note that some concrete achievements had come out of the project, including development of new solid-rocket motors, construction of telemetry receiving stations, and new experience with electronics, telemetry systems, and the handling and launching of large aircraft-carried rockets.[12]

Many additional claims have been made for NOTSNIK. One is that two

View of the NOTSNIK satellite with the diagnostic payload installed.
Courtesy of Dick Boyd

satellites possibly or definitely made orbit. Another is that the television scanner was in fact the payload and the Project Argus connection was only a cover story. These claims were put forward by John Nicolaides in a 1996 interview.[13] None of these achievements, however, is supported by the declassified records or by the recollections of most project veterans.

It is commonly reported that further signals were received from the August 22 satellite, either on the third orbit or over a longer period. Frank St. George, who manned the Christchurch, New Zealand, tracking station during all NOTSNIK launch attempts, is certain he heard only one signal from one launch. Some NOTSNIK veterans do believe that the first launch also may have made orbit.[14] According to NOTS communications engineer Dick Boyd, there was difficulty in getting good telemetry at China Lake itself because a commercial FM station in Santa Monica, transmitting at 107.9 MHz, interfered with the low-power 108 MHz transmissions from the satellite.[15]

This frame from a 16mm film shows a NOTS vehicle being launched in July 1958. The first two HOTROCs have just ignited. NOTS LHL 245728. Courtesy Official U.S. Navy Photograph/China Lake Photographic Archive

The odds against NOTSNIK were long. The compressed schedule forced shortcuts and truncated ground testing, which apparently resulted in a launch vehicle that had only a marginal chance of surviving the stresses created when the first stage ignited. A slower-paced project may well have allowed for diagnosis and correction of structural weaknesses.

The entire concept also depended upon the launch sequence working perfectly. If the release of the third, fourth, or fifth stages imparted unwanted motion in the wrong direction, the error would be compounded during the fifth stage's long journey around the Earth to its ignition point. The satellite could neither detect whether it was oriented incorrectly, nor correct for any pointing error. The relatively high orbit allowed for some margin of error, but apparently not enough. It may be that the signal detected at Christchurch on August 22, 1958, came from a vehicle that was working well but which ignited its final stage while pointed in a fatally erroneous direction.

No one knew—nor will we ever know for certain—whether this shoestring project put a satellite into orbit. As noted above, the NOTS staffers themselves were divided in their assessments.

It may be that NOTSNIK was just too simple; perhaps another kind of horizon sensor in an upper stage, combined with a directional thruster, could have made the difference. Or it may be that the rocket as built could have worked, but that the resources available and the murderous development schedule simply prevented the concept from being properly tested and debugged. The launcher-as-munition idea never made it to operational status.

The design did spawn a sequel, however, the Caleb or NOTS EV-2. (EV-1 was a name applied only retroactively to the original vehicle.)[16] This was a larger, four-stage design using a more powerful F-4 Phantom as the launch aircraft. The first stage was a single 24-inch motor called the NOTS 500, and the X-248 was the second stage. The 3,000 pound Caleb theoretically could place a twenty-pound satellite in a 1,000-mile high orbit.

Beyond 1960, the fate of NOTS' satellite effort becomes murky. There were at least three tests, involving both one- and two-stage versions, and in 1962 a Caleb suborbital flight carried instruments to a height of 726 miles.[17] These launches were carried out in a scientific project called Hi-Hoe (for Hydrogen, Helium, and Oxygen Experiment).[18]

It appears the program's further incarnations were split into numerous projects with very odd names. These included a suborbital tactical reconnaissance vehicle called Yo-yo (reportedly canceled in 1962), and a design called Dixie-Pixie (a biomedical satellite carrying two rats). A project named Cerebus may have involved an ASAT (antisatellite) weapon.[19] According to the history office at China Lake, another project was called Solar Instrument Probe (SIP), but the acronym actually stood for "Satellite Interceptor Program."[20] Dixie-Pixie lost out in the battle for funding, as did a recoverable Earth photography experiment called Vertical Probe (VP)-1.[21]

The facts concerning whatever ASAT work was done are obscured in a welter of names, stories, and rumors. The final results of any such efforts are still classified. Due either to funding difficulties, technical hurdles, or the never-ending roles-and-missions disputes with other services concerning space, the ASAT-related programs might well have been killed before any operational hardware was built. It will probably be many years before the full story of the NOTSNIK program and its successors is told.

While no direct descendants of NOTSNIK operate today, the air-launched satellite booster was to resurface three decades after the 1958 NOTS launches. The Pegasus, a much larger booster operating on the same principle, became the leading American small-satellite launcher in the 1990s.[22] In 1998, Brian Wilcox, son of the late Howard Wilcox and an engineer at JPL, suggested a rocket based on the simple NOTS design for the Mars-to-orbit portion of NASA's Mars Sample Return mission. The effort was benched when NASA postponed the mission for several years.[23]

In 1999 the Air Force Research Laboratory began studying a micro-satellite launch vehicle to be dropped from a fighter plane. The idea was to give the service the capability to rapidly orbit microsatellites in order to complement existing satellite coverage when a crisis erupted or a particular area needed increased surveillance. At the time this account is being written, the project has been moved to DARPA (Defense Advanced Research Projects Agency), where it has morphed into a system known as RASCAL (Rapid Access, Small Cargo, Affordable Launch).[24] The concept would have seemed very familiar to the Naval Ordnance Test Station crews of 1958.

■ *Chapter 9*

Storming the Heavens
Satellites of 1958–59

After the initial flurry of U.S. activity in the wake of *Sputnik 1*, America began examining its space, missile, and satellite programs more seriously. President Eisenhower resisted calls for a Manhattan Project–style crash program. He stood by his decision to limit the government's immediate actions to supplementing funding for missile programs while investigating what the country needed to do in space and what it could spend on such endeavors.

There were no questions in the government about one topic—reconnaissance satellites. America's space reconnaissance efforts got a triple boost from *Sputnik:* the Soviets had proven that satellite launch was possible, had established the right to overflight in space, and had intensified the determination of American intelligence analysts to find out what else their adversary might be up to. Everything about these satellites remained highly classified, but word quickly leaked out. The *New York Times* mentioned an American reconnaissance satellite program in an article dated October 14, 1957, and a *Newsweek* diagram, published on February 17, 1958, showed a spacecraft labeled "Air Force or Army TV reconnaissance satellite."[1]

In February 1958, Eisenhower approved a revamped reconnaissance satellite program. The WS-117L designation was eliminated, but the Air Force would continue with its efforts to develop a satellite that would radio images to Earth. (This program became known as SAMOS.) The Air Force also began a "biomedical" satellite program called Discoverer, with a recoverable capsule that would return specimens to Earth.

Discoverer, though, was a cover story. The Air Force was actually developing technology for an effort led by the CIA: a crash program to build an "interim" reconnaissance satellite to return exposed film from orbit by dropping capsules into the atmosphere. This effort, based on an Air Force concept called Program IIA, was named CORONA (supposedly an analyst considering possible code names, at that critical moment, happened to look down at his Smith-Corona typewriter).[2] In the years to come, CORONA, not SAMOS, would prove to be the preferred solution. CORONA ended up providing the main U.S. satellite reconnaissance capability from its first launch in 1959 until the last satellite with a CORONA designation made orbit in 1972.

All this activity sparked a more concentrated effort to improve the nation's space boosters as well. The SAMOS satellites were to be built into an upper stage called the Agena, which would weigh over two tons—a staggering figure for the American rockets available in 1958. In addition to the revamping of reconnaissance satellite projects, the two years following *Sputnik 1* saw critical changes in the organization of America's space efforts, the emergence of several new satellite programs, and an explosion of new applications for spacecraft.

On the organizational side, the administration opted to push for two new agencies. The first came into being when DoD directive 5105.15 establishing the ARPA was signed on February 7, 1958. The secretary of defense gave ARPA authority to coordinate all military space programs, an arrangement destined to last only until September 1959. Meanwhile, the Army pressed ahead in organizing for a continued and expanded space mission. In March 1958, the Army Ordnance Missile Command (AOMC) was created, with Medaris as commander. AOMC included ABMA, the Army Rocket and Guided Missile Agency, White Sands Missile Range, and JPL.[3]

The administration wanted a second new organization to execute the civilian space program. While there was some sentiment for giving all space research to the military, Eisenhower wanted a civilian agency to handle space projects not directly related to defense. The President's Science Advisory Committee, headed by Presidential Science Advisor James Killian, examined the subject and concluded the simplest course was to create a new agency based on NACA.[4]

Eisenhower agreed. Under the National Aeronautics and Space Act, signed into law on July 28, NACA became the core component of the National Aeronautics and Space Administration (NASA). The new agency would assume control of NACA's four laboratories and 8,000 personnel. In August, President Eisenhower picked T. Keith Glennan, president of Case Institute of Technology, to be NASA's first Administrator. Hugh L. Dryden, the former director of NACA, became his deputy.

The creation of NASA resulted in a drastic reduction in the military's space ambitions. First, NASA immediately acquired Project Vanguard. While John Hagen retained his leadership and Vanguard was still supported by and housed at the NRL, on May 1, 1959, Vanguard was reassigned to the new Goddard Space Flight Center (GSFC). Although subsequently renamed the GSFC Vanguard Division, it remained housed at NRL until the program's completion.[5] Vanguard's key personnel, however, along with forty-six others from the Rocket Sonde Section, moved to the new agency. Some played prominent roles in NASA: John Hagen was the agency's first Assistant Director of Spaceflight Development, and Milt Rosen later became Director of Launch Vehicles and Propulsion in the NASA Office of Manned Space Flight.

NASA also requested and eventually acquired the Army's two major centers of space expertise. General Medaris did not want to lose either JPL or the von Braun organization. However, it was difficult for him to argue that JPL's mission was uniquely military, especially given the organization's enthusiasm for scientific projects such as lunar probes and its diminishing contribution to Army missile development. Medaris quickly realized JPL was a lost cause.

On December 3, 1958, JPL was transferred from the Army to NASA and was given responsibility for robotic lunar and planetary exploration programs. The move was greeted by JPL staffers with "considerable enthusiasm," despite the lab's accomplishments as part of the Army's missile and space team. As William Pickering put it, "JPL argued for, and received, a charter to develop the deep space missions. As a personal aside, I was delighted to hold a contract that said in essence 'go out and explore the depths of the solar system.'"[6]

Ever since that date, JPL has been a NASA center under the continuing management of Caltech. JPL went on to become NASA's (and the world's) premier developer of planetary and deep space probes.

General Medaris and the Army tried harder to retain the ABMA, knowing the Army's hopes for continuing a major role in space rested on keeping the von Braun team. In 1958, von Braun was already working on designs for a giant launcher with 1.5 million pounds of thrust. The super-booster was originally called the Juno 5, then the Saturn (as von Braun pointed out, Saturn is the next planet after Jupiter, so the name was a logical progression).[7] Ambitious plans developed in Project Horizon, led by Hermann Koelle of ABMA's Future Projects Office, forecast soldiers stationed in orbiting outposts and even on lunar bases.

In September 1959, however, the Eisenhower administration considered the options for further reorganization and decided to centralize military launcher development in the Air Force. The Saturn, which had no apparent military utility (if the Army's plans for manned outposts were to be disregarded—and they were), was assigned to NASA, along with the ABMA team.

On July 1, 1960, the organization that had launched America's first satellite became the core of the new George C. Marshall Space Flight Center in Huntsville, Alabama. Von Braun was named the center's first director. Medaris still thought it a mistake to shift von Braun and Saturn to NASA when the Army space effort had posted a record of success, but there were no substantive arguments left to muster against the proposal. Medaris took some comfort in seeing the group transferred intact and in his own certainty they would go on to make major contributions to the nation.[8]

Another American reaction to *Sputnik*, one with long-term repercussions, came in the field of education. Criticism in Congress and elsewhere bombarded the American education system, a traditionally decentralized system in which the Federal government had played almost no role. Three days after *Sputnik*, Elmer Hutchison, director of the American Institute of Physics, even warned that the American way of life was "doomed to rapid extinction" unless students were taught to value science.[9]

John Hagen joined the chorus in a speech delivered on February 1, 1958, in which he claimed the nation had "gone soft." He called for stricter high-school curricula, higher educational standards, and a crusade to create the future "intellectual elite" needed to move the nation forward again. He also blamed the United States' "loss" to *Sputnik* on insufficient funds and other support for Project Vanguard.[10]

Hagen's crusade was widely taken up inside and outside the government. Many in Congress wanted the Federal government to take a major role in education. Eisenhower, always reluctant to expand Washington's size and power, endorsed a more limited initiative providing for a seven-year program of Federal assistance to students enrolled in science, engineering, and foreign-language programs. In September 1958, he signed this idea into law as the National Defense Education Act (NDEA). The Department of Health, Education, and Welfare was authorized to provide a billion dollars over the program's first four years for everything from college scholarships to high school laboratory equipment. In a related act, the National Science Foundation (NSF) found its budget tripled.

The drive for improved science education was a broad one, going beyond the obvious areas of physics and mathematics. Every area of the hard sciences benefited from the NDEA. The Committee on Educational Policies (CEP), established by the NAS, had been working on a revamped biology curriculum for secondary education since 1954, but had made little headway. When *Sputnik* opened the floodgates of Federal funding, however, the biology effort caught the wave of NDEA and NSF funding and soon brought forth new curricula across the country.[11]

Federal funding was not the only significant change wrought by Korolev's little satellite. The scientific establishment, represented by the NAS and NSF, had had long been battling against educators over the amount of hard science to be included in curricula that, since the war, had increasingly favored social sciences, along with a student-centered focus as opposed to the traditional model based on classical subjects and memorization. In 1957–59, the hard-science advocates climbed to an ascendant position and have had permanent effects on the content of the education system.[12]

The Federal government's role in education would not, as Eisenhower intended, be temporary and limited. Walter McDougall and others have chronicled how *Sputnik 1*, like a pebble rolling downhill in an avalanche zone, led to unforeseeable and enormous consequences.[13] The American national government's post-*Sputnik* involvement in education and civil space programs facilitated its massive expansion into almost every field of public activity, completely changing the balance of power in America's federal system.

Before any new changes in government organization could be implemented, there was a great deal of momentum still remaining in the existing Vanguard and Explorer programs. While the future of the respective services in space was uncertain, the two programs were already in place and funded. There was no reason to stop either effort to wait for national policy to be sorted out.

NRL engineers had not been standing idly by while the Army rushed into the breach created by TV-3. A hurried effort to analyze the causes of that failure and to prepare TV-3BU (Test Vehicle 3 Back-Up) for launch ensued immediately. By January 22, 1958, the Vanguard staff was at the Cape to try again. The rocket, however, was apparently not ready to be rushed. The countdown was started and stopped repeatedly, once getting down to 14 seconds. Technical problems, mainly with the second stage, caused one delay after another. After four days of effort and frustration, the Navy had to yield the range to the Jupiter C team.

By February 3, 1958, TV-3BU, its second stage now replaced, was being readied for another shot. A reporter assured *New York Times* readers that, "The feeling around Cape Canaveral is that the Vanguard 'is going to make it' this time."[14]

It was not to be. On February 5, 1958, at 2:33 in the morning, the countdown reached zero. The booster ignited and rose beautifully into the night, climbing vertically for ten seconds and then arcing out over the Atlantic. Fifty seconds after that, the rocket veered off course to the right and began to break up. The range safety officer, Air Force Lt. Col. Raymond Stevens, threw the switch sending a "destruct" signal to the rocket's flight termination system. The pieces of Vanguard TV-3BU tumbled into the ocean.

Admiral Bennett stoically told the press, "I'm disappointed but not downhearted. The troubles of the Vanguard are the kind that are normal in any development project."[15]

The Vanguard project was finally vindicated on March 17, 1958, when TV-4 was ignited at 7:16 p.m. and hurled itself into a calm evening sky. Some long-suffering staffers credited the success to a technician who affixed a Saint Christopher medal to the guidance package of the second stage. The launch was only slightly delayed due to a coincidence no one had foreseen: *Explorer 1* was passing overhead, and it was feared the two satellites' signals might interfere with one another.[16]

Once the world's first satellite "traffic jam" had passed and the vehicle was launched, everything went as planned. The first stage exhausted its fuel when the vehicle had reached an altitude of thirty-six miles and a velocity of 3,700 mph. That stage splashed into the Atlantic some 230 miles downrange, while the 7,500-pound thrust Aerojet General engine on the second stage took over. When the second stage burned out its fuel, the vehicle remained together so that the guidance system in the second stage could continue directing the vehicle's trajectory. The rocket's "brain" started the vehicle spinning and then sent the commands for third-stage separation and ignition. Finally, a mechanical timer actuated a spring mechanism to release the satellite.[17]

Kurt Stehling wrote of the almost intolerable tension as the staff jammed into the teletype room at the Cape, waiting for the message that

NRL engineers place *Vanguard 1* atop the third stage of the launch vehicle. Shown here *(from left to right)* are Roger L. Easton, Sandy J. Smith, Robert C. Baumann, and Joseph B. Schwartz. NRL photo 04-04. Courtesy Naval Research Laboratory

the satellite's signal had been received from orbit. After over ninety minutes had passed since the last signal was detected, Stehling had given up on the launch and was heading for his car when, "I heard a tremendous roar, as if a fire had started. Suddenly, books, shoes, and other things flew over the balcony down into the hangar."[18] A Minitrack station in San Diego had picked up a signal. The orbit was higher than expected (the perigee was 404 miles, the apogee almost 2,466), giving it a period of 134 minutes.

In response to all who thought this achievement had taken too long and involved too many missteps, John Hagen later wrote, "Vanguard started with virtually nothing in 1955, completed vehicle design in March 1956, and had a fully successful flight two years later. One can challenge any other new rocket program in the United States to demonstrate a completely successful launching within such a short time."[19]

Vanguard 1 struck another blow for the scientific utility of satellites.

Vindication at last for the Vanguard program. Launch vehicle TV-4 succeeds on March 17, 1958. NRL Photo 04-06. Courtesy Naval Research Laboratory

(In the Vanguard program, only those satellites reaching orbit were given numbers.) While the only instrumentation squeezed into the tiny vehicle were two radio transmitters and two thermistors, tracking this long-lived satellite produced significant knowledge of the Earth and its atmosphere. *Vanguard 1* had less instrumentation than *Explorer* or *Sputnik,* but also a key advantage: a much longer transmitting life span. Accordingly, it could be precisely tracked over a long period of time. Studying the satellite's orbit produced

1. Major advances in geodesy, establishing the exact shape and size of the Earth. It had been presumed the planet was a globe slightly flattened at the poles: *Vanguard 1* taught us it had a bulge in the southern hemisphere, meaning the Earth was slightly "pear-shaped."
2. The first information on the degree and timing of the expansion of the upper atmosphere when warmed by the sun, which helped plan the orbits of future satellites to account for the resulting atmospheric drag.
3. The knowledge that satellite orbits are affected by the pressure of light radiation from the sun and by the gravity of the Sun and Moon. This tiny force was sufficient to lower the perigee of *Vanguard 1* by 1.2 miles per year.[20]

Vanguard 1 was the first spacecraft to use solar cells for onboard power, providing a maximum output of five milliwatts. While the satellite's batteries died within three months, the minute trickle of electricity from the solar cells kept *Vanguard 1* transmitting for over six years. It is still in orbit, the oldest surviving satellite to date.

Explorer 2 was launched on March 5, 1958. It carried the payload that JPL called *Deal 2*—the radiation counter plus George Ludwig's tape recorder, which had been successfully modified for the harsh conditions. Unfortunately, the fourth stage failed to ignite.

General Medaris immediately requested and received permission to fire the backup booster and payload, already in place at the Cape. *Explorer 3* reached orbit on March 26th. It also carried the *Deal 2* payload. The tape recorder worked perfectly, keeping all the data gathered during the periods the satellite was out of contact with the ground and sending it down on command. This was the first data recorder of any type on a satellite.

Explorer 3 went into a more eccentric orbit than expected, varying in altitude from 117 to 1,740 miles.[21] As Van Allen noted, the wide-ranging path turned out to be "splendid for cosmic ray research."[22] *Explorer 3* reinforced its predecessor's radiation findings. As Van Allen described it, "The counting rate at low altitudes was in the expected range of 15 to 20 counts per second. There was then a very rapid increase to a rate exceeding 128 counts per second. . . . A few minutes later, the rate decreased rapidly to zero."[23]

Explorer 1 had provided 850 telemetry signals containing usable cosmic-ray data. *Explorer 3* successfully played back recordings from 408 complete orbits.[24] With the greatly increased database to work from, Van Allen and his colleagues were able to plot what was happening with the cosmic radiation. It became clear that, at certain altitudes, there was a field of particles a thousand times stronger than predicted.

Van Allen announced the discovery of Earth's radiation belt on May 1. The zone of radiation he described was actually the inner belt of what subsequent probes have shown is a double "girdle" of radiation around the planet. The inner zone, made up largely of electrons and protons, begins above 250 miles from the Earth (higher at most latitudes) and reaches maximum density at an altitude of approximately 2,000 miles.[25] The term "Van Allen belts" quickly entered the scientific lexicon.

A year later, *TIME* magazine wrote, "Today he [Van Allen] can tip back his head and look at the sky. Beyond its outermost blue are the world-encompassing belts of fierce radiation that bear his name. No human name has ever been given to a more majestic feature of the planet Earth."[26]

The belts are maintained by the force exerted by the Earth's magnetic field. In 1959, the term magnetosphere was coined to describe the vast region, extending out to at least ten times the radius of the Earth, in which this field exercises its influence.[27]

Explorer 3 was the only spacecraft to reach orbit carrying the *Deal 2* payload. Van Allen was next asked to provide radiation instruments to observe the effects of several nuclear bombs to be detonated at high altitudes in classified tests. Van Allen, assisted by George Ludwig and Carl McIlwain, provided the hardware on schedule.[28]

Between the requirements of the bomb tests and the desire to understand the new phenomenon of radiation belts, the decision was made by the Van Allen team to take out the data recorders in their last three Explorers. Instead, the satellites would be packed with more radiation detectors. They also dispensed with the troublesome whip antennas and replaced them with a dipole antenna, which was built into the body of the satellite.

When *Explorer 4* was launched on July 26, 1958, it went into a 50-degree orbit instead of the 34-degree inclination used by its predecessors.[29] This let the satellite record radiation over a broader range of latitude.

By this time, the debate over the future scope and organization of the nation's space program was in full swing. ARPA had been created, and NASA was about to be born. The Explorer program, however, was carried on by von Braun's team, even though ARPA was nominally in charge at this point and the Army's future in space was very much in question.

Thanks to continual improvements by JPL and ABMA, *Explorer 4* could be heavier than the satellites used on the first three launches. *Explorer 4* weighed 37.16 pounds and its payload 25.76 pounds.[30] This satellite carried a package of four detectors: a Geiger tube with light shielding, a heavily shielded tube that would pick up only the most energetic particles, and two types of scintillation counters. The Geiger tubes had cross-sections 100 times smaller than those on the first *Explorer*s, thus screening out more of the radiation and allowing for a better picture of the total rise and fall in intensity as the satellite's altitude and latitude changed.

The *Explorer 4* instruments provided the most detailed information yet on the Van Allen belts and enabled the study of the artificial radiation belts produced by the Argus series of nuclear bursts. As Van Allen wrote in a 1990 article, "Analysis of our *Explorer 4* data on the natural radiation belt as well as on the artificial radiation belts from the Argus bursts propelled the entire subject to a new level of understanding and broad scientific interest." This data disproved fears that the fields discovered by *Explorers 1* and *3* were the results of clandestine Soviet nuclear tests in space. It also became clear that the belts, while restricting activities at certain altitudes, did not begin low enough to preclude robotic or manned flights in low Earth orbit (LEO).

More changes were made to the detectors on the *Explorer 5* package to allow for the detection and classification of a wider range of particles. As with *Explorer 2*, however, the booster failed, and the satellite went into the ocean on August 24, 1958. The reason for *Explorer 5*'s demise was a fluke. When the upper section separated from the first stage, the propellants for the A-7 engine had not yet been entirely exhausted. The first stage overtook the second, bumping it off course.[31]

By the end of 1958, Explorer and Vanguard were no longer the only scientific satellite programs in the United States. On October 22, another Jupiter C went aloft with NASA's first satellite, *Beacon 1*. This was the latest version of an experiment proposed by NACA first for Vanguard and then for Explorer. *Beacon 1* was a sphere of thin plastic, coated with aluminum foil, which would be inflated in space to a diameter of twelve feet. The launch failed 110 seconds into flight when unusual vibrations developed, apparently causing the entire upper-stage unit to break loose from the first stage.[32]

By this time, the Army's second major space project was underway. In March 1958, ARPA had approved the launch of two JPL-developed lunar probes. JPL had first proposed a lunar mission in October, 1957. JPL's idea, conceived by William Pickering, would fly a small camera to the moon in a mission called Project Red Socks. But even this project had not quite been JPL's first excursion into studies of lunar missions: in 1950, JPL engineers on the Bumper project had calculated that a Corporal missile and Loki upper stages could theoretically land an empty beer can on the moon.

The Red Socks idea languished until it was presented to ARPA early in 1958. The new agency's director, Roy W. Johnson, showed an interest in sponsoring space firsts that might trump the Soviet advances.[33] When this emphasis became known, the agency received more space proposals than it could handle. Johnson's deputy, Rear Adm. John E. Clark, later summed up the atmosphere by saying, "It seemed to me that everybody in the country had come in with a proposal except Fanny Farmer Candy, and I expected them at any minute."[34]

As it turned out, both American and Russian decision makers quickly agreed the moon was the logical next step beyond Earth orbit. It was not only an exciting destination from a scientific point of view, but reaching it carried obvious prestige. It was not like a tiny, invisible satellite beeping overhead. People all over the world would be able to look up at the Earth's companion and marvel at the thought that space engineers had reached out and touched it.

The American lunar probes received the name Pioneer. AOMC was told to launch two of these spacecraft, while the Air Force was given the responsibility for three more. The way the launch order eventually shaped up, the Army launched *Pioneer 3* and *4* while the Air Force launched *Pioneer 1, 2,* and *5*.

Upon receiving the lunar assignment from ARPA, von Braun's team worked rapidly to develop a booster they hoped would be up to the task.[35] The upper stages from the Jupiter C were mated to a modified version of the Jupiter IRBM to produce a launch vehicle christened the Juno 2.

The Juno 2 had a very different appearance from its predecessor, thanks to the much heavier first stage and the addition of a fairing over the "washtub," which was jettisoned by a small rocket motor shortly after the first-stage separation. The third and fourth stage motors also used an improved propellant. The main engine was the 150,000-pound thrust Rocketdyne S-3D from the Air Force's Navaho program. The Navaho, rendered obsolete by ICBMs even before it became operational, was canceled on July 13, 1957. Given the technology it contributed to other programs, Navaho might be called the most successful missile never deployed.

The fins and steering vanes used on the Juno 1 were eliminated in Juno 2 in favor of small steering rockets (called verniers) and gimbaled engines. All these changes resulted in a rocket that could accelerate a 15-pound payload to escape velocity. Ten of the 76-foot-high vehicles were eventually built for the lunar probe missions and for NASA satellite launches.[36]

The first launch of the Juno 2 was on December 6, 1958. The rocket carried *Pioneer 3*, which weighed 13 pounds. The flight time to the moon was estimated at 33 hours, 45 minutes. On this flight, however, the first stage exhausted its propellant too quickly, and the terminal velocity was about 1,000 fps too low. While the Juno 2 was thus unable to loft *Pioneer* into a lunar flyby trajectory, the probe did reach 70,000 miles from Earth and mapped the outer limits of the Van Allen belts.[37]

Also in 1958 came the first space launches by the Air Force, involving the three Pioneer probes assigned to the service by ARPA. *Pioneer 1* and *2*, each weighing 85 pounds, were boosted by modified Thor IRBMs. *Pioneer 5* was a very different spacecraft, which weighed 370 pounds and went aloft on an Atlas. Both types of launch vehicles used Able second stages—derived from the Vanguard second stage—and carried Vanguard-developed X-248 solid-fuel third stages. Unfortunately, all three launches (in August, October, and November, 1958) failed to reach the target, although *Pioneer 1* yelded more information on the Earth's radiation belts. (*Pioneer 1, 3,* and *4* carried radiation detectors prepared by Van Allen's group at the University of Iowa.)[38]

The last Army launch in the Pioneer program came in March 1959, when *Pioneer 4*'s Juno 2 achieved the required velocity but was still slightly off in its orientation. That spacecraft missed the moon by 37,000 miles and went into a permanent orbit around the sun. The first American lunar program—which included the first and last space probes to be launched by the Army—closed out with only limited success.

Before the end of 1958, though, United States had one more space enterprise in store: a spectacular public-relations mission unrelated to any of the existing satellite programs.

Soon after the Soviets scored again with the May, 1958, launch of *Sputnik 3*, ARPA Director Roy Johnson visited Convair. Johnson's interest in surpassing the Soviets had already led to his approval of the JPL lunar probe proposal. Now he asked whether Convair's powerful Atlas missile could perform some feat that would strengthen American prestige in the wake of the latest Soviet accomplishment. "We've got to get something big up," he said.

Jim Dempsey, Atlas Program Director, had a quick answer: "Well, we could put the whole Atlas in orbit."[39]

One of Convair's experts, Peenemunde veteran Krafft Ehricke, had already worked out speculative plans for sending an entire Atlas into orbit.

Dempsey hadn't discouraged the outlandish thought, even though there was no requirement to do such a thing. Now Johnson took the idea to Washington. The President approved it—provided the mission was kept secret until it succeeded.

Thus was born the classified Project SCORE (Signal Communication by Orbiting RElay). Only eighty-eight of the men who worked on the project knew what the objective assigned to Atlas test missile 10-B was.[40] Even Curt Johnston, the director of the launch crew, was initially kept in the dark about the missile's true purpose.

The Atlas, still a year short of entering service as an ICBM, was a unique three-engine design. Rocketdyne had developed a side-by-side arrangement for the two booster and one sustainer engines. All three main engines were ignited at takeoff. This scheme somewhat resembled Tikhonravov's parallel staging design for the R-7, although in the Atlas the booster engines were not self-contained units but, instead, drew propellants from the same tanks as the sustainer engine.

The booster engines produced 154,000 pounds of thrust each; the sustainer, 57,000 pounds. Steering was accomplished with two 1,000-pound thrust verniers. All the engines burned lox with a type of high-grade kerosene called RP-1. The total thrust of the three large engines was far greater than any other American rocket of the time. The Atlas remained less powerful than Korolev's R-7, but compensated for this with its lighter, more efficient design.

The height of the Atlas was 76 feet (or greater, depending on the nose cone used). Its body diameter was 10 feet, broadening to 16 feet at the base. The weight of a fully fueled Atlas was around 260,000 pounds. For this flight, the Army Signal Corps built a 130-pound package including a radio transmitter and receiver. *Atlas 10-B* was to become the world's first communications satellite.

Johnston and the other "uninitiated" crew members soon figured out something was up. The day before launch, Johnston was let in on the plan and told to take the standard blunt Atlas nose off the missile and install a special streamlined nose with no separation system. This was no small feat, since the missile was already on the launch pad. The work began at 4:30 P.M. on December 16. At 5:30 the next morning, after some frantic juryrigging, the job was done.

At 6:02 p.m. on December 18, 1958, the missile left the pad. *Atlas 10-B* soared flawlessly into orbit, dropping the booster engines en route. The 8,700-pound satellite broadcast Christmas greetings to the world in the taped voice of President Eisenhower. SCORE transmitted for thirteen days before its batteries expired.

Krafft Ehricke would go on to design the Centaur upper stage, the first large rocket to use lox and liquid hydrogen. Centaur proved the contention, advanced decades before by Tsiolkovsky, Oberth, and Goddard, that hydrogen was a practical and powerful fuel for space flight.

The U.S.S.R. attempted two more satellite launches in the never-officially-named Sputnik series. The third launch, on April 27, 1958, was the first failure. The booster rose less than ten miles into the atmosphere. The satellite was ejected from the rocket and eventually recovered, some of its instruments reportedly still functioning.

Sputnik 3 made it into orbit on May 15, 1958, atop an R-7 8A91 booster. This was Korolev's original Object D design, the "automatic laboratory" in space. *Sputnik 3* had an apogee of 1,167.5 miles and took 106 minutes to circle the Earth. The satellite was conical in shape, 5 feet 8 inches in diameter at the base and 11 feet 7 inches in height, excluding the protruding antennae. It weighed 2,925 pounds, of which the instrumentation, radio, and power systems took up 2,134 pounds. The satellite had both chemical batteries and solar cells. The twelve experiments on board studied the pressure and composition of the upper atmosphere, the electrical charges that built up on the satellite, solar and cosmic radiation, the Earth's magnetic field, and micrometeorites.

Sputnik 3 continued the Soviet tradition of sending high-power, low-frequency transmissions, easily received by observers around the world and useful in the study of the ionosphere. Signals lasting 150–300 milliseconds were continually transmitted at 20.005 MHz.

Sputnik 3's payload of instruments included Geiger counters that could and did detect the radiation of the Van Allen belts. The spacecraft's tape recorder malfunctioned, though, and Soviet scientists didn't know whether high radiation readings were being received throughout the orbit or only during the brief period when the satellite was in contact with their ground stations. They were not sure what to think of the fragmentary data until Van Allen announced the existence of the radiation belts. *Sputnik 2*, it turned out, had also detected the belts, but the data had not been analyzed properly and the discovery was thus missed.

In a clumsy and rather humorous attempt to save face, Soviet physicist Sergey Vernov claimed in 1959 that he had discovered the radiation belts first, based on information from the *Sputnik*s. James Harford, in his biography of Korolev, wrote: "Afterwards, a Russian joke circulated that the belts were to be called the Van Allen-Vernov radiation belts. 'What did Vernov do? He discovered the Van Allen belts.'"

With so little known about upper-atmosphere and space conditions, every satellite of this period offered opportunities for knowledge to scientists not even connected with the particular spacecraft. George W. Swenson, Jr., of the University of Illinois, later recorded the work his team in the Astronomy Department was able to do by listening to *Sputnik 3*.

> It transmitted for nearly two years on 20 MHz, providing opportunity to observe seasonal effects and to accumulate statistically significant numbers of observations. These satellites were in high-inclination orbits, covering the entire band of latitudes from plus to minus 65 degrees. This was useful, as it gave good geographical coverage. *Sputnik 3* was in a rather eccentric orbit, so that at times it passed over us above the region of maximum ionization, and at times below. This permitted an approximate determination of the height at which the scintillation-producing irregularities existed.[41]

Western space researchers and intelligence officers generally thought of the Soviet program as a well-planned and integrated enterprise. They would have been surprised to learn *Sputnik 3* was, at the time of launch, the only authorized space effort in the U.S.S.R.[42] Korolev's bureau had been doing design work on a "manned sputnik" (designated Object OD-2), a reconnaissance satellite (Object OD-1), and lunar probes since 1956.[43] However, the chief designer had to go back to the government after *Sputnik 3* to request permission to build any of these systems. Thanks in part to Khrushchev's belief in the propaganda advantages of space successes, approval was forthcoming.

The first result was that the Soviet Union also launched lunar probes in 1958. On September 23, October 11, and December 4, three attempts were made to get a Luna spacecraft to the vicinity of the moon. All three launch vehicles failed early in flight. In 1959, three probes in the Luna series would succeed. Their achievements included impacting on the moon *(Luna 2)* and photographing its dark side *(Luna 3)*. The Soviet probes were much larger than any of the American ones, with *Luna 2* the heaviest at 858 pounds.[44]

Meanwhile, the staff of Project Vanguard was trying to get the remainder of their satellites into orbit. Like their Army counterparts, the Vanguard engineers did not know their future, but they were excited by the present, and the team went ahead with the planned TLV and SLV launches.

After the success of *Vanguard 1*, though, the project hit another rough patch. The next Vanguard attempt came on April 28, 1958. Booster TV-5 was loaded with a full-sized Vanguard satellite, pushing its payload capacity to the limit. The results of this risk were never to be learned, though, because an electrical failure prevented the third stage from separating or igniting.[45]

Following the failure of TV-5, the first three SLVs were launched without a success. Of the remaining rockets built as test vehicles, TV-2BU was deemed unusable and is now a museum exhibit. The TV-4BU was converted to a SLV.

On May 27, 1958, SLV-1 suffered a control failure and pointed its third stage in the wrong direction. One month later, SLV-2's second stage shut down only eight seconds after ignition. On September 26, SLV-3 looked like a success, but the second-stage performance was below par. SLV-3's ultimate velocity was a mere 250 fps lower than required, and the satellite flew a long ballistic arc back into the atmosphere.[46]

In February 1959, another Vanguard finally reached orbit. *Vanguard 2* carried the photocells of William Stroud's meteorological experiment. This was the first Vanguard orbited under the imprimatur of NASA. Unfortunately, the spacecraft's time in orbit was brief. In a near-repeat of the *Explorer 5* failure, residual propellant in the third stage reignited and bumped the satellite, imparting to it a tumbling motion that all but wiped out the mission's scientific utility. *Vanguard 2* stayed aloft only eighteen days.

The next two Vanguard launches were failures. SLV-5 carried the inflatable sphere originally proposed by NACA scientists as well as a satellite-mounted magnetometer. On April 13, 1959, the second stage went out of control after separation. On June 22, SLV-6 suffered from a problem in pressurizing the second-stage tanks. It quickly lost power and never came close to orbiting.

The last Vanguard launch was perfect. The booster was the remodeled TV-4BU, now known as SLV-7. With the lighter ABL fiberglass-cased third stage, this vehicle put up *Vanguard 3* on September 18, 1959. *Vanguard 3* weighed over 52 pounds. The upper hemisphere had a shell of fiberglass and a protruding cone 23 inches high to accommodate its main experiment, the NRL magnetometer designed by James Heppner.

With the completion of this mission, NASA closed down the Vanguard Division, and one of the most turbulent chapters in American space exploration came to a close. John Hagen considered the Vanguard budget well spent. The $110 million cost of the program "included the design and the construction of the launching vehicle and the support of all the scientific work that went into the design and construction of the experiments. It also covered all of the radio tracking, the establishment of overseas sites,

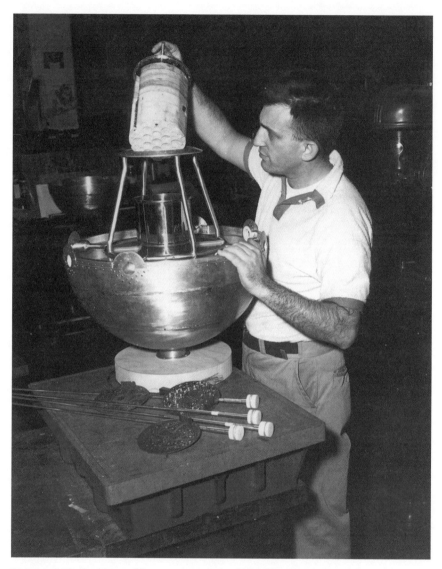

Vanguard 2 before assembly. Note circuit boards and antenna sections on bench. NRL photo 81968 (2). Courtesy Naval Research Laboratory

and the construction of extensive facilities at Cape Canaveral and its down-range stations. At the time, it seemed a rather large figure. In retrospect, when one compares the cost of other missile and follow-on space programs, it does not appear excessive."[47]

There were other Explorer flights in 1959, although the satellites were

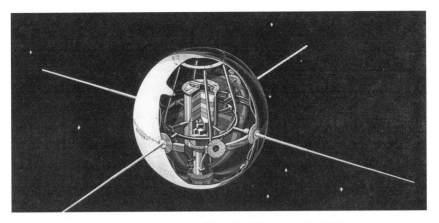

NRL illustration of the *Vanguard 2* satellite. NASM Photo 7B 33736. Courtesy
National Air and Space Museum

larger than their predecessors and had different origins. After the Army-
launched series closed out with *Explorer 5*, NASA picked up the Explorer
name for a long series of small science satellites with a variety of missions.

The first NASA *Explorer* was a 91-pound satellite that failed to orbit on
July 16. It was another casualty of a Juno 2 failure. (NASA followed the
Vanguard precedent of assigning numbers only to the successfully-orbited
Explorers.) The 141-pound *Explorer 6,* launched on August 7 on a Thor
booster, was built by the Space Technology Laboratories (STL), part of the
company later known as TRW. *Explorer 6* was the first satellite orbited in
the Explorer series to use solar cells, and it was the first to be deliberately
launched into a highly eccentric orbit.

To make the most complete measurements possible of the extent of the
radiation belts, *Explorer 6* had an inclination of 47 degrees, a perigee of 152
miles, and an apogee of 26,346 miles.[48] *Explorer 6* radioed back the first
photograph of Earth taken from orbit. This flight also marked the first Explorer payload not prepared by Van Allen's group: the detectors on *Explorer
6* were built by the STL, the University of Minnesota, and the University of
Chicago. *Explorer 6* showed that the Van Allen belts were more complex
and variable than discovered so far, and it also provided the first study of
the activities of solar energetic particles over the Earth's poles, where
"holes" in the Van Allen belts existed.[49]

Explorer 6 also served a unique function: that of a target. In a classified
project named Bold Orion, an antisatellite (ASAT) missile was launched
from a B-47 bomber with *Explorer 6* as its objective. On October 13, 1959,
the interceptor passed within four miles of the satellite, close enough for a

kill if a nuclear warhead had been carried on the missile.[50] The ASAT, however, was not pursued further.

Explorer 7, built at the ABMA and then turned over to NASA, was successfully launched by a Juno 2 on October 13, 1959. This 91-pound satellite functioned for almost two years, sending back data on cosmic rays, solar energetic particles, and Earth's radiation.

The Juno 2 got another tryout when it launched the second Beacon inflatable satellite on August 14, 1959. Unfortunately, *Beacon 2* also failed when the booster's first stage shut down prematurely.[51]

Before the busy year of 1959 came to an end, two other American satellite programs made their first launch attempts. The first of these progrmas was Transit. *Transit 1A*, the ARPA/NRL pathfinder for the highly successful Transit navigation satellites, failed to orbit on September 17 when its Thor booster malfunctioned. The second program was Discoverer.

No fewer than eight satellites in the Discoverer series, the first fruits from the long reconnaissance satellite development program, were launched by the Air Force between February 28 and November 20 of 1959. *Discoverer 1* became the first satellite to enter a polar orbit. The Discoverer satellites were the public face of this still–top-secret effort, now renamed CORONA and directed by the CIA. Discoverer launches were publicly announced as scientific missions, although they were intended to photograph the Soviet Union and return film capsules from orbit. The Discoverers were massive by American satellite standards of the day, weighing over 1,500 pounds.

Discoverer 1 was not only the first polar orbiter, it also marked the debut of a new U.S. space launch site. Cape Canaveral was not ideal for launches into polar orbit, as the flight path would require passage over populated areas. The task of finding a suitable location went to two officers with the WS-117L program. In the spring of 1956, Navy Capt. Robert Truax, along with Air Force Capt. James Coolbaugh, made an aerial tour of the California coast.

Traux was one of the pioneers of the military space and missile programs. He had been encouraging or directing rocket, missile, and satellite programs since the 1930s. At the time of his real estate hunting trip, he was on loan to the Air Force, serving as deputy director of the secret WS-117L program. He was the obvious choice to lead the search for a new launch site.

The site that stood out was an Army base called Camp Cooke. This training base, which also hosted a Navy radar station, was located on Point Arguello, a site north of the city of Santa Barbara where the coastline jutted out into the Pacific. Camp Cooke was a perfect choice: it was not only well located for polar launch trajectories, but was relatively isolated, controlled a large area of land, and was no longer required by the Army. The Air Force had no problems obtaining approval to start a missile and space launch facility, and by 1957 had taken possession of what became Cooke Air Force Base. By the time of the Discoverer launches, it had been re-named Vandenberg Air Force Base, a nod to the late Gen. Hoyt Vanden-berg. It was an appropriate choice of names, given Vandenberg's action a decade earlier to claim the space mission for the Air Force.[52]

Six of the first eight Discoverer satellites made it into orbit, although none of the return capsules was retrieved. The series did eventually pro-duce successful missions and proved the utility of the photoreconnaissance satellite—a concept which, at least in part, had inspired the American gov-ernment to support satellite programs in the first place.

As the new decade dawned, the world was a very different place. American and Soviet satellites circled the globe continually, trying out a variety of tasks in addition to the original mission of gathering scientific data. Eleven probes had been hurled toward the moon, with one making contact. Both spacefaring nations were gearing up programs to put human beings into orbit.

The First Space Race was over. It was destined to be eclipsed by the even more dramatic race to the moon, but its impact would continue. As von Braun said, we would never give up our foothold on the newest frontier.

■ *Chapter 10*

Final Assessment

Despite the limitations and failures of the first three satellite programs, all were, by any measure, successful. By the end of 1959, scientists assembling data from all three programs had unprecedented knowledge of the environment around Earth. The concepts of space flight had been proven, and space enthusiasts' dreams for the future had been unleashed. The seed planted by Johannes Kepler and nourished by Isaac Newton, Konstantin Tsiolkovsky, Hermann Oberth, Robert Goddard, and countless others had borne fruit these visionaries could only have imagined.

If the drive into space is considered a race to be first, then of course the U.S.S.R. was the winner. While many reasons were advanced for this when *Sputnik 1* went up, such as the capability of totalitarian societies to focus their resources and the ridiculous claim that the Soviets "got the best Germans," the bottom line is that Korolev was able to get his superiors to support his determined efforts to launch first.

In the United States, ensuring a victory was simply never given priority. The pre-*Sputnik* feelings of American leaders ranged from the assumption the United States would never be beaten in any technological endeavor to Secretary Wilson's "I don't care" philosophy. The people like von Braun who felt launching first should be the primary objective lacked the influence to shape national priorities. One cannot but wonder whether anything would have changed had von Braun been granted the kind of direct access to President Eisenhower that Korolev had to Khrushchev.

On both sides of the space race, though, the efforts exerted by would-be space pioneers were little short of magnificent. Korolev had top-level sanction, but he also had to deal with layers of centralized bureaucracy, competition from other organizations that sought many of the same scarce resources and trained personnel he needed, and the inefficiencies and shortages that plagued the entire Soviet economy. A dedicated staff and the limitless energy and drive of the Chief Designer overcame all obstacles. The American programs, both before and after the launch of *Sputnik,* performed near-miracles of their own. Project Vanguard engineers and technicians worked tirelessly to perfect their advanced technology, while Army personnel rushed their satellite and launch vehicle to completion, and the China Lake entrepreneurs made heroic (if less fruitful) efforts to build a space launch system and satellite from almost nothing.

The themes common to all these projects were improvisation and the willingness to ignore proper procedure. Veterans of the Explorer and NOTSNIK programs, in particular, told the authors that their "just get it done" approach would not be possible today. This is worth remembering when drawing lessons about program management and execution from these early space efforts.

In the late 1950s, e-mail and cellular phones did not exist, and long-distance telephone and fax service was nowhere near as cheap and reliable as it is today. Routine high-speed jet travel was just being born (the first domestic all-jet passenger service began between New York and Miami in 1958), and only few segments of the Interstate highway system authorized in 1956 were in existence. Accordingly, micromanagement of programs from Washington (or Moscow, for that matter) was physically impossible. Tele-type messages and mailed reports were the most common means of keeping headquarters informed of what was happening in remote laboratories and at launch sites hundreds or thousands of miles away. Local managers thus had great flexibility in moving people, equipment, and money around compared with their twenty-first–century counterparts, and they used it, often brilliantly, to get the nation into space. When Vanguard, Explorer, NOTSNIK, and Sputnik programs ended, the talent and dedication still existed, but bureaucratic and political influences were destined, for better or worse, to have an increasing impact on future space projects.

There were still many milestones ahead for the Soviet Union, including putting the first human into space and establishing the first space station.

In the long run, though, if the first space race had a victor, it was the United States. Aroused by the sting of defeat, America embarked on a massive expansion of its space capabilities that led to the walk on the Moon, a huge commercial space industry, and the world's most capable network of military spacecraft for support of all types.

The programs involved in the first space race had varying destinies. After 1958, no satellite based on *Sputnik 1* or NOTSNIK was ever orbited again. The Explorer program continued, at least in name. While the failed *Explorer 5* was the last Earth satellite built by the Army-JPL team, NASA science satellites called Explorers continued probing the heavens. NASA's current Small Explorer program continues this tradition, and over seventy spacecraft with Explorer designations have now been launched.[1]

The Explorer success did not secure for the Army its hoped-for place in space exploration. Army engineers worked on a few more spacecraft programs, notably an early communications satellite called Courier. Within a few years of Explorer, though, with the von Braun team and JPL transferred to NASA, the Army's space role was refocused on the development of ground terminals and systems to work with satellites built by the Air Force and Navy.

The Vanguard program finished with three satellites orbited. The program's staff members, then and now, bristle at any suggestion that Vanguard was a failure. The objective of Project Vanguard was to orbit one satellite within the IGY. Three spacecraft made it to orbit, and they contributed significantly to scientific discovery. Moreover, the program developed booster designs and technology that are still, in modified form, in use today.

In 1998, Milt Rosen affirmed that, regardless of the schedule slips and other problems, he had never second-guessed the booster's design.[2] Despite the Vanguard booster's spotty record for getting payloads into orbit, this belief is justified. Vanguard's second and third stages, modified to become the upper stages of the Thor-Able and Atlas-Able, would evolve into the upper stages of the extremely successful Delta launch vehicle family. The X-248 would also be used over the course of two decades in NASA's Scout, the agency's workhorse small launcher. The direct descendant of the Minitrack system (the Naval Space Surveillance System or NAVSPASUR) is still in service today, and almost every spacecraft carries solar cells.

When Vanguard was transferred to NASA, the Navy almost gave up its space capability altogether. Marty Votaw, however, convinced the NRL hierarchy that the lab should stay in the space business. He reformed the remaining small contingent into the new Satellite Techniques Branch.[3]

The Vanguard name, unlike that of Explorer, was not used for additional satellites by NASA or anyone else. The spherical satellite body or "bus" built for Vanguard had a second life, however, in the next NRL-sponsored space program, the SolRad/GRAB series of satellites. These spacecraft, first launched in 1960, had a dual mission. Their publicly announced purpose was the study of solar radiation, hence the official name of SolRad. The unannounced (if still innocuous-sounding) name of GRAB (Galactic Radiation and Background) referred to their second, highly classified mission. The SolRad/GRAB series were the world's first electronic intelligence satellites, used to pick up transmissions from Soviet radars and send the data to Navy ground stations for analysis. The NRL and other Navy organizations continued to play an important role in American military satellites, although since the mid-1960s the Air Force has built the lion's share of military spacecraft.

It would be more accurate to say the Air Force's contractors build most military satellites, since the services have outsourced almost all of their satellite work to the private sector. The NRL has maintained some of its heritage and today is the only American military organization capable of building spacecraft in-house. Modern satellites built by the NRL, by itself or in partnership with other organizations, have included the highly successful 1994 Clementine lunar probe and the 1996 Tether Physics Experiment (TiPS), two satellites connected by a tether two and a half miles long.

Some other 1950s programs and proposals have direct descendants. RCA's Janus reconnaissance satellite concept was reoriented toward weather observation. It contributed to two projects, NASA's TIROS weather satellite and its classified Air Force counterpart, Project 417. The other predecessor to TIROS, which was developed with the help of S. Fred Singer, was Singer's 1952 design for MOUSE. Singer became the first director of the U.S. Weather Bureau's satellite office.[4]

Sergey Korolev never achieved his ultimate goal of leading Russia to the moon and the planets. He did have many other successes, though, of which the most significant was launching a human being into orbit in 1961. Korolev called the Soviet cosmonauts his "little eagles," and he hand-picked Yuri Gagarin for the mission that would earn the cosmonaut a place in history.

Korolev went on to design the giant N1 booster, intended to get cosmonauts to the moon. The N1 failed in three launches beginning in 1969, and no Soviet ever stood on the lunar surface. The chief designer himself did not live to see the N1's failure. While Korolev had been an excellent athlete in his youth, he never fully recovered from the gulag years. By 1965, the decades of driving his body and his weak heart (he survived a heart attack in 1960) beyond their limits finally caught up to him. He had difficulty with any physical exertion and talked for the first time of looking forward to retirement. On January 14, 1966, doctors performing a relatively minor surgical procedure on Korolev discovered a large, cancerous tumor in his abdomen. What was supposed to be a brief operation stretched into eight hours. Their patient survived the surgery but died without regaining consciousness.

By order of Leonid Brezhnev, first secretary of the Communist Party, the identity of the chief designer was revealed to the world. Brezhnev himself helped carry Korolev's ashes to a place of honor in the Kremlin Wall. In death, Korolev finally received widespread recognition; his achievements were publicized, and his legacy was enshrined in museums. After the fall of the Soviet Union, Podlipki, the Moscow suburb that housed OKB-1, was renamed Korolev.[5]

In 1993, Korolev's slide rule—nicknamed the "magic wand" by his colleagues—was consigned to an auction in New York. It sold for $21,000 to the Perot Foundation, which loaned it to the National Air and Space Museum in Washington. There it is displayed along with the slide rule used by Wernher von Braun. Ironically, they are almost identical. Both were made by Albert Nestler A.G., a German company.[6] The same exhibit holds yet another artifact Korolev would recognize: an arming key removed from *Sputnik 1* just before launch. It shares a case with the battered satellite salvaged from the Vanguard TV-3 disaster.[7]

Vassily Mishin, one of Korolev's top assistants for many years, took over as head of his design bureau. Despite the setback of the N1 fiasco, the engineers Korolev trained and the descendants of his rockets—not greatly changed in design from the R-7—soldiered on to place hundreds of satellites into orbit and to establish the first long-term crewed space station, *Mir*, in 1986. After the fall of Communism, the organization that Korolev had built from OKB-1 eventually became the private Russian space giant RSC Energia.

Mikhail Tikhonravov survived his collaborator by eight years. He died in 1974, shortly after the government had belatedly granted him public recognition by bestowing on him several of the U.S.S.R.'s highest civilian and scientific honors.[8]

Of the three great theorists of the early twentieth century, only Hermann Oberth lived to see the launch of both satellites and men into space. Oberth, who was not part of the initial German exodus to the United States, did join von Braun in 1955 to work on orbital calculations, advanced spacecraft concepts, and other projects with ABMA. In 1958, he retired and re-

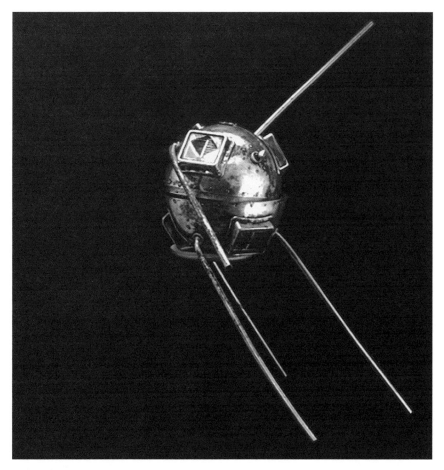

Relics of the first space race. This is the actual Vanguard TV-3 satellite. It is displayed in the National Air and Space Museum along with an arming key removed from *Sputnik 1* just before launch. NASM Photo 97-16258. Courtesy National Air and Space Museum

turned to Germany. Eleven years later, Oberth had the satisfaction of see-ing humans land on the moon using the lunar-orbit rendezvous approach he had conceived of in the 1920s.

Oberth continued pursuing his interest in space, but branched out into other subjects as well. In the 1970s, he designed alternative-energy sys-tems, including a power plant driven by the winds of the jet stream. He then turned to the study of theology and political philosophy. At the age of ninety, he wrote *Primer for Those Who Would Govern*, a book collecting a lifetime of insights about the workings of successful democratic governments and the need to educate voters.

Oberth died in Nuremberg on December 29, 1989. The elder statesman of space travel was ninety-five years old. Always concerned with the place of space exploration within the greater meaning of human existence, he chose a Biblical quotation for his tombstone. It read, "Blessed are those who hunger and thirst for justice."

The home of Konstantin Tsiolkovsky and the New Mexico workshop of Robert Goddard are now maintained as museums. Goddard was remembered in 1959 by the creation of NASA's Goddard Space Flight Center in Greenbelt, Maryland. The following year, the U.S. government acknowledged the debt its rocket and missile programs owed to Goddard by paying his estate and the Guggenheim Foundation $1 million for the use of Goddard's patents.

In 1969, Goddard received an unusual post-mortem accolade when the *New York Times* printed a retraction of its critical editorial published in 1920. The new editorial stated, "It is now definitely established that a rocket can function in a vacuum as well as in an atmosphere. The *Times* regrets the error." This item ran three days before Neil Armstrong set foot on the Moon, an event to which Goddard, Tsiolkovsky, and Oberth had all contributed, and for which Wernher von Braun had, drawing on the ideas of these men, developed the world's most powerful rocket.

Like Korolev, von Braun also had an ultimate goal—sending Americans to Mars. In 1961, his Redstone booster, nicknamed "Old Reliable" for its successful service in so many roles, launched the first American, Alan Shepherd, into space. As developer of the giant Saturn V booster, whose Rocketdyne engines were based on the design of the 1950s Redstone and Jupiter power plants, and as director of NASA's Marshall Space Flight Center, von Braun was instrumental in landing the first humans on the moon. Mars, however, was beyond his reach. Budgetary pressures and shifts in political priorities after the Apollo landings crippled von Braun's hope of taking the next great step into the solar system.

In 1970, von Braun became deputy associate administrator of NASA in charge of strategic planning. Frustrated by the agency's post-Apollo course, he worked less than two years in the agency's Washington headquarters before retiring from NASA. Von Braun spent his last years with Fairchild Industries. In 1974, he founded and became first president of the National Space Association (later National Space Institute), a private group dedicated to increasing public support for space exploration. This organization merged with the L5 Society in 1987 to form the National Space Society, which remains active today.[9]

Von Braun died on June 16, 1977. Again like Korolev, he was a man who had accomplished great things in space travel, although he had greater dreams he could not fulfill. (Each man had voiced the wish he could have met and worked with the other.)[10]

General Medaris, after less than two years as AOMC commander, retired from the Army in January 1960. Somewhat like Hermann Oberth, he turned his thoughts to higher affairs. In 1970, he was ordained an Episcopal priest. He served as a pastor in Maitland, North Carolina, and passed away in 1990.

John Hagen stayed in NASA until 1962. When he left government service, he became a professor of astronomy at Pennsylvania State University in State College. He also died in 1990.

Wernher von Braun in a formal portrait taken in the 1960s. NASA Marshall #9131095. Courtesy NASA/MSFC Archives

William Pickering retired from JPL in 1976, after twenty-two years as director. He served for many years as CEO of Lignetics, a California energy company. He died on March 15, 2004.

Most of the surviving veterans of the 1950s satellite programs have gone into well-deserved retirement, but a few remain active and continue to make their contributions to science.

James Van Allen went on to design instruments and conduct experiments on thirty-six missions, including those probes to six other planets.[11] He headed the Department of Physics and Astronomy at the University of Iowa from 1951 to 1985. In 1961, he and his students built the first university satellite, Injun 1. He chaired working groups for JPL, which developed the Voyager and Galileo planetary missions.[12] Today he is Regent Distinguished Professor of Physics and Astronomy at the University of Iowa, where he has his office in the Van Allen Building.[13] He continues to write, lecture, and study the results of the Galileo and Pioneer probes.

Ernst Stuhlinger co-authored a biography of von Braun in 1994 and still writes on space. S. Fred Singer heads the Science and Environmental Policy Project in Arlington, Virginia, and is one of the most prominent scientific critics of the global warming hypothesis.[14]

Sputnik, Vanguard, and *Explorer,* in countless ways, paved the road into space. The knowledge they sent back is still as pertinent as ever, and every satellite that has gone up since owes some debt to these pioneers. Every astronaut, space scientist, satellite operator, and everyday user of space technology can likewise trace his or her opportunities back to those dreamers who undertook the first race toward the stars.

Notes

All Internet sources were checked before this book went to press and were valid at that time. Future availability of Internet resources cannot be guaranteed.

CHAPTER 1

1. Details on Tsiolkovsky, Korolev, and other Soviet pioneers, if not otherwise footnoted, are mainly from James Harford, *Korolev* (New York: John Wiley and Sons, 1997), and Asif Siddiqi, *Challenge to Apollo: The Soviet Union and the Space Race, 1945-1974* (Washington, D.C.: NASA SP-2000-4408, 2000).

2. Boris Rauschenbach, *Hermann Oberth: The Father of Space Flight* (New York: West-Art, 1994), 26–27.

3. Harford, *Korolev*, 14; Siddiqi, *Challenge to Apollo*, 2.

4. Walter A. McDougall, *The Heavens and the Earth: A Political History of the Space Age* (Baltimore: The Johns Hopkins University Press, 1986), 27.

5. Harford, *Korolev*, 38-39.

6. Peter Alway, "The Rockets of GIRD," *Quest* 4, no. 1 (Spring, 1995): 24.

7. Ibid.

8. Harford, *Korolev*, 44.

9. Ibid., 40-41.

10. Peter Gorin, "Rising from the Cradle: Soviet Perceptions of Space Flight Before Sputnik," in *Reconsidering Sputnik: Forty Years Since the Soviet Satellite*, ed Roger D. Launius, John M. Logsdon, and Robert W. Smith, (Amsterdam: Harwood Academic Publishers, 2000), 21.

11. Shirley Thomas, *Men of Space*, vol. 1 (Philadelphia: Chilton, 1960), 28.

12. Homer E. Newell, *Beyond the Atmosphere: Early Years of Space Science* (Washington, D.C.: NASA SP-4211, 1980). See chapter 3 in on-line version, http://www.hq.nasa.gov/office/pao/History/SP-4211/ch3-1.htm.

13. Thomas, *Men of Space*, 1:28.

14. Ibid., 39.

15. Robert H. Goddard, "The Past Revisited," previously unpublished manuscript printed in *Quest* 5, no. 2 (Summer, 1996): 4.

16. The *Times* writer was a victim of the still-popular fallacy that reaction engines (jets and rockets) need something for their exhaust to "push against." He seemed not to understand what scientists knew since Newton's day—if an engine accelerates a mass in one direction (in this case, by burning fuel and oxidizer and expelling the products at high speed), the engine will move in the other.

17. Robert H. Goddard, *A Method of Reaching Extreme Altitudes* (Washington, D.C.: Smithsonian Institution Press, 1919); David A Clary, *Rocket Man: Robert H. Goddard and the Birth of the Space Age* (New York: Hyperion, 2003), 97.

18. Robert A. Braeunig, *Rocket and Space Technology*, 1997, http://users.commkey .net/Braeunig/space/propel1.htm.

19. Thomas, *Men of Space*, 1:34–35.

20. The *Times* editorial rankled Goddard for a long time. In 1936, he showed a copy to Frank Malina, a visitor from the California Institute of Technology, who wrote, "He appeared to suffer keenly from all the nonsense directed at him." Frank J. Malina, "Memoir on the GALCIT Rocket Research Project, 1936–38," June 6, 1967, http:// www.olats.org/OLATS/pionniers/memoir1.shtml.

21. Harford, *Korolev*, 35.

22. Ibid.

23. Bainbridge, William S. *The Spaceflight / Revolution.* (Malabar: Kreiger Publishing, 1983), 132–36.

24. Burrows, William. *This New Ocean* (New York: Random House, 1998), 85.

25. Malina, "Memoir on the GALCIT Rocket Research Project, 1936–38."

26. Frank J. Malina, "Origins and First Decade of the Jet Propulsion Laboratory," in *History of Rocket Technology: Essays on Research, Development, and Utility,* ed. Eugene Emme (Detroit: Wayne State University Press, 1964), 52.

27. The account of JPL's early years is from Malina in *History of Rocket Technology,* ed. Emme; and Clayton R. Koppes, *JPL and the American Space Program: A History of the Jet Propulsion Laboratory* (New Haven and London: Yale University Press, 1982).

28. Ernst Stuhlinger and Frederick Ordway III, *Wernher von Braun: Crusader for Space* (Malabar: Kreiger Publishing Company, 1994), 159.

29. Goddard once wrote out a feature-by-feature comparison between the V-2 and his own rockets. He argued there were no significant differences other than the choice of fuel (Goddard preferred gasoline to alcohol). German researchers may have examined Goddard's patents (before they were classified in 1942), but this is essentially a striking example of engineers independently studying the same problems and coming to similar solutions. Milton Lehman, *This High Man: The Life of Robert H. Goddard* (New York: Farrar, Straus and Co., 1963), 385. Von Braun was later asked to examine the question of whether German and U.S. government rocketry had infringed on Goddard's patents, and he found they did. Von Braun was later instrumental in having the first marker placed at the site of Goddard's pioneering rocket launch. Stuhlinger and Ordway, *Wernher von Braun*, 159–60.

30. The production of operational V-2 missiles was supervised, not by von Braun or his army superiors, but by the Armaments Ministry, with labor supplied by what historian Michael Neufeld calls the "rent a slave" operation of the Nazi Party's military arm, the SS. Thousands of slave laborers were worked to death in missile plants. Von Braun

denied any complicity in the use of slave labor, although he admittedly knew it existed. A thorough investigation of the topic is beyond the scope of this book. For the most thorough treatment of this subject, see Michael Neufeld, *The Rocket and the Reich* (New York: The Free Press, 1995).

31. Stuhlinger and Ordway, *Wernher von Braun*, 23.

32. Michael Neufeld, "The Reichswehr, the Rocket, and the Versailles Treaty: A Popular Myth Reexamined," *Journal of the British Interplanetary Society* 53 (2000): 163. Minutes of Army Ordnance meetings in 1930 and 1932 show one of the main influences was the thought that rockets, inaccurate though they were, would be highly suitable for the delivery of poison gas.

33. Michael Neufeld, "The Excluded: Hermann Oberth and Rudolf Nebel in the Third Reich," *Quest* 5, no. 4 (1996):

34. Harford, *Korolev*, 49.

35. John B. Medaris, *Countdown for Decision* (New York: Putnam, 1960), 38.

36. Walter Dornberger, "The German V-2," in Emme, *History of Rocket Technology*, 42.

37. Frederick I. Ordway and Mitchell R. Sharpe, *The Rocket Team* (New York: Thomas Y. Crowell, 1979), 242.

38. Quoted in Frederick C. Durant III, "Some Recollections of Early I.A.F. Congresses," n.d., in authors' possession.

39. The German term for Dornberger's rank at this point was *Generalmajor,* but this is equivalent to a brigadier, not a major, general. The designation for Kammler's rank of major general was *Gruppenfuhrer.* The American terms are used here for clarity. See Neufeld, *The Rocket and the Reich*, 215.

40. Ordway and Sharpe, *The Rocket Team*, 81.

41. Ibid., 1–2.

42. Various sources give the number of Paperclip émigrés at anywhere from 115 to 127. A few men came over after the initial group, so part of the discrepancy lies in whether these are counted.

43. Harford, *Korolev*, 66.

44. Ibid., 49. Historians have never discovered what happened to the flow of information to the U.S.S.R. from Peenemunde after 1938. Presumably, the agent inside Peenemunde was compromised or reassigned.

45. G. A. Tokaty, "Soviet Rocket Technology," in Emme, *History of Rocket Technology*, 276; Siddiqi, *Challenge to Apollo*, 27.

CHAPTER 2

1. John L. Rudolph, *Scientists in the Classroom: The Cold War Reconstruction of American Science Education* (New York: Palgrave, 2002), 87–88.

2. Josef Stalin, speech to industrial managers, February 1931. Speech reprinted in Joseph V. Stalin, *Problems of Leninism* (Moscow: Foreign Languages Publishing House, 1953), 454–58.

3. Quoted by General Bernard Schriever (USAF, ret.), interview by Carol L. Butler, April 15, 1999, NASA Johnson Space Center Oral History Project, http://www.jsc.nasa .gov/history/oral_histories.htm. The full transcript of the General Schriever's interview is available at http://www.jsc.nasa.gov/history/oral_histories/NASA_HQ/Ballistic/ SchrieverBA/BAS_4015099.pdf.

4. R. Cargill Hall, "Early U.S. Satellite Proposals," in *History of Rocket Technology*, ed. Emme, 73.

5. Harvey Hall, "The Navy's Pioneering Venture into the Space Program," *Quest* 8, no. 3 (Fall, 2001): 33.

6. Project RAND, *Preliminary Design of an Experimental World-Circling Spaceship* (1946; reprint, Santa Monica: RAND Corporation, 1999), v-viii.

7. Ibid., "Introduction," 1, 2, 10.

8. Ibid., "The Importance of a Satellite Vehicle," 9-16.

9. Roger E. Bilstein, *Stages to Saturn* (Washington, D.C.: NASA History Office, 1996), chap. 1.

10. Dwayne A. Day, in *Exploring the Unknown: Selected Documents in the History of the U.S. Civil Space Program*, ed. John M. Logsdon et al., vol. 2 (Washington, D.C.: NASA SP-4407, 1996), 236.

11. R. Cargill Hall, "Early U.S. Satellite Proposals," in *History of Rocket Technology*, ed. Emme, 86.

12. Harvey Hall, "The Navy's Pioneering Venture into the Space Program," 33.

13. White Sands Missile Range Museum, "White Sands Missile Range History," http://www.wsmr-history.org/History.htm, no date; and Arnie Crouch, e-mail to Matt Bille, 17 May 2002.

14. Redstone Arsenal, "Corporal," n.d., http://www.redstone.army.mil/history/systems/corporal/welcome.html. While "Without Attitude Control" was the most common translation of WAC, some sources use "Without Altitude Control" or state the definition was an after-the-fact addition to a name based on the Women's Army Corps.

15. Bumper speed, altitude from Lloyd S. Swenson, Jr., James M. Grimwood, and Charles C. Alexander, *This New Ocean: A History of Project Mercury* (Washington, D.C.: NASA SP-4201, 1989), also available at http://www.hq.nasa.gov/office/pao/History/SP-4201/ch1-4.htm. (This publication bears no relation to William Burrows' book *This New Ocean*.)

16. NASA, *Aeronautics and Astronautics Chronology*, 1955–1957, http://www.hq.nasa.gov/office/pao/History/Timeline/1955-57.html. The Aerobee had a storied career, ending with the 1,037th launch in January 1985.

17. Newell, *Beyond the Atmosphere*, chap. 2, http://www.hq.nasa.gov/office/pao/History/SP-4211/ch4-2.htm.

18. James A. Van Allen, "What is a Space Scientist? An Autobiographical Example," 1990, http://www-pi.physics.uiowa.edu/java/.

19. G. K. Megerian, "V-2 Report #2, Minutes of Meeting," General Electric Company, February 27, 1946.

20. Ibid.

21. Newell, *Beyond the Atmosphere*, chap. 4, http://www.hq.nasa.gov/office/pao/History/SP-4211/ch4-2.htm.

22. Ralph Roberts, *Leo White: Mountain Rocket Man* (Alexander, N.C.: WorldComm, 1977), 31.

23. David DeVorkin, *Science with a Vengeance* (New York: Springer-Verlag, 1992), 171.

24. Milton Rosen, telephone interview by Matt Bille, October 25, 1999.

25. Milton Rosen, telephone interview by Matt Bille, November 1998; and Milton Rosen, *The Viking Rocket Story* (New York: Harper & Bros., 1955).

26. Keith Scala, "The Viking Rocket: Filling the Gap," *Quest* 2, no. 4 (Winter, 1993), 34.

27. DeVorkin, *Science with a Vengeance,* 171.

27. The ONR had advertised the Viking's utility as a testbed for missile technology to the Pentagon's Research and Development Board as early as June 1947. The NRL's internal "Rocket Research Report No. VI," dated April 1, 1951, was titled, "Conversion of Viking Into a Guided Missile." See DeVorkin, *Science with a Vengeance,* 181–83.

29. Scala, "The Viking Rocket," 34.

30. William B. Harwood, *Raise Heaven and Earth: The Story of Martin Marietta People and Their Pioneering Achievements* (New York: Simon and Schuster, 1993), 257.

31. NASA Glenn Research Center, Propulsion Systems Analysis Office, "AeroQuiz," November, 1999, http://www-psao.grc.nasa.gov/psao.quiz/november.99.html.

32. M-15 as test vehicle only. Milton Rosen, telephone interview by Matt Bille, October 25, 1999.

33. Earnst A. Steinhoff, interview with Frederick Ordway, August 19, 1971. Quoted in C. M. McCleskey and D. L. Christensen, "Dr. Kurt H. Debus: Launching a Vision," 52nd International Astronautical Congress, Toulouse, France, October 1-5, 2001, paper IAA-01-IAA-2.1.08.

34. Harford, *Korolev,* 68.

35. Paul H. Satterfield and David S. Akens, *Historical Monograph: The Army Ordnance Satellite Program,* (Huntsville: ABMA, November 1, 1958), 47. Also available online at http://www.redstone.army.mil/history/pdf/welcome.html.

36. Army Missile Command History Office, "Redstone Arsenal Complex Chronology: The Redstone Arsenal Era, 1950-55," http://www.redstone.army.mil/history/cron2a/cron2a.html.

37. DeVorkin, *Science with a Vengeance,* 61.

38. Medaris, *Countdown for Decision,* 63.

39. Wernher von Braun and Frederick Ordway, *History of Rocketry and Space Travel* (New York: Crowell, 1969), 94.

40. Wernher von Braun, "The Redstone, Jupiter, and Juno," in *History of Rocket Technology,* ed. Emme, 109.

41. Swenson, et al., *This New Ocean: A History of Project Mercury.*

42. Convair was a name created by General Motors when it bought the company and made it a GM division in 1954. See company history at http://www.gd.com/overview/history/aviation/.

43. Milton Rosen, telephone interview by Matt Bille, March, 2001.

44. John L. Chapman, *Atlas: The Story of a Missile* (New York: Harper & Bros., 1960), 34.

45. James M. Grimwood, *Project Mercury: A Chronology* (Washington, D.C.: NASA SP-4001, 1963). Also available at http://history.nasa.gov/SP-4001/p1a.htm.

46. Ibid.

47. Andrew LePage, "The Beginnings of America's Man in Space Program," *SpaceViews,* November, 1998, http://www.spaceviews.com/1998/10/article1a.html.

48. Frederick C. Durant, "Some Recollections of Early I.A.F. Congresses," n.d., in authors' possession.

49. Frederick Durant, personal communications to Matt Bille, June 3, 2002. The Russian name for the "Commission on Interplanetary Communications" is translated "Commission on Interplanetary Flight" in some sources.

50. Ibid.

51. Stuhlinger and Ordway, *Wernher von Braun*, 94.

52. "What Are We Waiting For?" *Collier's*, March 22, 1952, 23.

53. Ron Miller, "To Boldly Paint What No Man Has Painted Before," *American Heritage of Invention & Technology* 18, no. 1 (Summer, 2002): 17.

54. Ibid., 18.

55. Fred Durant took the first of the Disney films, "Man in Space," to the 1955 IAF Congress in Copenhagen. The Soviet representative, Leonid Sedov, begged for permission to borrow it to show "at the highest level" in his home country. He was allowed to do so, but the film was never returned to Disney. Durant wrote, "I suspect the film simply wore out." Durant, "Some Recollections of Early I.A.F. Congresses."

56. Stuhlinger and Ordway, quoting Disney archivist David R. Smith, in *Wernher von Braun*, 116.

57. While popular films increased interest in space travel, they did not present all science and technology as good. The science fiction films of the 1950s gave American audiences the stereotype of the clean-cut hero astronaut (always a young white male, in accordance with the predominant culture of the time) but also those of the radiation-spawned monster, the evil alien, and the mad scientist bent on world domination. For a thorough treatment of the interplay between entertainment and space travel in this era, see Howard McCurdy, *Space and the American Imagination* (Washington, D.C.: Smithsonian Institution Press, 1997.)

58. Grimwood, *Project Mercury*. By the time this project was killed in 1958, it had acquired the name Man In Space Soonest, giving it the unfortunate acronym MISS.

59. Ibid.

60. S. Fred Singer, "My Adventures in the Magnetosphere," in *Discovery of the Magnetosphere: History of Geophysics*, vol. 7 (American Geophysical Union, 1997), 165–71.

61. Singer's 1953 paper was expanded in 1955 to include discussion of the preferred orbit (polar) and techniques for storing and downlinking data. See S. Fred Singer, "Studies of a Minimum Orbital Unmanned Satellite of the Earth," *Astronautica Acta* 1 (1955): 171–84. This was reprinted in *Exploring the Unknown: Selected Documents in the History of the U.S. Civil Space Program*, ed. John M. Logsdon et al., vol. 1 (Washington, D.C.: NASA SP-4218, 1995), 314–24.

62. James Van Allen, interview by Erika Lishock, April 6, 2001.

63. Grimwood, *Project Mercury*.

64. Ted Wilbur, "Let George Do It," *Naval Aviation News*, December 1971, 17.

65. "Explorer Launching Was Preceded by Years of Work, Planning Here," *Redstone (Ala.) Rocket*, February 19, 1958, 9.

66. Wernher Von Braun, *A Minimum Satellite Vehicle based on components from missile developments of the Army Ordnance Corps* (Huntsville: Guided Missile Development Division, Redstone Arsenal, September 15, 1954).

67. Wilbur, "Let George Do It," 17.

68. George W. Hoover, "U.S. Navy Developments Leading to Space Flight: A Memoir," AIAA 7th Annual Meeting and Technical Display, Houston, Texas, October 19-22, 1970, AIAA Paper No. 70-1256.

69. Wernher von Braun, "The Story Behind the Explorers," *This Week*, April 13, 1958.

70. Dwayne Day, "Invitation to Struggle: The History of Civilian-Military Relations in Space," in *Exploring the Unknown*, ed. Logsdon et al., 2:238.

71. Carolyn Noon, "James Van Allen: Renowned astrophysicist got start in Mount Pleasant," *The Hawk Eye,* December 4, 1999, http://www.thehawkeye.com/specials/millennium/mm04127.html.

72. Van Allen, "What Is a Space Scientist?"

73. "Reach into Space," *TIME,* May 4, 1959, 64.

74. James Van Allen, interview by Erika Lishock, April 6, 2001.

75. "Reach Into Space," *TIME,* May 4, 1959, 64.

76. Quoted in Burrows, *This New Ocean,* 169.

77. Newell, *Beyond the Atmosphere,* chap. 5. http://www.hq.nasa.gov/office/pao/History/SP-4211/ch5-1.htm.

78. Hoover, "U.S. Navy Developments Leading to Space Flight: A Memoir."

79. For an example of a reference to "Project Orbit," see Captain W. C. Fortune and Colonel C. W. Eifler, to Chief, Office of Naval Research, "Conference on Project ORBIT," memorandum, December 14, 1954, in authors' possession. "Orbiter" appears in all documents dated January 1955 and later.

80. Grimwood, *Project Mercury.*

81. R. Cargill Hall, "Origins and Development of the Vanguard and Explorer Satellite Programs," *Airpower Historian* 9, no. 4 (October 1964): 104–105.

82. *New York Times,* December 17, 1954, quoted in Merton E. Davies and William R. Harris, *RAND's Role in Evolution of Balloon and Satellite Observation Systems and Related U.S. Space Technology,* (Santa Monica: RAND Corporation, September 1988), 58.

83. Hoover, "U.S. Navy Developments Leading to Space Flight: A Memoir."

84. John O'Keefe paper in *On the Utility of an Artificial Unmanned Earth Satellite,* American Rocket Society, November 24, 1954.

85. "Interplanetary Commission Created: Russians Planning Space Laboratory for Research Beyond Earth's Gravity," *Washington Post,* April 17, 1955.

86. William Pickering, interview by Michael Q. Hooks, October 20, 1989, JPL Oral History, provided to authors by JPL Archives, Pasadena, Calif.

87. Constance McLaughlin Green and Milton Lomask, *Vanguard—A History,* (Washington, D.C.: NASA SP-4202, 1970), 27.

88. McDougall, *The Heavens and the Earth,* 118–34.

89. William S. Bainbridge, *The Spaceflight/Revolution,* 4-6. Bainbridge's argument that liquid-fuel missile development was pushed primarily by enthusiasm for space flight is weakened by the fact that, until the mid-50s, there was little confidence the smaller solid rockets could be made powerful enough for long-range missiles. Soviet missiles remained predominately liquid-fueled for over a decade after *Sputnik.*

90. George W. Hoover, "Why an Earth Satellite," presentation to the Engineers' Society of Milwaukee, Milwaukee, Wisconsin, 22 February 1956. There is an interesting note on the author's copy of this paper, provided by George W. Hoover II. The typed text closes with the statement that, "We may not fly them (spaceships), but our sons may. " A penciled change reads "sons and daughters," indicating Hoover was a forward-looking thinker by 1956 standards.

91. Fred Durant, e-mail to Matt Bille, 1 May 2002.

CHAPTER 3

1. Newell, *Beyond the Atmosphere,* chap. 3, http://www.hq.nasa.gov/office/pao/History/SP-4211/ch3-1.htm.

2. Harford, *Korolev*, 45.

3. Aleksandr Glushko, "Ivan T. Kleimyonov," *Quest* 8, no. 1 (Spring, 2000): 24; and Harford, *Korolev*, 47.

4. Harford, *Korolev*, 57; Siddiqi, *Challenge to Apollo*, 14.

5. Ibid., 61.

6. Ibid., 63.

7. Jonathan Sanders, "A Socialist Moon Program Made by Moscow's Mystery Man," http://www.pbs.org/redfiles/moon/inv/moon_inv_ins.htm; and interviews in documentary film, *Red Files: The Secret Soviet Moon Race*, directed by Greg Barker (Orlando: Invision Digital & Media Arts, 1999). The entire script of the documentary *Red Files* is available at http://www.pbs.org/redfiles/moon/.

8. Harford, *Korolev*, 65.

9. Ibid., 74.

10. Ibid., 63.

11. Ibid., 97.

12. Sergey Khrushchev, "The First Earth Satellite: A Retrospective View from the Future," in *Reconsidering Sputnik*, ed. Launius et al., 277.

13. Harford, *Korolev*, 94.

14. Kerim Kerimov, interviewed in documentary film, *Red Files: Secret Soviet Moon Race*.

15. Greg Goebel, "Space History: The Fall & Rise of the Space Race," February, 2001, http://vectorsite.tripod.com/v2001m04.html#m2.

16. William P. Barry, "Sputnik and the Creation of the Soviet Space Industry," in *Reconsidering Sputnik*, ed. Launius et al., 98.

17. Barry, "Sputnik and the Creation of the Soviet Space Industry," 99.

18. Wm. Robert Johnson, "U.S. Nuclear Warheads and Applications," September, 2000, http://www.johnstonsarchive.net/nuclear/wrjp159u.html; James M. Grimwood and Frances Stroud, *History of the Jupiter Missile System* (Huntsville, Ala.: Army Ordnance Missile Command, July 27, 1962); and Peter Stickney, e-mail to Matt Bille, 23 May 2002.

19. "R-7—SS-6 Sapwood," 2000, http://www.fas.org/nuke/guide/russia/icbm/r-7.htm. Payload weights for both Soviet and American missiles vary depending on the documentation cited. This occurs because most of these rockets had more than one version, with differing capabilities, and due to discrepancies about what components (e.g., guidance equipment) are counted as part of the payload. For example, some authors give the R-7 payload as 12,000 lbs.

20. Harford, *Korolev*, 17, 48.

21. Mikhail Tikhonravov, "A Report on an Artificial Earth Satellite," memorandum, May 26, 1954, http://www.hq.nasa.gov/office/pao/History/sputnik/ussr.html; Sergey Korolev, "A Report on the Feasibility of Development of an Artificial Earth Satellite," memorandum, May 26, 1954, http://www.hq.nasa.gov/office/pao/History/sputnik/ussr.html. Other articles on this website are: "Announcemnt of the First Satellite," from *Pravda*, October 5, 1957, and "Proposals of First Launches of Artificial Earth Satellites."

22. Harford, *Korolev*, 125.

23. Asif A. Siddiqi, "Korolev, Sputnik, and the International Geophysical Year," http://www.hq.nasa.gov/office/pao/History/sputnik/siddiqi.html; Barry, "Sputnik and the Creation of the Soviet Space Industry," 101.

24. Greg Myre, "Sputnik Marked Exciting Time for Russian Scientist," Associated Press, September 3, 1977.

25. Sergey Kryukov, interviewed in *Red Files: Secret Soviet Moon Race.*

26. James Oberg, *OMNI Magazine* (October, 1990): 96–102. Also available online at http://www.rocketry.com/mwade/articles/inskonur.htm.

27. Mark Wade, "Sputnik 3," http://www.rocketry.com/mwade/craft/sputnik3.htm; Siddiqi, *Challenge to Apollo,* 162.

28. Sergey Korolev, "Proposals of First Launches of Artificial Satellites Before the Beginning of the International Year of Geophysics," memorandum, January 5, 1957, http://www.hq.nasa.gov/office/pao/History/sputnik.html. The confusion of Vanguard with Redstone is inexplicable, since a review of the open literature published in the U.S. would have made it clear there was no relationship.

29. Harford, *Korolev,* 126

30. Mark Wade, "Sputnik 1," http://www.rocketry.com/mwade/craft/sputnik1.htm.

31. Mikhail Tikhonravov, "The Creation of the First Artificial Earth Satellite: Some Historical Details," in *History of Rocketry and Astronautics,* AAS History Series, vol. 8 (Amsterdam: Univelt, 1974), 210.

32. This is very clear in diagrams published in Robert Godwin, ed., *Rocket and Space Corporation Energia* (Burlington, Ont.: Apogee Books, 2001), 35.

33. Mikhail Tikhonravov, "The Creation of the First Artificial Earth Satellite," 207–13.

34. Ibid., 211.

35. Ibid., 210.

36. Siddiqi, *Challenge to Apollo,* 163.

37. Harford, *Korolev,* 127.

38. Ibid., 128.

39. Andrew LePage, "Sputnik: The First Man Made Earth Satellite," *SpaceViews,* October, 1997, http://www.seds.org/spaceviews/9710/articles.html. The reentry section of the first two missiles flown broke up before reaching the target area, and there were several serious problems with subsequent tests. The SS-6, as fearsome as it was, took years to develop into a reliable system. Korolev would no doubt have been grimly amused by American projections that the Soviets would deploy 1,000 ICBMs by 1962. See Curtis Peebles, *Shadow Flights: America's Secret Air War Against the Soviet Union* (Novato: Presidio Press, 2000), 173.

40. An American U-2 spyplane had actually photographed the launch site on August 5, 1957. This, of course, did not prove a successful flight had taken place, although it did convince U.S. leaders the ICBM program was real. A week after the launch, another U-2 mission photographed the site again. Norman Polmar, *Spyplane: The U-2 History Declassified* (Osceola: Motorbooks International, 2001), 108–109.

41. Harford, *Korolev,* 108.

42. An alternate translation of this idiom is "Little Number 7." In an odd coincidence, the missile's American counterpart, the Atlas, was called the Model 7 by Convair.

43. Robert Christy, "Sputnik—The Soviet Union's Traveller in Space," 1999, http://www.zarya.freeserve.co.uk/Diaries/Sputnik/.

44. Harford, *Korolev,* 127.

CHAPTER 4

1. Robert L. Perry, "Origins of the USAF Space Program 1945–1956," 1961; reprint, 1997, from History Office, Air Force Space and Missile Systems Center, http://www.fas.org/spp/eprint/origins/index.html.

2. Neufeld, *Beyond Horizons,* 41.

3. Barton Beebe, "Law's Empire and the Final Frontier: Legalizing the Future in the Early *Corpus Juris Spatialis," The Yale Law Journal* 108 (1999): 1761.

4. Ibid., 1764.

5. McDougall, *The Heavens and the Earth,* 109, 118, 187, 192; Beebe, "Law's Empire and the Final Frontier," 1749–50; R. Cargill Hall, "Origins of U.S. Space Policy: Eisenhower, Open Skies, and Freedom of Space," in *Exploring the Unknown,* ed. Logsdon et al., 1:219. Even after the first satellites were orbited, the National Security Council noted, "There is as yet insufficient basis for legally deciding that air space extends so far and no farther: that outer space begins at a certain point above the earth." National Security Council, NSC 5814, "U.S. Policy on Outer Space," June 20, 1958, reprinted in *Exploring the Unknown,* ed. Logsdon et. al., 1: chap. 2. Indeed, no exact demarcation between sovereign airspace and free space has ever been agreed upon.

6. In an episode resembling the plot of a bad spy thriller, the Genetrix project produced its most important results a year after the launches ended. One balloon's gondola somehow drifted in the Pacific until it washed up in the Aleutian Islands in 1957. It turned out to contain the first photographs of the enormous facility at Krasnoyarsk where uranium for Soviet nuclear weapons was mined, separated, and refined. Curtis Peebles, *Shadow Flights* (Novato, Calif.: Presidio Press, 2002), 173.

7. R. Cargill Hall, "Origins of U.S. Space Policy," 216.

8. Feed Back is often spelled as one word, but it was a two-word title. See Davies and Harris, "RAND's Role in the Evolution of Balloon and Satellite Observation Systems and Related U.S. Space Technology," 53.

9. Robert L. Perry, "Origins of the USAF Space Program 1945–1956."

10. Green and Lomask, *Vanguard—A History,* 32.

11. National Security Council, "Draft Statement of Policy on U.S. Scientific Satellite Program," NSC 5520, May 20, 1955.

12. Ibid.

13. The IGY program fit so well with the national security goal of establishing free transit of space that historian R. Cargill Hall believes Quarles may have contacted the National Committee for the IGY and suggested satellite proposals be submitted so he could promote them to advance the NSC 5520 agenda. There is, however, no documentation to prove this scenario took place. R. Cargill Hall, "The Eisenhower Administration and the Cold War: Framing American Astronautics to Serve National Security," *Prologue* 27, no. 1 (Spring 1995): 59–72; R. Cargill Hall, telephone interview by Matt Bille, January 19, 2000.

14. Green and Lomask, *Vanguard—A History,* 35.

15. Fred Durant, telephone interview by Matt Bille, May 27, 2002. Durant also recalled, "Fred Whipple and I celebrated for two weeks, convinced it (the U.S. satellite program) was the Army project, then we learned the sad news."

16. Siddiqi, "Korolev, Sputnik, and the International Geophysical Year"; John Hillary, "Soviets Planning Early Satellite," *New York Times,* August 3, 1955.

17. Michael Neufeld, "Orbiter, Overflight, and the First Satellite: New Light on the Vanguard Decision," in *Reconsidering Sputnik,* ed. Launius et al., 238.

18. Green and Lomask, *Vanguard—A History,* 43.

19. Ibid., 43.

20. Von Braun, in *History of Rocket Technology,* ed. Emme, 111.

21. "A Scientific Satellite Program," NRL Memorandum Report No. 487, July 5, 1955, 3.

22. Ibid., 18.

23. Technically, as Kepler showed, all orbits are ellipses, and a circle is a type of ellipse. Circular orbits are often used in planning, although a perfect circle is almost impossible to attain in practice.

24. "A Scientific Satellite Program," NRL Memorandum Report 487, 6–7.

25. Ibid., 27.

26. Office of the Assistant Secretary of Defense (Research and Development), *Report of the Ad Hoc Advisory Group on Special Capabilities,* RD 263/9, Log no. 55-1067A, August, 1955, 4. (hereafter cited as *Stewart Committee Report*)

27. Michael Neufeld, "Orbiter, Overflight, and the First Satellite," 241.

28. Milton Rosen, telephone interview by Matt Bille, November 6, 1998.

29. Fred Durant, personal communication to Matt Bille, May 13, 2002.

30. Milton Rosen, telephone interview by Matt Bille, November 12, 1998.

31. Green and Lomask, *Vanguard—A History,* 54.

32. Ibid., 52. The proposed super-Redstone was never built, although the later Jupiter missile and Juno 2 satellite launcher developed by ABMA used a version of this engine, the S-3D.

33. Neufeld, "Orbiter, Overflight, and the First Satellite," 249.

34. Grimwood, *Project Mercury.*

35. Siddiqi, "Korolev, Sputnik, and the International Geophysical Year."

36. Green and Lomask, *Vanguard—A History,* 51.

37. Von Braun, "The Story Behind the Explorers."

38. *Stewart Committee Report,* 6, 15; Green and Lomask, *Vanguard—A History,* 49–50.

39. Green and Lomask, *Vanguard—A History,* 51.

40. William Pickering, telephone interview by Matt Bille, June 2, 1999.

41. Green and Lomask, *Vanguard—A History,* 48.

42. Milton Rosen, telephone interview by Matt Bille, November 1998.

43. "A Scientific Satellite Program," NRL Memorandum Report No. 487. The NRL engineers worked out that each degree of pointing error changed the apogee and perigee by approximately 75 miles. See also "Secrecy Covers Army's Satellite," *New York Times,* February 1, 1958, 7B.

44. McDougall, *The Heavens and the Earth.* See especially pages 120–24. Helen Gavaghan, in a 1998 work of popular history describing the origins of the first applications satellites, accepts it as a given the dice were loaded in favor of the Navy's "less militaristic" proposal. Helen Gavaghan, *Something New under the Sun* (New York: Springer-Verlag, 1998), 27.

45. Len Cormier, personal communication with Matt Bille, October 5, 2002.

46. National Security Council, "Discussion at the 339th Meeting of the National Security Council," October 10, 1957, Washington, D.C., http://www.eisenhower.utexas.edu/dl/Sputnik/Sputnikdocuments.html.

47. *Stewart Committee Report,* 1.

48. Neufeld, "Orbiter, Overflight, and the First Satellite," 243.

49. For a description of the events between the two Stewart Committee votes, see Green and Lomask, *Vanguard—A History,* 52-56.

50. McDougall, *The Heavens and the Earth,* 130.

51. Hoover, "Why an Earth Satellite."

52. Green and Lomask, *Vanguard,* 129-30.

53. Medaris, *Countdown for Decision,* 135.

54. Milton Rosen, telephone interview by Matt Bille, November 1998.

55. Ibid.

CHAPTER 5

1. Hoover was promoted to full Commander in January 1955.

2. Green and Lomask, *Vanguard—A History,* 55.

3. Milton Rosen, telephone interview by Matt Bille, October 25, 1999.

4. Green and Lomask, *Vanguard—A History,* 74.

5. Ibid., 55.

6. Roger Easton, interview by David Van Keuren, March 8, 1996, NRL Oral History, provided to authors by History Office, Naval Research Laboratory.

7. Green and Lomask, *Vanguard—A History,* 58.

8. Ibid., 59.

9. Ibid., 60–65.

10. Ibid., 66.

11. Roger Easton, interview by David Van Keuren, March 8, 1996, NRL Oral History.

12. Green and Lomask, *Vanguard—A History,* 145.

13. All Minitrack information here is from Roger Easton's interview by David Van Keuren, March 8, 1996, NRL Oral History.

14. Air University, "Space Handbook," AU-18, http://www.fas.org/spp/military/docops/usaf/au-18/part01.htm.

15. Green and Lomask, *Vanguard—A History,* 154.

16. Grimwood, *Project Mercury;* and Neufeld, "Orbiter, Overflight, and the First Satellite," 241.

17. James Van Allen, *The Scientific Uses of Earth Satellites* (Ann Arbor: University of Michigan Press, 1956).

18. James Van Allen, *Origins of Magnetospheric Physics* (Washington, D.C.: Smithsonian Institution Press, 1983), 41-42.

19. Ibid., 42.

20. Ibid., 42.

21. Green and Lomask, *Vanguard—A History,* 121–22.

22. Ibid., 120–23: Durant, personal communication to Matt Bille, June 3, 2002; Percival Brundage, Director, Bureau of the Budget, memorandum for the President, "Project Vanguard," April 30, 1957, http://www.hq.nasa.gov/office/pao/History/sputnik/ii4.html.

23. Dwayne Day, "Invitation to Struggle: The History of Civilian-Military Relations in Space," in *Exploring the Unknown,* ed. Logsdon et al., 2:245. Presumably, someone in the agency thought the establishment of "freedom of space" sufficiently important to ensure the Vanguard project was funded.

24. LePage, Andrew, "Vanguard: America's Answer to Sputnik," *SpaceViews,* 1997,

http://www.seds.org/spaceviews/9712/articles3.html; John Hagen, "The Viking and the Vanguard," in *History of Rocket Technology,* ed. Emme, 129.

25. Green and Lomask, *Vanguard—A History,* 80-82, 89-90.

26. Ibid.

27. John Perlin, "Solar Power: the Slow Revolution," *American Heritage of Invention & Technology* 18, no. 1 (Summer, 2002): 22.

28. Green and Lomask, *Vanguard—A History,* 89-90.

29. Ibid., 177.

30. Ibid., 72.

31. This was an industry-standard 100-inch wide sheet rolled into a cylinder. William Harwood, *Raise Heaven and Earth,* 256.

32. Green and Lomask, *Vanguard—A History,* 89.

33. Ibid., 72.

34. NASA, *Dictionary of Technical Terms for Aerospace Use,* http://roland.grc.nasa.gov/~dglover/dictionary/m.html.

35. Kenneth Gatland, *Development of the Guided Missile* (London: Illiffe and Sons, 1954), 178.

36. Green and Lomask, *Vanguard—A History,* 116.

37. Ibid., 125.

38. The account of the facilities at Canaveral is from Green and Lomask, *Vanguard—A History,* 137–42.

39. Grimwood and Stroud, *History of the Jupiter Missile System,* 108. Also available at http://www.redstone.army.mil/history/systems/jupiter/chapter8.html.

40. Percival Brundage, memorandum for the President, "Project Vanguard."

41. National Security Council, memorandum, Discussion at the 322d Meeting of the NSC, May 19, 1957.

42. Ibid.

43. "Project Vanguard: Past, Present, and Prospects," *Missiles and Rockets* (July, 1957): 117.

44. Roger Easton, interview by David Van Keuren, March 8, 1996, NRL Oral History.

CHAPTER 6

1. "Project Vanguard: Past, Present, and Prospects," *Missiles and Rockets* (July, 1957): 117.

2. Allen W. Dulles, memorandum to Donald Quarles, July 5, 1957, reprinted in *Exploring the Unknown,* ed. Logsdon et al., 1: chap 2.

3. William Pickering, telephone interview by Matt Bille, July 10, 2001; Koppes, *JPL and the American Space Program,* 82.

4. Len Cormier, personal communication with Matt Bille, October 5, 2002.

5. Valdimir Khilchenko, in *Roads to Space,* ed. John Rea, vol. 3 (Washington, D.C.: Aviation Week Group, 1995), 380–81.

6. Vladimir Yastrebov, in *Roads to Space,* 3:444.

7. Harford, *Korolev,* 129.

8. A surprising number of translations of the word "sputnik" have been offered. The detailed explanation in Willy Ley's *Rockets, Missiles, and Men in Space,* (New York: Viking Press, 1968), 385, is accepted here.

9. "Soviet Satellite Sends U.S. into a Tizzy," *LIFE* 43, no. 16, October 14, 1957. Available online at http://www.life.com/Life/space/giantleap/sec1/sec1.htm.

10. Robert W. Smith, "A Setting for the International Geophysical Year," in *Reconsidering Sputnik,* ed. Launius et al., 130.

11. "Soviet Satellite Sends U.S. into a Tizzy," *LIFE* 43, no. 16, October 14, 1957. Available online at http://www.life.com/Life/space/giantleap/sec1/sec1.htm.

12. William Pickering, telephone interview by Matt Bille, July 10, 2001.

13. James R. Killian, *Sputnik, Scientists, and Eisenhower* (Cambridge: MIT Press, 1977), 2–3.

14. "Dr. Vannever Bush Talks," *Newsweek,* October 21, 1957, 30.

15. Dave Cravotta, "What Sputnik Meant to Me," *Final Frontier* 10, no. 5 (September/October, 1997): 23.

16. Neil McAleer, "Where Were You When the Space Age Began?" *The Scientist,* October, 1987, http://www.the-scientist.com/yr1987/oct/opin_871005.html.

17. "Announcement of the First Satellite," *Pravda,* October 5, 1957. Reprinted in *Florida Today,* http://www.flatoday.com.space/.

18. Tikhonravov, "The Creation of the First Artificial Earth Satellite," 212.

19. Michael Wright, "Here Comes Sputnik!" August 30, 1997, http://www.batnet .com/mfwright/sputnik.html.

20. "From Legends to Science of Space Travel," *Pravda,* October 11, 1957. Reprinted in *Soviet Writings on Earth Satellites and Space Travel* (New York: Citadel Press, 1958); "They've Got—We Plan," *Newsweek,* October 14, 1957, 38.

21. M. Vassilev, *Sputnik into Space,* (New York: Dial Press, 1958).

22. Ron Miller, e-mail to Matt Bille, April 4, 2001.

23. Ernst Stuhlinger, "Russian Comments to the American Satellite Project," memorandum, October 29, 1957, in Satterfield and Akens, *Historical Monograph.*

24. Ibid. It is not clear when Soviet intelligence corrected the earlier belief, committed to paper by Korolev, that the Vanguard booster was based on the Redstone.

25. "Man's Awesome Adventure," *Newsweek,* October 14, 1957, 37.

26. Roger Launius, "Prelude to the Space Age," in *Exploring the Unknown,* ed. Logsdon et al., 1:16.

27. "Satellites and Our Safety," *Newsweek,* October 21, 1957, 33.

28. Central Intelligence Agency, "Comments on Various Military Factors Affecting Soviet Capabilities and Intentions over the next Five Years," memorandum, October 28, 1957, http://www.foia.cia.gov.

29. Eisenhower's staff secretary, then-Colonel Andrew Goodpaster, had warned Eisenhower in advance that a Soviet satellite would have serious effects on the American public, but the President did not agree. Andrew Goodpaster, interview by Dwayne Day, March 19, 1996, cited in Dwayne Day, "Invitation to Struggle," 245.

30. W. H. Lawrence, "President Voices Concern on U.S. Missiles Program, But Not on the Satellite," *New York Times,* October 10, 1957.

31. Robert Divine, *The Sputnik Challenge* (New York: Oxford University Press, 1993), 12.

32. Andrew Goodpaster, interview by John Costello, December 23, 1998, http:// www.doingoralhistory.org/students/coldwar/costello.html.

33. Divine, *The Sputnik Challenge,* 68–69.

34. Rodger A. Payne, "Public Opinion and Foreign Threats: Eisenhower's Response to Sputnik," *Armed Forces & Society* 21 (Fall, 1994), 89–111.

35. Gretchen J. Van Dyke, "Sputnik: A Political Symbol and Tool in 1960 Campaign Politics," in *Reconsidering Sputnik,* ed. Launius et al., 377.

36. John Foster Dulles to James C. Hagerty, memorandum, October 8, 1957, with attached "Draft Statements on the Soviet Satellite," October 5, 1957, http://www.hq.nasa.gov/office/pao/History/sputnik/15.html.

37. McDougall, *The Heavens and the Earth,* 134.

38. Divine, *The Sputnik Challenge,* 12; Beebe, "Law's Empire and the Final Frontier," 1763. To Beebe, "By 1960, the failure of any nation to protest Sputnik I and its successors had effectively suspended the debate over the altitudinal extent of national sovereignty."

39. McDougall, *The Heavens and the Earth,* 192.

40. Ibid., 260.

41. Roger Launius, NASA History Office, telephone interview by Matt Bille, April 16, 1999.

42. Walter Sanders, "The Seer of Space," *LIFE* 23, no. 31 (November 18, 1957): 133.

43. Wernher von Braun, "The Story Behind the Explorers."

44. William Pickering, interview by Michael Q. Hooks, November–December, 1989, JPL Oral History, provided to authors by JPL Archives, Pasadena, Calif.

45. McDougall, *The Heavens and the Earth,* 153.

46. "The Russians—And the 'Losers'," *Newsweek,* October 14, 1957, 39.

47. "Satellites and Our Safety," *Newsweek,* October 21, 1957, 33.

48. "The Russians—And the 'Losers'," 39.

49. "Soviet Satellite Sends U.S. Into a Tizzy," *LIFE* 43, no. 16, October 14, 1957.

50. "The Calamity. . . Why," *Newsweek,* December 16, 1957, 65.

51. "Course Recorded," *New York Times,* October 5, 1957.

52. Green and Lomask, *Vanguard—A History,* 195.

53. "Device is 8 Times Heavier Than One Planned by U.S.," *New York Times,* October 5, 1957.

54. Ibid.

55. Richard Witkin, "U.S. Delay Draws Scientists' Fire," *New York Times,* October 5, 1957.

56. "Device is 8 Time Heavier," *New York Times,* October 5, 1957.

57. Van Allen, *Origins,* 46.

58. Grimwood, *Project Mercury.*

59. Ibid.

60. Ibid.

61. Ibid.

62. Khrushchev, Sergey, "The First Earth Satellite," 273.

63. Robert Christy, "Sputnik—The Soviet Union's Traveller in Space"; and Siddiqi, *Challenge to Apollo,* 174.

CHAPTER 7

1. Walter Sanders, "The Seer of Space."

2. Grimwood, *Project Mercury.*

3. Stuhlinger and Ordway, *Wernher von Braun,* 104.

4. Medaris, *Countdown,* 119. Many sources say there were six such missiles. The figure of twelve is given by Medaris and confirmed by the Army's "History of the Jupiter

Missile Program," http://www.redstone.army.mil/history/systems/jupiter/chapter8.html. Also, the booster's name is often written "Jupiter-C," even in some official documents. In writings by von Braun and Medaris, as well as the Army history just cited, there is no hyphen, and this appears to be the original designation.

5. Von Braun, "The Redstone, Jupiter, and Juno," in *History of Rocket Technology,* ed. Emme, 113.

6. Von Braun, "The Story Behind the Explorers."

7. "Explorer Launching Was Preceded by Years of Work, Planning Here," *The Redstone Rocket,* February 19, 1958, 9. One version of this satellite idea featured a large disk extending around the center of the cylindrical craft to increase its visibility. This was dropped when radio tracking made it unnecessary. Michael Neufeld, Email to Matt Bille, December 3, 1998.

8. "Satellite Policy," transcript of discussion between MG John B. Medaris, Dr. Wernher von Braun, Colonel John C. Nickerson, Jr., Dr. Eberhardt Rees, Dr. Ernst Stuhlinger, April 20, 1956, copy located in AMCOM Historical Office inquiry files, Huntsville, Ala.

9. Medaris, *Countdown,* 120. For photograph of Missile 27 proving the fourth stage was installed, see http://www.redstone.army.mil/history/archives/jupiter/jupiter_c_rs27 .jpg. No actual order concerning the prevention of an "accidental" satellite has been located by the Army Missile Command historian or other researchers, so presumably this was a telephoned instruction to Medaris.

10. Stuhlinger, telephone interview by Matt Bille, July 9, 2001. Kurt Debus recalled many years later that he jokingly proposed an unauthorized satellite launch several times to General Yates, whose response was a heated "No, we cannot do that!" Interview by McCleskey and Christensen, January 20, 1983, quoted in their paper, "Dr. Kurt H. Debus."

11. Von Braun, "The Story Behind the Explorers."

12. Dwayne Day, "Cover Stories and Hidden Agendas: Early American Space and National Security Policy," in *Reconsidering Sputnik,* ed. Launius et al., 175–78.

13. Dwayne Day, "Cover Stories and Hidden Agendas,"180.

14. Von Braun and Ordway, *History of Rocketry and Space Travel,* 129.

15. "History of the Jupiter Missile System," chap. 8, http://www.redstone.army.mil/ history/systems/jupiter/chapter8.html.

16. Ibid.

17. Medaris, *Countdown,* 155.

18. Satterfield and Akens, *Historical Monograph,* 60–61. Also available online at http://www.redstone.army.mil/history/pdf/welcome.html.

19. Ibid., 62.

20. Stuhlinger and Ordway, *Wernher von Braun,* 131.

21. Emme, Eugene M., *Aeronautics and Astronautics: An American Chronology of Science and Technology in the Exploration of Space, 1915-1960,* NASA, 1961, http://www.hq.nasa .gov/office/pao/History/timeline.html. Another possible contender for this honor was a V-2 launched on December 17, 1946, that carried explosives to create "artificial meteors." James Van Allen, letter to the authors, March 10, 2003.

22. Milton Rosen, telephone interview by Matt Bille, July 9, 2001.

23. Martin Votaw, telephone interview by Matt Bille, November 27, 1998.

24. Milton Rosen, telephone interview by Matt Bille, November 12, 1998.

25. Green and Lomask, *Vanguard—A History,* 197. After the failure, Hagerty denied the executive branch had overly publicized the planned launch. See "'Bird Watchers' Diary," *Newsweek,* December 16, 1957, 25.

26. Kurt Stehling, "Vanguard," in *The Coming of the Space Age,* ed. Arthur C. Clarke (New York: Meredith Press, 1967), 19.

27. Ibid.

28. Martin Votaw, telephone interview by Matt Bille, November 27, 1998.

29. Roger Easton, interview by David Van Keuren, March 8, 1996, NRL Oral History.

30. Milton Bracker, "Vanguard Rocket Burns on Beach; Failure to Launch Test Satellite Assailed as Blow to U.S. Prestige." *New York Times,* December 7, 1957.

31. Green and Lomask, *Vanguard—A History,* 209–10.

32. Ibid., 201–202.

33. Medaris, *Countdown,* 166.

34. Lockheed Martin Communications and Power Center, "Early RCA History," excerpt from *The RCA Engineer* 28, no. 2 (Mar./Apr., 1983), http://www.payloads.com/pay/earlyrca.htm; Andrew LePage, "TIROS: The First Weather Satellite," *SpaceViews,* 2000, http://www.spaceviews.com/2000/04/article3b.html.

35. Medaris, *Countdown,* 187-89.

36. "The Target—Space," *Newsweek,* December 9, 1957, 57.

37. "Explorer Launching Was Preceded by Years of Work, Planning Here," *The Redstone Rocket,* February 19, 1958, 9.

38. Sources on the appearance and materials used on the casing of Explorer 1 include: Al Hibbs, telephone interview by Matt Bille, March 1, 1999; Walter Downhower, telephone interview by Matt Bille, April 1, 1999; Gerhard Heller, "The Explorer," in *Ten Steps into Space* (Philadelphia: Franklin Institute, December 1958), 98–108; "Satellite Will Provide Much Scientific Data," *Huntsville Times,* February 1, 1958, 2; Jet Propulsion Laboratory (JPL) photographs #293-3322B and 293-3325, JPL Archives, Pasadena, Calif. According to Downhower, there was no engineering reason why the metal casing was sandblasted. It was done to remove fingerprints that became highly visible when the spacecraft was tested in a thermal-vacuum chamber.

39. Kurt Debus, "From A-4 to Explorer 1: A Memoir," presented to International Academy of Astronautics, Baku, U.S.S.R., 1973; also in *History of Rocketry and Astronautics,* ed. Von Braun and Ordway, chapter 15.

40. Von Braun, "The Story Behind the Explorers."

41. "Up There—At Last," *Newsweek,* February 10, 1958, 28; Debus, "From A-4 to Explorer 1: A Memoir."

42. Medaris, *Countdown,* 214.

43. Ibid., 215.

44. The account of the launch sequence is from Medaris, *Countdown;* see also "Up There—At Last," *Newsweek,* February 10, 1958, 29.

45. Medaris, *Countdown,* 217; Ernst Stuhlinger, "Launching of Explorer 1," unpublished paper, May 29, 1998.

46. NASA, "Explorer 1 and Jupiter-C," no date, http://history.nasa.gov/sputnik/expinfo.html.

47. NASA, "Explorer 1 and Jupiter-C;" Debus, "From A-4 to Explorer 1: A Memoir."

48. Von Braun, "The Story Behind the Explorers"; and "Up There—At Last," *Newsweek,* February 10, 1958, 30.

49. Al Hibbs, telephone interview by Matt Bille, July 9, 1998. Hibbs also gave Medaris a guess at Explorer's orbital lifetime—ten years. Given the data at hand, this was impressively close to the actual figure of twelve years.

50. Koppes, *JPL and the American Space Program*, 90.

51. Von Braun, "The Story behind the Explorers."

52. William Pickering, e-mail to Matt Bille, September 18, 2000.

53. Henry Magill, e-mails to Matt Bille, March 30 and 31, 1999. Magill wrote, "No, the note that I passed did not say 'Goldstone.' I said Earthquake Valley has heard the signal." Other sources on the location of the tracking station include: William Corliss, *A History of the Deep Space Network* (Washington, D.C.: NASA CR-151915, May 1, 1976); Curtis Emerson, personal communication to Matt Bille, March 25, 1999; Jet Propulsion Laboratory, "Description of World Network for Radio Tracking of Space Vehicles," JPL publication no. 135, July 1, 1958; Jet Propulsion Laboratory, "Deep Space Network: History," March 26, 1999, http://deepspace1.jpl.nasa.gov/dsn/history; Cliff Lethbridge, e-mail to Matt Bille, April 3, 1999; William Pickering, telephone interview by Matt Bille, June 2, 1999; and Medaris, *Countdown*, 224. No contemporary media account examined, including *LIFE* magazine for February 10, 1958, which has a photograph of Medaris holding the famous note, reports the "Goldstone" phrase. The only source for this quote that does not cite Medaris' account is Ernst Stuhlinger, of the von Braun team. (Stuhlinger and Ordway, *Wernher von Braun*, 138; Stuhlinger, telephone interview by Matt Bille, May 27, 1999). Stuhlinger recalled this statement being made as an announcement by Charles Lundquist to the crew assembled at the Cape, not as a note. If he is correct, the reason Lundquist would have said "Goldstone" is unknown.

54. Stuhlinger and Ordway, *Wernher von Braun*, 138.

55. Burrows, *This New Ocean*, 209.

56. "Up There—At Last," *Newsweek*, February 10, 1958, 28.

57. Medaris, *Countdown*, 225.

58. Ibid., 226.

59. "Up There—At Last," *Newsweek*, February 10, 1958, 33.

60. Ibid., 34.

61. "The Space Patrol," *Newsweek*, February 10, 1958, 21.

62. Kurt Debus, "From A-4 to Explorer 1: A Memoir."

63. Stuhlinger and Ordway, *Wernher von Braun*, 117.

64. Van Allen, *Origins*, 49–50.

65. Ibid., 50–53.

66. James Van Allen, telephone interview by Matt Bille, April 29, 1998; Van Allen, *Origins*, 54; James Van Allen, interview by Erika Lishock, April 6, 2001.

67. Medaris, *Countdown*, 202-03: Debus, "From A-4 to Explorer 1: A Memoir," 252.

68. Walter Downhower, telephone interview by Matt Bille, April 1, 1999.

69. Van Allen, *Origins*, 55.

70. Ibid.

71. Gladwin Hill, "Radioed Data of Satellite Ease Fear of Space Trips," *New York Times*, February 4, 1958, 1.

72. Van Allen, *Origins*, 64-65.

73. Van Allen, *Origins*, 62; James Van Allen, letter to the authors, March 10, 2003.

74. Van Allen, *Origins*, 67.

75. J. E. Froelich, *Contributions of the Explorer to Space Technology,* External Publication no. 526 (Pasadena: Jet Propulsion Laboratory, July 7, 1958).

76. Al Hibbs, *Notes on Project Deal,* External Publication no. 471 (Pasadena: Jet Propulsion Laboratory, March 14, 1958).

77. ABMA, "Army Contributions to the nation's space research," fact sheet, n.d. [1958?].

78. ABMA, "Army Contributions to the nation's space research."

CHAPTER 8

1. Milton Rosen, telephone interview by Matt Bille, November 6, 1998.

2. Frank Cartwright, telephone interview by Matt Bille, November 16, 1997.

3. Mark Pahuta, producer, *Secret City: A History of the Navy at China Lake,* video documentary (China Lake, Calif.: China Lake Museum Foundation, 1995); Mikey Strang, "Interview with Dr. Howard Wilcox; re: The NOTS Project" (May 25, 1967): 1, reprinted in a notebook titled *NOTSNIK,* compiled by Hardold D. Parode, Public Information Officer, Office of Information, U.S. Naval Weapons Center, China Lake, Calif., December 9, 1976. A copy of this notebook was provided to the authors by Dwayne Day, of the Space History Division, National Air and Space Museum. The notebook is hereafter refered to as *NOTSNIK* Notebook. Dr. Wilcox recalled that he suggested the air-launched concept: it has also been credited to Dr. Bill McLean, then Technical Director of NOTS.

4. Robert "Bud" G. S. Sewell, telephone interview by Matt Bille, 1998; Frank Knemeyer, "Astronautics Test Schedule," NOTS internal memorandum, March 18, 1960, in *NOTSNIK* Notebook.

5. Joel W. Powell, "The NOTS Air-Launched Satellite Programme," *Journal of the British Interplanetary Society* 50, 1997, 433. Due to the hurried nature of the NOTS program, as well as its classification, many aspects of the effort are not well documented.

6. Robert G. S. Sewell, "An Exploratory Program Leading to Military Meteorological Observations From Television Satellites," NOTS Document 2056, June 27, 1958, 7, 12, in *NOTSNIK* Notebook.

7. Naval Weapons Center Technical Information Department, "Summary of Informal Interviews," in *Project Pilot: Informal Research Package,* 1960, reprinted in *NOTSNIK* Notebook.

8. Given the ambiguous results of the NOTSNIK program, the Scout can still be called the first all-solid launcher proven to be successful.

9. Joel Powell, e-mail to Matt Bille, May 6, 01.

10. Keith Scala, "Rocket's Red Glare," *Quest* 3, no. 1 (Spring, 1994): 60.

11. Scala, "Rocket's Red Glare"; Knemeyer, "Astronautics Test Schedule."

12. Robert G. S. Sewell, "Informal Thoughts on the NOTS Project," memorandum to Head, Weapons Development Department, Naval Ordnance Test Station, China Lake, Calif., September 2, 1958, in *NOTSNIK* Notebook.

13. Peter Pesavento, "U.S. Navy's Untold Story of Space-Related Firsts," *Spaceflight* 38 (July, 1996): 239–45.

14. Pesavento, "U.S. Navy's Untold Story of Space"; Powell, "The NOTS Air-Launched Satellites Programme"; Knemeyer, "Astronautics Test Schedule"; Parode, "Project Pilot"; Strang, "Interview with Dr. Howard Wilcox," in *NOTSNIK* Notebook; Knemeyer, "Astronautics Test Schedule," in *NOTSNIK* Notebook; Andrew LePage, e-mail

to Matt Bille, March 2, 1999; Frank St. George, telephone interview by Matt Bille, May 7, 1999; Leroy Doig, e-mail to Matt Bille, Mar 29, 2001.

15. Richard (Dick) Boyd, NOTSNIK, telephone interviews by Matt Bille, May 21 and June 2, 1999.

16. EV-1: Joel Powell, e-mail to Matt Bille, May 7, 2001.

17. Keith Scala, "A History of Air-Launched Space Vehicles," *Quest,* 3, no. 1 (Spring, 1994): 38.

18. Hi-hoe: Leroy Doig, e-mail to Matt Bille, May 7, 2001.

19. Yo-yo: Joel Powell, e-mail to Matt Bille, May 7, 2001; ASAT: Joel Powell, e-mail to Matt Bille, May 7, 2001; and Leroy Doig, e-mail to Matt Bille, May 7, 2001.

20. SIP: Leroy Doig to Matt Bille, May 7, 2001.

21. Powell, "The NOTS Air-Launched Satellite Programme."

22. While Pegasus proved the NOTSNIK air-launch concept was viable, there was no direct connection between the two programs. Antonia Elias, who conceived Pegasus, was unaware of the NOTSNIK project at the time. His inspiration was the Vought ASM-135A, a two-stage suborbital antisatellite vehicle which had been successfully fired from an Air Force F-15 in 1985. Bob Richards, Orbital Sciences, interview by Matt Bille, August 13, 2001.

23. Howard Wilcox, telephone interview by Matt Bille, 2001: "The One-Pound Problem," *Air & Space,* (October/November 1999): 50–57.

24. DARPA RASCAL briefing, April 2003, unclassified, provided to authors by Preston Carter, RASCAL Program Manager, Devense Advanced Research Projects Agency.

CHAPTER 9

1. Jack Raymond, "500-Pound Space Vehicle Planned to Survey Earth," *New York Times,* February 2, 1958, 1A.

2. Dwayne Day, John M. Logsdon, and Brian Latell, eds., *Eye in the Sky: The Story of the CORONA Spy Satellites* (Washington, D.C.: Smithsonian Institution Press, 1998), 6. Another version of the story has the program named after a brand of cigar. Also, CORONA is not an acronym, but all intelligence program code names at the time were written in all capital letters.

3. Satterfield and Akens, *Historical Monograph,* 78. Also available online at http://www.redstone.army.mil/history/pdf/welcome.html.

4. Roger Launius, *Sputnik and the Origins of the Space Age,* http://www.hq.nasa.gov/office/pao/History/sputnik/sputorig.html.

5. NASA History Office, "Vanguard Division," http://www.hq.nasa.gov/office/pao/History/nara/vandiv.html.

6. William Pickering, telephone interview by Matt Bille, July 10, 2001; Brian Sweenn and Kevin Roberts, "William Pickering, Rocket Man," http://www.nzedge.com/heroes/pickering.html.

7. Stuhlinger and Ordway, *Wernher von Braun,* 153.

8. Medaris, *Countdown to Decision,* 266-9.

9. Harold M. Schmeck, "Nation is Warned to Stress Science," *New York Times,* October 8, 1957.

10. "Vanguard Chief Urges U.S. Elite," *New York Times,* February 1, 1958.

11. Rudolph, *Scientists in the Classroom,* 108–109.

12. Ibid., 52–54.

13. McDougall, *The Heavens and the Earth,* chaps. 7–8, and section 5.

14. Milton Bracker, "Vanguard Firing Expected Soon; Army Roots for Navy Success," *New York Times,* February 3, 1958.

15. Milton Bracker, "Vanguard Fired But Fails Again; Destroyed in Air," *New York Times,* February 5, 1958, 1A.

16. Green and Lomask, *Vanguard—A History,* 218.

17. Naval Research Laboratory, *Project Vanguard and the Scientific Earth Satellite Program,* NRL, May, 1958.

18. Kurt R. Stehling, *Project Vanguard,* (Garden City, New York: Doubleday and Company, 1961), 216.

19. Hagen, "The Viking and the Vanguard," in *History of Rocket Technology,* ed. Emme, 138.

20. Robert Jastrow, "Results of Experiments in Space," Lecture to the Institute of Aerospace Sciences, December 18, 1961.

21. Satterfield and Akens, *Historical Monograph,* 69. Also available online at http://www.redstone.army.mil/history/pdf/welcome.html.

22. Ibid.

23. Van Allen, *Origins,* 66.

24. Ibid., 67–70.

25. Robert G. Keesee "Earth's Magnetic Field," http://www.albany.edu/faculty/rgk/atm101/magnet.htm; NASA, "Space Radiation and Astronaut Safety," http://srag-nt.jsc.nasa.gov/FAQ/SpaceRadiation.htm.

26. "Reach into Space," *TIME,* May 4, 1959, 4.

27. Van Allen, *Origins,* 72.

28. Van Allen, "What Is A Space Scientist?

29. Army Ballistic Missile Agency, "Army Contributions to the Nation's Space Research," fact sheet, no date [1958?].

30. NASA History Office, "Explorer 1 and Jupiter C," http://history.nasa.gov/sputnik/expinfo.html.

31. Medaris, *Countdown,* 229.

32. NASA, "Explorer 1 and Jupiter C"; Mark Wade, "Beacon," http://www.rocketry.com/mwade/craft/beacon1.htm; Satterfield and Akens, *Historical Monograph,* 73. Also available online at http://www.redstone.army.mil/history/pdf/welcome.html.

33. Johnson was plucked by Eisenhower from his job as a vice president for General Electric. He was so enthused about the position that he took a salary reduction from $160,000 (a princely sum in 1958 dollars) to $18,000.

34. R. Cargill Hall, *Lunar Impact: A History of Project Ranger* (Washington, D.C.: NASA History Office, 1977), chap. 1.

35. ARPA approval: Joel W. Powell, "Juno 2," *Quest* 5, no. 1 (Spring, 1996), 58.

36. Medaris, *Countdown,* 241.

37. Mark Wade, "Juno 2," http://www.rocketry.com/mwade/lvs/junoii.htm.

38. Van Allen, "What Is a Space Scientist?"

39. John L. Chapman, *Atlas: The Story of a Missile* (New York: Harper & Brothers, 1960), 153.

40. Thomas, *Men of Space,* vol. 1, 65.

41. George W. Swenson, Jr., "Reminiscence: At the Dawn of the Space Age," 1994, http://www.ece.uiuc.edu/pubs/reminisc/space/space4.html.

42. Siddiqi, *Challenge to Apollo,* 175.

43. Mikhail Tikhonravov, "The Creation of the First Artificial Earth Satellite: Some Historical Details," *Journal of the British Interplanetary Society* 47, no. 5 (May, 1994): 191–94; Peter A. Corbin, "Rising from the Cradle: Soviet Perceptions of Space Flight Before Sputnik," in *Reconsidering Sputnik,* ed. Launius et al., 38.

44. The impact of Luna 2 brought up another new point of space law: was the U.S.S.R. claiming ownership of the moon? When asked by a reporter, Khrushchev responded that the question "reflects capitalist psychology" and that Socialist countries thought of the flight "as a victory not only of our country but of all countries of all mankind." Beebe, "Law's Empire and the Final Frontier," 1759.

45. Green and Lomask, *Vanguard—A History,* 223.

46. Ibid., 226.

47. Hagen, "The Viking and the Vanguard," in *History of Rocket Technology,* ed. Emme, 135.

48. Van Allen, *Origins,* 113.

49. Ibid., 114.

50. Cliff Lethbridge, "Bold Orion Fact Sheet" (1998), at http://www.spaceline.org/rocketsum/bold-orion.html.

51. Mark Wade, "Beacon," *Encyclopedia Astronautica,* December 22, 2000, http://www.rocketry.com/mwade/craft/beacon1.htm.

52. Office of the Assistant Secretary of the Air Force for Acquisition, "The AFSCN History," no date, http://www.safaq.hq.af.mil/aqsl/afscn/history/history.html; "Space Firsts," *Air Force,* www.afa.org/magazine/space/96space/t-02.html.

CHAPTER 10

1. Ed Bell, NASA Goddard Space Flight Center, "NASA's Explorer Missions," National Space Science Data Center, June 7, 2001, http://nssdc.gsfc.nasa.gov/multi/explorer.html; NASA Goddard Space Flight Center, "Explorers: Searching the Universe Forty Years Later," NASA Fact Sheet FS-1998(10)-018-GSFC, 1998.

2. Milton Rosen, telephone interview by Matt Bille, November 6, 1998.

3. Ron Potts, telephone interview by Matt Bille, December 2, 1998: Roger Easton, interview by David Van Keuren, March 8, 1996, NRL Oral History; Ivan Amato, *Pushing the Horizon: Seventy-Five Years of High Stakes Science and Technology at the Naval Research Laboratory* (Washington, D.C.: Government Printing Office, 1998), 197–99.

4. S. Fred Singer, "Origins of the MOUSE Proposal," presented to the International Academy of Astronautics symposium, Washington, D.C., 1992.

5. James Oberg, e-mail to Matt Bille, June 27, 2001. The city had also been known as Kaliningrad.

6. Stuart Schneider, "The Russian Space Auction at Sotheby's in New York," *Quest* 2, no. 4 (Winter, 1993): 28; Dwayne Day, "Exhibiting the Space Race," *Quest* 7, no. 1 (Spring, 1999): 52.

7. Day, "Exhibiting the Space Race," 52.

8. NASA History Office, "Mikhail Tikhonravov," biography sheet, http://www.hq.nasa.gov/office/pao/History/sputnik/mikhail.html.

9. National Space Society, "History of the National Space Institute," http://hiwaay.net/~hal5/HAL5/NSI-history.shtml.

10. Ernst Stuhlinger, "Sputnik 1957: Memories of an Oldtimer," unpublished manuscript, October 4, 1997.

11. University of Iowa, "UI Space Pioneer James A. Van Allen celebrates 40th Anniversary of Explorer 1," press release, January 26, 1998; Van Allen, "What Is A Space Scientist?"

12. Van Allen, "What Is A Space Scientist?"

13. University of Iowa, "James A. Van Allen to receive honorary degree from Johns Hopkins," press release, May 24, 1999.

14. Science and Environmental Policy Project, http://www.sepp.org.

Suggested Reading

There are two valuable works on Project Vanguard. Green and Lomask's book is an authoritative history of the project, while Kurt Stehling was Vanguard's lead propulsion engineer and wrote a compelling first-person account.

Green, Constance McLaughlin, and Milton Lomask. *Vanguard-A History.* Washington, D.C.: NASA SP-4202, Smithsonian Institution Press, 1969.
Stehling, Kurt. *Project Vanguard.* Garden City, N.Y.: Doubleday, 1961.

Surprisingly, there are no books devoted entirely to the Explorer program. There are, fortunately, some valuable works on spaceflight history that include this period and cover Explorer and/or Sputnik. The best include:

Burrows, William E. *This New Ocean: The Story of the First Space Age.* New York: Random House, 1998.
Dickson, Paul. *Sputnik: Shock of the Century.* New York: Walker & Co., 2001.
Emme, Eugene M., compiler. *Aeronautics and Astronautics: An American Chronology of Science and Technology in the Exploration of Space, 1915–1960.* Washington, D.C.: NASA, 1961.
McDougall, Walter A. McDougall. *The Heavens and the Earth: A Political History of the Space Age.* New York: Basic Books, 1985.
Harford, James. *Korolev: How One Man Masterminded the Soviet Drive to Beat America to the Moon.* New York: John Wiley & Sons, 1997.
Koppes, Clayton R. *JPL and the American Space Program.* New Haven: Yale University Press, 1982.
Launius, Roger, John Logsdon, and Robert Smith, eds. *Reconsidering Sputnik: Forty Years Since the Soviet Satellite.* Amsterdam: Harwood Academic Publishers, 2000.
Ley, Willy. *Rockets, Missiles, and Men in Space.* New York: Signet, 1969.
Siddiqi, Asif. *Challenge to Apollo: The Soviet Union and the Space Race, 1945-1974.* Washington, D.C.: NASA SP-2000-4408, 2000.

Stuhlinger, Ernst, with Frederick Ordway III. *Wernher von Braun: Crusader for Space.* Malabar, Fl.: Krieger Publishing Co. 1994.

Van Allen, James. *Origins of Magnetospheric Physics.* Washington, D.C.: Smithsonian Institution Press, 1983.

There are many Internet sites with space history information, but two stand out. Mark Wade's *Encyclopedia Astronautica,* http://www.astronautix.com, has information on every program, booster, engine, and satellite ever built (and many which were never built.) The NASA History Office's Web site, http://history.nasa.gov, is the central point for all NASA historical information, including the many books NASA has sponsored. Numerous books and reports, including the McLaughlin/Green history of Vanguard, are available free on-line.

A unique Internet resource can be found at http://www.amsat.org/amsat/features/sounds/firstsat.html. Here Roy Welch of the Radio Amateur Satellite Corporation (AMSAT) has placed sound recordings of signals from *Sputnik 1, Explorer 1,* and *Vanguard 1.*

Finally, there is *Quest,* the only magazine devoted entirely to space history. *Quest* is produced by the Space Studies department of the University of North Dakota. A subscription to this quarterly magazine costs $29.95 for recipients in the United States. Write to: Quest Subscriptions, P.O. Box 5752. Bethesda, MD, 20824-2824 or see the information on the Space Studies Web site at http://www.space.edu.

Index

Pages with illustrations indicated by italic typeface

ISBN 1-58544-374-3